Music and Citizenship

OXFORD THEORY IN ETHNOMUSICOLOGY

Martin Clayton, Series Editor
Martin Stokes, Series Editor

Music Theory in Ethnomusicology
Stephen Blum

Music and Citizenship
Martin Stokes

Music and Citizenship

MARTIN STOKES

OXFORD
UNIVERSITY PRESS

Oxford University Press is a department of the University of Oxford. It furthers the University's objective of excellence in research, scholarship, and education by publishing worldwide. Oxford is a registered trade mark of Oxford University Press in the UK and certain other countries.

Published in the United States of America by Oxford University Press
198 Madison Avenue, New York, NY 10016, United States of America.

© Oxford University Press 2023

All rights reserved. No part of this publication may be reproduced, stored in a retrieval system, or transmitted, in any form or by any means, without the prior permission in writing of Oxford University Press, or as expressly permitted by law, by license, or under terms agreed with the appropriate reproduction rights organization. Inquiries concerning reproduction outside the scope of the above should be sent to the Rights Department, Oxford University Press, at the address above.

You must not circulate this work in any other form
and you must impose this same condition on any acquirer.

Library of Congress Cataloging-in-Publication Data
Names: Stokes, Martin, author.
Title: Music and citizenship / Martin Stokes.
Description: [1.] | New York : Oxford University Press, 2023. |
Series: Oxford theory in ethnomusicology series |
Includes bibliographical references and index.
Identifiers: LCCN 2023021926 (print) | LCCN 2023021927 (ebook) |
ISBN 9780197555194 (paperback) | ISBN 9780197555187 (hardback) |
ISBN 9780197555200 | ISBN 9780197555217 (epub) | ISBN 9780197555224
Subjects: LCSH: Music—Political aspects. | Music—Social aspects. |
Citizenship. | Ethnomusicology.
Classification: LCC ML3916 .S86 2023 (print) | LCC ML3916 (ebook) |
DDC 306.4/842—dc23/eng/20230524
LC record available at https://lccn.loc.gov/2023021926
LC ebook record available at https://lccn.loc.gov/2023021927

DOI: 10.1093/oso/9780197555187.001.0001

Dedicated to the memory of Neil May, 1962–2018.

Contents

Acknowledgments   ix

1. Introduction: How Musical Is the Citizen?   1
   1.1 Sly civilities   8
   1.2 Citizen audience   14
   1.3 Citizen media   20
   1.4 Citizen voice   27
   1.5 Citizen performance   33
   1.6 Conclusion   37

2. Ethnomusicology of Citizenship, Ethnomusicology as Citizenship   49
   2.1 Identity   50
   2.2 Technocracy   57
   2.3 Intimacy   67
   2.4 Conclusion   76

3. Citizenship Resounding   87
   3.1 The citizen on his bike   88
   3.2 The citizen in the crowd   102
   3.3 The citizen in the square   116
   3.4 Conclusion   128

4. Conclusion   140

Bibliography   159
Index   177

Acknowledgments

The idea for *Music and Citizenship* took shape, in the first instance, in the Institute of Musical Research Distinguished Lecture Series at the University of London in May 2017. I am grateful to Geoff Baker for inviting me to deliver the lectures, and to those who came along to them and participated in the seminars, including Georgina Born, Matt Brennan, Anna Bull, James Butterworth, Katia Chornik, Byron Dueck, Ed Emery, Michael Fend, John Finney, Luis-Manuel Garcia, Dave Hesmondhalgh, Peyman Heydarian, Tom Hodgson, Jasmine Hornabrook, Angela Impey, Samuel Llano, Fred Moehn, Keith Negus, Tom Perchard, Ian Richie, Merav Rosenfeld, Shzr Ee Tan, Ilana Webster-Kogen, and Stephen Wilford. This is the very definition of a peer group. I am still processing what I heard and learned that month.

There followed a long—embarrassingly long—period of gestation. I revisited the Senate House lectures in various talks and conference presentations, and some short, published essays sprang from them. I am particularly grateful for the interest and support during this period of John Baily, Steven Cottrell, Christine Galliard, Fırat Kutluğ, Fiona Magowan, Eric Samothrakis, Hikmet Toker, and Özlem Doğuş Varlı. Ideas accumulated during this period, even as other things claimed my time and energy. Some took shape in the effort to translate them into French and Turkish. Some were connected to the fallout from the Trump presidency in the United States and the Brexit referendum in the United Kingdom. Some sprang from the feedback I was getting from the talks and the essays. The more the ideas grew, the harder I was finding it to return to the original lectures.

In the event, the Covid-19 pandemic forced the issue. Lockdown and travel restrictions meant an interruption of my 2019–2022 Leverhulme Major Research Project ("Urban Song of the Upper Euphrates"), much of which I had intended to spend in Turkey. I had to abandon fieldwork just as it was getting going, and, like everybody else, kick my heels for over a year. This proved to be exactly the space I needed to fundamentally reconceive and write this book. I am very grateful to the Leverhulme Trust, then, for making this possible, and for their flexibility.

I gave various sections of this book an outing in colloquia and public lectures at various institutions. I would like to thank Ayfer Bartu, Zeynep Bulut, Andy Fry, Salvatore Morra, Eckhard Pistrick, Suzel Reily, Kamal Salhi, Jonathan Shannon, and Zafer Yenal for those invitations, and to all involved in the discussions on each occasion. Various other friends contributed along the way with comments, recommendations for reading or viewing, or just turns in the conversation that ended up being hugely important, including Beyza Boyacıoğlu, Cüneyt Çakırlar, Giuliano Danieli, Ziad Elmarsafy, Michael Gilsenan, Denis Laborde, Davide Martello, Steven Millar, Yara Salahiddeen, and Harvey Whitehouse. The first full drafts of the book were read by Lucy Baxandall, Martin Clayton, Dafni Tragaki, and Gavin Williams. At OUP, Suzanne Ryan-Melamed set this volume in motion; Norm Hirschy kept it moving forward with a subtle and patient hand. Leslie Safford, Bala Subramanian, and Madison Zickgraf cared for the text, the cover, and the timeline. The anonymous reviewers' comments were helpful and instructive, provoking some real self-questioning on occasions. Mez Dubois-Van Slageren helped at the last minute with the music examples. I am deeply grateful to everybody mentioned above.

Finally, I would like to remember Neil May. Neil was a pioneer in the field of sustainable building technologies, for which he received an MBE in 2016. He was appointed around then to a post in the Institute for Environmental Design and Technology at University College London. I hoped that might offer us an opportunity to rekindle a conversation that had begun in our teenage years, but that had dwindled as we pursued our separate paths in life. We had plans, among many other things, to form a group in London to discuss sound and building. That would certainly have had a direct impact on this book. But he died in 2018, after a short illness. He will always be in my thinking. I dedicate this book to his memory.

1
Introduction

How Musical Is the Citizen?

People are arguing about a garbage incinerator near where I live in East London. Some would call it a classic case of environmental racism—the positioning of dirty urban infrastructure in a racially mixed neighborhood, one that, moreover, tends not vote for the current government. Others would say it has to go somewhere. Why not here, next to the—if anything even dirtier—North Circular, the unloved and much-complained-about northern section of Central London's ring road?[1] A "Citizens' Assembly" has been proposed to break the deadlock. I catch a community group representative discussing the matter with a BBC reporter on the car radio. It seems to her like a step in the right direction. "What we really need," she says, warming to her theme, "is to be able to get together and talk about this over a cup of tea."

Pioneered in Canada in 2004, Citizens' Assemblies have been attracting attention across Europe. They seem to have delivered both progressive and representative thinking on some notoriously intractable issues, as in Ireland's same-sex marriage and abortion referendums.[2] Political leaders in Belgium, France, and the United Kingdom have discussed making Citizens' Assemblies a routine component of government decision-making. Many are skeptical about them, though. Political analyst Naomi O'Leary, for instance, observes that governments can use Citizens' Assemblies to say they are listening, but also to distance themselves, if not simply ignore them, when they prove to be inconvenient. The Irish case is symptomatic, she suggests. The Irish Citizens' Assembly's much-vaunted results would probably have been achieved by other means. The various other things that Assembly discussed have simply been forgotten (O'Leary 2019).[3]

It is the "cup of tea" that sticks in my head. As the community representative utters those words, the conference facility acoustics, the rattle of the tea trolley, the clinking of spoons in white cups, the gentle crescendos and diminuendos of break-time conversation come, unbidden, to my ears. My first instinct is to smile at the banality of it all.[4] But the image persists. It rests, after all, on something larger—a fantasy of civility that is simultaneously powerful and precarious. The power of that fantasy lies in the alternative it offers to the dominant soundscape of democratic politics in the United Kingdom—the ferocious roar of the Westminster parliament in session. Its precariousness lies in the questions that increasingly attach to that soundscape—the advantage it is understood to confer on those reared in the debating societies of our elite private schools and its capacity to silence others. A palpable anxiety attaches to it.

The community representative and I have lived, as millions of others have, through an era of referendums in Western Europe, offered by those who have peddled them as solutions to the question of political audibility. The Brexit referendum in the United Kingdom, to take just one example, proved only the opposite. Most people, we learned, prefer to shout rather than listen, given the opportunity to do so. An election was subsequently won, and won in a landslide, by a party that offered to put an end to that shouting. The shouting has, of course, not only not stopped but also intensified.[5] In the course of it, fundamental changes to the structure of British citizenship—drawing radical new lines of separation between those born on these islands and those not, empowering governments to withdraw citizenship from those it considers unworthy—have been proposed and passed, more or less unopposed, by Parliament.

I switch off the radio, suddenly feeling the need for silence. The road swishes beneath me; autumnal countryside slips by. But the community group representative's words continue to reverberate.

I am being hailed, as Althusser would have it, as a resident of my East London borough and as a UK citizen. I am also being hailed, it would seem, as a musicologist—as somebody professionally invested in questions about sound and listening and the struggles over them. This conjuncture does not strike me as particularly strange. Questions about democracy, citizenship, and music have long been related, after all. In the thinking of classical antiquity, music and civic order were closely linked. For Plato and the Pythagorean philosophers, music would lead people astray if it failed to reflect the principles of order and proportion that held things together. These principles—and the responsibilities they entailed—would need to be clearly understood by musicians and, more importantly perhaps, by those who governed them. For Aristotle, music was valued ethically in the context of the virtues that make for social flourishing—'eudaimonia' (see Hesmondhalgh 2013). Musicians—and those who ruled over them—would need to consider how these positive effects might be harnessed for the broader good. By the time of the French Revolution questions such as these, deeply rooted in the traditions of thinking and talking about music in earlier centuries, had become more distinct and more urgent. Music and citizenship would be directly linked, as the revolution's leaders experimented with the technologies and architectures of revolutionary listening.

A nascent musicology was soon to make "ideal citizens" of its composers, Beethoven chief among them. The myth of Citizen Beethoven is still very much with us. I encountered it while I was tackling the slow movement of the "Pathetique" at the piano as a twelve-year-old, as I recall. My teacher took the opportunity to deliver a homily on the responsibilities of adult musicianship, making a present for me of his old copy of the Piano Sonatas, complete with Stieler's well-known portrait of the composer on its second page, as he did so. Another homily, on Beethoven's *Eroica* symphony dedication, duly followed. Here was the very essence of art's relationship to politics, emblematized in the conjoined figure of the citizen eternally vigilant against tyranny, the composer eternally defiant of convention. The memories are muddled—did this all, really, happen in the same lesson? With the same teacher? Like all myths, they fuse into solid matter if the environment is conducive—and it certainly was.

And to an extent, so it remains. From a scholarly perspective the myth of Citizen Beethoven might have been entirely debunked.[6] But in the popular culture accompanying the 250th anniversary of his birth, it is rampant. Jan Caeyers's biography (Caeyers 2020) for instance, one of many to take advantage of this anniversary, describes Beethoven in its advertising blurb as "the prototypical modern citizen, who, regardless of his background or origin, can take control of his life in order to achieve greatness."[7] It is a confused matter, certainly. A model citizen of what, exactly? Of Bonn, Germany, Europe? Of the world? Ottmar

Hörl's 700 identical green and gold statues of Beethoven, dotted around Bonn to celebrate the anniversary year, offer a wry commentary on what would seem to be a crisis of citizenship semiosis. A miniature Beethoven for everybody. We no longer know what single thing he stands for, when once it seemed terribly clear.

The case of Beethoven's near-contemporary, Luigi Cherubini, arguably provides the more revealing commentary on the citizen-composer myth today. The Italian conductor Riccardo Muti recently mounted a campaign to exhume Cherubini, who was buried in the Père Lachaise cemetery in Paris in 1844, and have him reinterred in his place of birth, Florence. Italy, united only in 1861, has been peculiarly dependent upon retrospective acts of claiming its widely scattered dead—just as it claims its plundered artworks (not entirely without justification) as national heritage. The case for making a posthumous Italian of Cherubini involves considerable ironies, as musicologist Michael Fend has noted (Fend 2018). The Declaration of the Rights of Man and of the Citizen of 1789 enabled the composer, along with other immigrants who had married or set up businesses in France, to acquire French citizenship— a unique opportunity in Europe at the time. He had plenty of reasons to feel grateful to France. And he had expressed no particular desire to return to Italy, least of all to be buried there. Muti, for his part, had failed to link his campaign to a revival of Cherubini's music, which might perhaps have enabled some public traction. After a flurry of publicity, it ran out of steam. Cherubini remains in Paris. The church in Florence designated as his final resting place contains only a memorial. Fend shows us that the questions at play today—linking the composer to the ideals of citizenship, democracy, and national identity—encounter recalcitrant material in the late eighteenth century. Scholars must approach them carefully, and populists like Muti would be well advised to stay clear of them.[8]

Thirty minutes with these thoughts pass by quickly. The outskirts of a town come into view. I apply brakes at a roundabout. I join the traffic and drive past pebble-dash houses, supermarkets, the railway station, the old town walls, the boarded-up high-street shops, the river that once marked a border. I've now got to find somewhere to park. Not home yet, by a long way. But it seems like a starting place.

* * *

A striking number of articles, chapters, and monographs in ethnomusicology published in recent years have prominently displayed the word 'citizen' in their titles.[9] Questions about democracy and music may have been beating a cautious retreat in the Western canon's musicology. In our field, the reverse would seem to be the case.[10] Strangely, the matter has not been the subject of much discussion, which is to say that the relationship between citizenship and music may well have been explored extensively though individual ethnomusicological case studies. But no thinking *across* these case studies has yet been undertaken. No answer to the questions "why ethnomusicology" and "why now" has yet been offered, in other words. Some assessment of this term 'citizenship,' some joining of the dots, is clearly overdue.

One answer to these questions might be that ethnomusicologists have only recently been reading and responding to a by now well-established "anthropology of citizenship." Sian Lazar's anthology (Lazar 2013) defined the field some time ago. It has important anthropological antecedents, as she herself points out. On the one hand there are the classic social theoretical texts defining the central critical questions about democratic participation in the modern nation-state system.[11] On the other, there is the "political anthropology" of the 1950s and 1960s, then largely preoccupied with sub-Saharan Africa's postcolonial transformations—its new nation-states, its emerging industries, its new cities.[12] The "citizenship turn" represented by Lazar and others has built on them, but focused on today's increasingly global social movements, insurgencies, and democracy-making projects. It has aspired to take into account not only the ravages of neoliberal programming, which played out across the world in the 1970s with a wide range of effects. It has also engaged with today's landscape of failed states, new authoritarianisms, neocolonial wars, climate emergency, struggles over reproductive rights, public health crises, and more.

Mainly, though, it has underlined the case for approaching citizenship ethnographically. Lazar and others have been emphatic that the question of citizenship involves rather particular challenges in this regard. Like anything else, the question of citizenship needs to be considered globally. The Global North is understood to have no special privileges, no special status as the driver of history these days. From a certain perspective indeed, it is the social movements and insurgencies of the Global South that define emergent global patterns regarding democracy. But the term citizenship is a highly normative one, and one associated with the ancient historical hegemonies of the Global North—which have been dependent, in the modern world, on colonialism and slavery. This normativity continually, and problematically, pulls the observer toward the question of what citizenship *should* be (rather than how it is being actively constructed in any particular situation). The risk in the study of citizenship, as Lazar stresses, is one of continually reinscribing that normativity, that hegemony, and of measuring others against it. But the payoff is the potential to invest it in its localized instantiations with new life, new creativity, new democratic potential, learned by global example. This is a matter of conceiving ethnography not only in terms of the "bottom-up" analysis of a concept routinely approached in "top-down" ways. It is also a matter of conceiving an ethnography of citizenship in conversational, multimodal, decolonizing, task-oriented terms. It is a commitment to the proposition that we all might learn from one another in such encounters and, step by step, shape collaborative democratic futures.

Lazar also stresses the ethnographic challenges citizenship poses as a concept of *practice*. We are peculiarly habituated to understanding the term citizenship as a legal category, as textual matter handed down from on high, of authority to be acknowledged, if not actively revered. This interpretation makes it all the more difficult to focus on the imagery, iconography, and symbolism of citizenship that surrounds us. It makes it all the more difficult to observe the ritual performances of citizenship, embedded as they often are in bureaucratic routine or in state ceremonial. It makes it all the more difficult to track discursive appropriations, inflections, and citations of legal and bureaucratic language about rights and responsibilities in everyday communication.[13] It makes it all the more difficult to track the *feeling* of citizenship, the particular ways in which the state addresses our bodies, emotions, and sensory apparatus.[14] Citizenship is clearly "made" in all of these ways. But the weighty associations of the word render this "making" hard to grasp—and hard to reflect in descriptive and analytical writing. Anthropology, Lazar and others suggest, has a particularly tough task on its hands with a word like citizenship, even if it is, in the final analysis, a familiar one. But she also implies that it also might have a particular kind of responsibility. Citizenship might, in the effort, be liberated from its problematic Enlightenment entanglements, in ways that keep collective and collaborative democratic futures open.

There would be some truth to this suggestion. The anthropologists central to Lazar's project—Renato Rosaldo, Aihwa Ong, and others—are often cited by the ethnomusicologists I will discuss in Chapter 2 of this book. But these citational habits would suggest a more systematic level of engagement with the field than I believe to be the case. It would also potentially frame ethnomusicology's central question as one of "what music adds"—to knowledge established elsewhere. This framing suggests a derivative and hierarchical relationship between ethnomusicological and anthropological theory. Many if not most ethnomusicologists, fully cognizant of the debt to anthropology, would nonetheless be unhappy with this characterization.

I would like to take several steps back and set the argument up differently. A great many traditions of thinking and writing in something we might broadly label 'music study' have been preoccupied with the relationship between music and democracy. Many indeed significantly predate "music study" and "ethnomusicology."[15] I will try to describe them in what remains of this introductory chapter. I do so mainly to establish the wider intellectual space within which today's ethnomusicological contributions—to be discussed in Chapter 2—resonate. This will also allow me to anticipate some of the ways in which I try to extend them in Chapter 3. It is a complex space, not an easy one to parse in terms of conventional disciplinary thinking, or conventional divisions of labor between humanities and social sciences. I will try to map this space in the following pages instead, then, around some rather broad sets of coordinates: audiences and assemblies; media systems and mediation; voice and vocality; sovereignty and the state. Two arguments spring from this regarding ethnomusicology's relationship to the anthropology of citizenship, perhaps worth signaling now. One is that the current ethnomusicological interest in citizenship draws on significantly deeper intellectual roots. The other is that music, sound, and listening have been significant indeed, central components of these discussions, and not incidental.

1.1 Sly civilities

Before I develop these arguments, though, it might be helpful, at the very outset, to describe the way my own research led me toward this topic. It began some years ago when I read a biography by Emine Aşan about a singer in Turkey who fascinated me, Zeki Müren (Aşan 2003). The last chapter was called, "He was the model citizen, him" ("*Örnek yurtaştı o*"). These three Turkish words puzzled me. The first part of the puzzle was the final *o* of the sentence, adding a 'he' or 'him' that initially seemed superfluous. The rhetorical spin it added to the sentence—"*the* model citizen, him," or "now *there's* a model citizen for you"—seemed clearer when I said it out loud. But why signal rhetoric here? To what ends, and for whose benefit? Why hint at the very outset that, as cases go, it was a counterintuitive one, one that might even require a little sophistry?

The other part of the puzzle was Aşan's choice of the word for "citizen" itself. As a Turkish speaker, you are often presented with a choice of words. You can choose a word of Arabic or of Persian derivation, a word that usually has a certain kind of historical resonance and emotional charge. Or you can choose a word of Turkish or Turkic derivation, usually one with a more modern and bureaucratic feel. Many words in this latter category were indeed invented by sometimes overzealous language reformers in the middle of the twentieth century. Such choices are ubiquitous. Sometimes they clearly signal political or religious identities. Sometimes (as with the corresponding bifurcation of the word for 'love' into *aşk* and *sevgi*) people may know only that *something* is at stake, if not exactly *what*. In everyday usage, citizen seems to fall in this latter category. It can be either *vatandaş* or *yurttaş*. The former is made of the Arabic *watan* (nation), the latter the Turkic *yurt* (home); both attached to the suffix *-daş/-taş* (roughly "sharing").

The more one thought about the singer, the more of a puzzle this sentence became. Queer, overweight, ill, an artist most at home in the old music and the old poetry, whose embrace of the commercial mass media eventually meant his exclusion from state radio and television, he flouted the norms of the modern Republic. Why should *he* have been celebrated as an iconic national citizen in the first place? And why would the more modern and bureaucratic word *yurttaş*, signifying kinship within the *yurt* rather than the *vatan*, have been considered the appropriate choice? The latter word, with its evocation of an older culture, sitting so uncomfortably within the modern state, seemed to me to be more obvious in Zeki Müren's case. It seemed worth asking native Turkish-speaking friends, many of them erudite academics. But, as so often with questions of this kind, I got no straight answer.

The question of the identification of Zeki Müren as an "ideal citizen" continued to grow in my mind, though. How, and when, for instance, did the term attach itself to this unlikely figure in the first place? The citizenship narrative seems to have taken off with his death in 1996. The presiding imam at his funeral, a media jamboree broadcast live on state television, may have been the first to speak of Zeki Müren in such terms in his eulogy. The citizenship narrative subsequently snowballed, in part because it spoke to a number of otherwise incompatible political oppositions—left/right, secularist/Islamist, modernist/traditionalist—in regard to each of which he could be said to have represented some category of exclusion, and thus enrolled in pleas for tolerance and open-mindedness. The citizenship narrative took shape in a post-mortem cult, then, that celebrated this combination of sincerity and social subtlety in his artistic persona, and his consequent enrolment as a representative of various categories of marginalization. Zeki Müren had, it would seem, mastered the art of living while wars raged, currencies collapsed, military juntas came and went, all the while dodging and deflecting the gaze of those in power. Homi Bhabha's description of the "sly civility" of the subaltern sprang to mind (Bhabha 2004). I started to see why this "slyness" might have mattered so much in 1996, and why it should have continued to matter in the decades ahead.

It also struck me that something might be gained by comparing Zeki Müren to two slightly later, but comparable, figures, Orhan Gencebay (in the 1970s) and Sezen Aksu (in the 1990s).[16] The citizenship narrative, in both cases, was neither as explicit nor as close to the surface, but it was there. The comparison between them suggested it might be possible to track the historical transformation of the idea of the 'ideal citizen' in the Turkish context, and its subtly shifting vocalizations and embodiments. Such transformations, I argued, could be linked to the successive crises of the Turkish "liberal period," punctuated as it was by successive military coups. They told an elusive story about what one might label, following Plummer and others, as *intimate* citizenship (Plummer 2003). As icons of that intimate citizenship, they could be differentiated by gender, sexuality, class, and body type as well as by association with particular structures of feeling (melancholy, world-weariness, resignation, *acı, hüzün*). It was a story of changes, then, as well as continuities, in which rich senses of participation in national community might be identified. One could point, thereby, to a history of endurance, of political ingenuity, of quiet and everyday spaces of resistance, one not often seen from outside, or in the terms Turkish cultural officialdom has provided.

Where, though, was such a history located? In what, materially speaking, could it be said to be grounded? An obvious answer was "voice," but this immediately ran the risk of piling weighty abstractions upon thin air. The methodological questions grew only more complex as one tried to think about their historical dimension. The case of Zeki Müren once again provided the cue. For this was a voice whose contradictions seemed to invite, over the decades, sustained bouts of *discussion*. This was a voice that was, over time, praised both for its traditional and its modern qualities, for its queerness and its capacity to build community, for its emotionality and its civility (*nezaket*). His handling of the microphone lay at the heart of these contradictory characterizations, which date back to the 1950s. Indeed, one particularly analytically minded commentator at the time devoted several pages of a book on Zeki Müren to the "microphonic" (*mikrofonik*) qualities of the singer's voice.[17] Here was a direct invitation, then, to think about voice in terms of embodiment, technology, governmentality, discourse, and affect, and its circulations and distributions in social space. Far from being elusive, a matter of "thin air," here was a Maussian "total social fact," tangibly present, it seemed, wherever I looked.[18]

The risks seemed worthwhile. Indeed, they seemed worthwhile extending both comparatively and historically. Beyond Turkey, ethnomusicologists at the time were looking at other mass-mediated scenes of contested emotion coupled with fraught figures of citizenly identification. In the background of many of these case studies lay the more or less global efforts by "developing nations" to juggle import-substituting industrialization with the demands of global trade, rural-urban migration, Cold War militarization, ethnic conflicts, authoritarianism, and state violence. Often, too, they involved comparably ambiguous figures of urbanity—typically portrayed in musical films as the peasant in the big city, put upon and out of their depth, hopelessly in love with a social superior, struggling to maintain decency under duress, with little to draw on other than deep feelings and fine voices. Alongside Turkish *arabesk*, the genre Zeki Müren was eventually to embrace, I began to notice similar scenarios in *rebetika* in Greece, *sevdalinka* in Bosnia, *enka* in Japan, *fado* in Portugal, *dangdut* in Indonesia, and *sertaneja* in Brazil, among others.[19] These and other cases displayed comparable patterns of official disdain, comparable cosmopolitan leanings toward the global soundscapes of the 1950s and 1960s, and those of neighbors, rather than those of cultural nationalism at home, comparable phantasmagorias of voice.[20]

Such comparisons relied heavily on the semiotic stability of such scenes. They assumed the *legibility* of such singers as citizens. Such assumptions soon appeared to me to be premature, and before long entirely unwarranted. In the case of Zeki Müren, the more pressing question began to appear to me not such much one of *what* he signified, but of *how* he signified. There was something perplexing about his voice—and his image, too—to those around him. A puzzle that might indeed require an entire book (like that of Edip Özışık) to answer.[21] And beyond all this lay the more troubling question about *whether* he "signified" at all. He seemed, to some observers, to mark the limits of meaning-making itself. This question lay at the heart of an interesting artwork I encountered recently, Erinç Seymen's *Bir Paşanın Portresi* ("A Pasha's Portrait") of 2007. This is an installation comprising a short video and two canvases. The top canvas displays Zeki Müren's head, facing the viewer in an iconic pose. In the video we see a marksman, wearing noise-baffling earphones, slowly shooting holes around Zeki Müren's outline with a pistol from a few meters' distance. We hear nothing on the video except the dull, repeated explosions of the gun. The task of shooting these holes is eventually completed, leaving a silhouette outline on the canvas behind. The video ends, the front canvas is disposed of (we assume), and the rear canvas remains for contemplation.

It is worth thinking about this, briefly. Critic and cultural theorist Cüneyt Çakırlar, who introduced both this artist and this installation to me, situates it cogently in the cosmopolitan queer universe of Seymen's art practice (Çakırlar 2015). Zeki Müren, Çakırlar explains, was a queer icon who, nonetheless, was never "out" and who, moreover, seemed to enjoy a cozy relationship with the military.[22] The question this implies is playfully evoked by the title—"Paşa" being both Zeki Müren's affectionate nickname and the military honorific conventionally used to address generals. The general in question here can only be General Kenan Evren. Evren led the 12 September 1980 coup, which set in train thousands of extrajudicial deaths and disappearances. The installation poses a set of questions about the relationship between the two paşa-s: which are we seeing; which are we hearing? How do we understand the relationship between the civility of the one and the violence of the other?

Seymen's piece also raises a question about the nature of icons, of popular cultural signification itself, as Çakırlar adroitly observes. In *Bir Paşanın Portresi,* where, exactly, has the icon gone? If we are to concentrate on the doubled canvas, which of the two? The underlying one, Çakırlar notes, is "done from behind" and this, in an important sense, grounds things for Seymen. It has, queerly, turned things upside down and inside out, substituting a voice with gunshots, and a beloved cultural icon for bullet holes. The 1980 coup, it implies, broke the chains of coherence that linked popular cultural icons to meanings, chains that were never, subsequently, to be restored.

As a meditation on Zeki Müren's strangeness, Seymen's installation is far from unique. A film from around about this time makes a point closely related to Seymen's, *Vizontele,* written and directed by Yılmaz Erdoğan in 2001. This describes the efforts of an ambitious mayor of a remote (and clearly Kurdish) town to bolster his prestige by introducing the village to television. Without electricity, or television signals, this is going to be a challenge. The first attempt to do so involves trekking up the nearest mountain to plant the antenna supplied by the Turkish government. A signal is located—but it turns out to be Iranian television. The mayor becomes a figure of ridicule, orchestrated by the owner of the local cinema. But he finally prevails, winning the viewer's respect for his perseverance and innate decency. The big day arrives, and he assembles the village ... to watch a televised Zeki Müren concert. Will we need to wear suits and ties to watch Zeki Müren? asks one of the villagers, slyly, an eye on the cinema owner. The committee behind the project wrestles frantically with the signal and the electricity supply. Until the very last moment it looks as though another humiliating disaster for the mayor was likely. The screen hums and crackles into life. But the Zeki Müren concert has been interrupted at the last moment to bring an important announcement by the government. Turkey has gone to war in Cyprus. And one of the very first casualties is the mayor's eldest son, whom we witness being conscripted earlier in the film.

An underlying point in this film relates closely to Seymen's. In *Vizontele* Zeki Müren is a sign of the state—the state as light entertainment, polite, undemanding, domestic. But what the situation ultimately reveals is the inability of modern media to deliver that sign, efficiently and coherently, to those the state seeks to address. Zeki Müren becomes, as a consequence, a fantasy of an unmoored modernity, with no grounding in local realities. Even worse, he seems to have an unfortunate capacity to reveal that modernity's dark underside—the state as monster, devouring, like Saturn, the village's children.

In such mediations and meditations on Zeki Müren as "model citizen," the question is not what and how he represents but one of *what he has done to the field of representation itself*. They show how the singer has become a screen onto which all sorts of compensatory fantasies are projected (singer as nation, singer as figure of sincerity, singer as beloved). They speak of a phantasmagoria of citizenship, of fragmentary, microperformative operations shoring up, in compensatory fashion, both idea and representation.[23] And they draw attention to the complex matter of what is at play when a singer is deemed to *model* or *exemplify* citizenship (which is, after all the implication of that word '*örnek*'). Where and on what, exactly, is that modeling taking place? Neither Zeki Müren's queer poses, nor his vociferous support for the Turkish military, seems to provide obvious symbolic material. The answer is, clearly, "his voice." But if so, which voice? He sang with many. Mediated how, heard how and by whom? What exactly in his voice made it a "model" or "exemplar" (örnek) of citizenship? Because citizenship is supposed, among various other things, to consist *of* voice, not simply be something represented *by* it. Zeki Müren, a musician I was never, sadly, able to meet, returns to haunt me time and time again, as indeed he does many of my Turkish interlocutors. This provokes conversations that have periodically challenged me, inspired me, and pushed me toward unexpected corners of the literature. It is time to return to this literature now, hoping the diversion will have alerted readers to some of the ways in which I am going to approach the question of citizenship. For my part, Zeki Müren will help me over the following pages in the ways he always has—to connect, puzzle, provoke. To smile, too, when things risk getting too heavy. Let us start, then, with the question of the citizen audience.

1.2 Citizen audience

An old story about Zeki Müren involves an unruly scene in a nightclub.[24] An uncouth demand emanates from a rural type at a table nearby. Zeki Müren brushes it aside wittily. But there is an angry riposte from across the hall. A fight, predictably, ensues. Plates and glasses fly across the room. Zeki Müren starts singing and stillness falls. The audience is charmed, its differences instantly forgotten. The story involves, in part, a distinct juncture in the history of nightclubs (then called '*gazino*') in Turkey in the 1950s. The gazino-s had expanded in size and ambition of programming to meet demand in a city population swelled by the wealthy rural-urban migrants, still, the story goes, poorly educated in the ways of the city. The question of the citizenly audience, of the resonant assembly, has a longer philosophical pedigree, though.

Rousseau was preoccupied with the links between audibility and political society, as is well known. A famous passage in the *Essai sur l'origine des langues* implies that democracy extends as far only as the last person in the crowd capable of hearing the orator's voice.[25] The problem for Rousseau was primarily one of language. It troubled him that the French language scarcely seemed capable of traveling to the back of the room, let alone filling the Place des Vendômes. Herodotus' recitations by contrast, he says, "were easily heard in the public square," and the air "resounded to applause." And if street hustlers ('*les charlatans des place*') constituted more of a problem in Italy than in France, filling the air with lies, the problem for Rousseau is not that they make more noise. It is just that they are speaking Italian, a language properly capable of being heard. "Every tongue in which one cannot be heard by the assembled people is a servile language," he observes, implying the problem with French. "It is impossible for people to remain free and speak that language."

Rousseau's contemporaries had the political responsibilities and agencies of listeners, as well as speakers, in mind (Rosenfeld 2011). Theories of the listening ear were changing. Medieval notions of resonance, whereby listening was imagined as an act of inner vibration, proportionate to the vibrations without, were being replaced by a conception of listening in the circulation of nerve liquid, sentiment, and tears. In such a conception, listening required knowledge of codes and the "mechanisms" by which they operate on the listener (Rouget 1985, 167–168). A particular melody might thus move some to tears (like "Ranz des vaches," beloved of the Swiss mercenaries Rousseau supposedly encountered in Savoy), but not others. Audition was a matter of understanding, not merely of vibrating sympathetically. And it was a public act, not a private one. Political community depended on an assembly of such listeners, capable of "resounding" in a public place, able to give credence to vital public narratives (like Herodotus' *histoires*), and to expose *les charlatans des places* for what they were.

It was also a matter of filtering. The removal of prepublication censorship in 1789 meant raised voices and the clamor for attention. The revolutionary assemblies were a cacophony. As Marat and others quickly realized, one could not dispense with basic rules and procedures to ensure that voices raised at these assemblies were also voices *heard*. Architectural and technological solutions, like megaphones and raised platforms, were proposed. Revolutionaries and counter-revolutionaries alike counseled a return to common sense ("*le bon sens*," Rosenfeld 2011), in which the ear was imagined not just as an organ for letting sound in, but also for keeping quite a lot of it out. A regime of censorship was reimposed in 1792. As a result of wavering revolutionary thinking about the relationship between what was said and what was heard, and how it might be regulated, an ideal of citizenship as "communicability"—of citizens having their own voice *and being listened to*—was to emerge.

In post-revolutionary France, the question of communicability within the assembly was soon to be complicated by the question of Otherness. Rousseau had anticipated the question in his *Essai sur les origines des langues*. The emerging colonial order would soon extend greatly extend it. The nineteenth century world fairs—brutal and unflinching demonstrations of the supremacy of the West's colonial and industrial order—galvanized thinking about citizenship and the arts. As Jan Pasler shows, this had an important history in France (Pasler 2009) in connection with the Exposition Universelle of 1889. Following defeat in the Franco-Prussian war, and the constant threat of a resurgent monarchy, the French Republican legacy needed reinvention and reinvigoration. The centenary of the Revolution provided an opportunity. This saw the emergence of a growingly French, and growingly anti-German, idea of the public utility of "The Arts." The Third Republic would indeed make the idea its own, and Parisian artistic worlds, lacking the patronage of state or church, of course, would cling to it. "Public utility" involved the composition and performance of large-scale works to animate public spaces (e.g., those of Gossec), and, as Katherine Bergeron has shown elsewhere, a growing national pedagogy surrounding song (Bergeron 2008). Public education in the arts would not only teach people how to be French, but also how to observe, compare, choose, and thereby develop taste and judgment. This, in turn, would lead citizens toward, and safeguard, democracy.

Over time, these ideas unraveled, and took other, quite volatile, shapes. The language of citizenship, here as elsewhere, responded to historical and political circumstance, and the fragmentation of positions within and between social classes. Pasler shows how the public utility arguments that emerged in 1889 became anxious and defensive. Indeed, they set in motion a ferocious reaction, one we mainly associate today with Baudelaire and the Symbolists. A powerful strand of French modernism was, and remains, fiercely opposed to public utility discourse, and thus found itself wedded to its opposite, a defiantly aloof aestheticism on the one hand, the flaneur's distracted cynicism on the other. The Third Republic's conceptual trinity of "people-nation-culture" had evolved from revolutionary "liberty, equality and fraternity," but would eventually lead to today's "identity, memory and heritage" (Pasler 2009, 49).

The 1889 Exposition Universelle structured, then, a space of citizenly imagining in which the sounds of Others—and acts of listening across difference—were central. Exotic sounds focused the citizenly call to judgment, discernment, scientific knowledge, and a historical sense of France's destiny in the world. A vital component of these sounds were the architectural spaces in which they reverberated. Such spaces were significant, naturally enough, in the ways in which they framed and ordered the exotica on display—both spectacularizing and naturalizing the regime of representation that Timothy Mitchell saw as fundamental to colonialism and the late-nineteenth century's emerging global order (Mitchell 1991). They were also significant in the awe-inducing size and resonance of the architecture, and their ability to gather huge crowds. These constituted a more complex, and, arguably, enduring challenge to the forging of an orderly relationship between citizenship and public listening.

Fear of the crowd has, for a long time, haunted the idea of the "citizen audience," and done so with a particular intensity in North America. As Butsch shows in *The Citizen Audience: Crowds, Publics and Individuals* (Butsch 2008), mid-nineteenth-century American theaters were a battleground setting pit against boxes. A struggle took shape that pitted the emerging American working class—the "b'hoys"—in the pit, boisterous, noisy, and unruly against those above them in the boxes—patrician, propertied, and "English." This struggle involved two distinct ideas about citizenship and civic virtue, opposing the claims of labor to those of property. Theaters were overtly political spaces; Federalists and Republicans had rival establishments, sometimes indicated by their names.[26] Attempts at neutrality on the part of theatre managers failed. Actors were subject to a constant barracking and heckling, pelting with rotten eggs and potatoes, shoes and chairs.[27]

There was initially admiration for these vigorous, masculine, and unruly democratic energies. But, as Butsch recounts, in 1849, English actor William Macready turned up to play his Macbeth in the Astor Place Opera House; American actor Edwin Forrest was, meanwhile, involved in a rival production a few blocks away. Forrest's supporters, the "b'hoys," succeeded in stopping Macready's first night. Macready and his supporters decided not to back down on the second night, however. There was a riot. Twenty-two people were killed, and over one hundred wounded (Butsch 2008, 29). The mood changed. Sections of the American middle classes began to react to the—populist and antiestablishment—Jacksonian citizenly ethics of the time in terms of new ideas of "respectable" citizenship. They placed a high level of responsibility on the performing arts—theater, music, and opera in particular—as well as on print journalism to cultivate this new sense of civic duty.

The core institutions of public entertainment were changing, too, and so was their architecture, in line with changing ideas about how sound circulates in public spaces. Opera houses and concert halls would be designed with orderly, seated, contemplative listening in mind. The new arts of "audiencing" would be born, of imagining, and practicing, listening silently, alone in the crowd (Cavicchi 2011). The theater of absorption would replace the theater of distraction; realism would replace melodrama; narrative would replace spectacle. Acoustics would develop as a science, or quasi-science, to support the new architectures of entertainment, architectures designed to permit audibility in ever-growing spaces of resonance—sound now being understood in terms of waves rather than rays. Materials would be developed to contain and direct resonance, noise reconceived as matter to be disciplined and regulated, the crowd tamed and civilized in the act of listening.[28]

Such anxieties would be reinvented and transformed in successive waves of social and technological change. With cinema and radio, the fear of the audience as "crowd" was quickly supplanted by a fear of the "mass." For American social theorists, the problem of the audience would become one of negotiating between the two. On the one hand lies the crowd—too much community. On the other, the mass—too little. The ideal audience was public, orderly, citizenly, rational, informed, and bound together by *discussion*. What was sought in the audience was not too much of a sense of community, and the unruly emotions that go with that, but not too little, either. Goldilocks style, something in the middle, mediated by critical discussion and reflection, would be just right.

The crowd, as imagined in North American debates at the beginning of the twentieth century, was an immigrant crowd, associated with unions and labor unrest (Butsch 2008, 41). The social cohesion provided by immigrant communities was being eroded by city life, or so it was thought. The arguments that took place around early cinema showed how such anxieties evolved. On the one hand, cinema was quickly understood as a means of taming the (immigrant) crowd. On the other, the idea of men and women isolated in their homes, meeting only as strangers in cinemas and other places of public entertainment, passively consuming nonsense, distracted and thus easy prey for ruthless advertisers, or enemy propaganda, was concerning.[29]

They were more quickly resolved as they concerned radio, particularly in the public settlements that took shape over radio's commercial regulation in the 1930s. The question of "the public good"—understood in terms of educating and informing the public, and maintaining diversity—was always paramount here, and later regarding television. The so-called "trustee model," guaranteeing such responsibility on the part of the corporations, was to last until the wave of Reaganite deregulation in the 1980s. The Internet and social media were to change the landscape significantly, as "others" opposed to which the citizenly capacities of radio, cinema, and television might be progressively reimagined. But the fundamental terms of the discussion—the threats constituted by new media to the ideals of citizenship—have, it would seem, remained remarkably steady.

The question of musical citizenship could be described, in the first instance, as a question about listening in an assembly. In Enlightenment political theory, as we have seen, the imperative of communication was central to the earliest debates about revolutionary community, a question not only of voice but of audibility. It was not enough for the citizen to speak. The citizen also needed to be heard. An important supplement to this question in more recent times has been one of the institutions, architectures, technologies, and media built over time both to support and contain political communicability. These soon had to expand to take account of hearing across lines of difference, specifically those constituted by colonized others and the urban crowd. Citizenship narratives consolidated themselves around these emergent figures of political alterity, but in doing configured new threats to the idea of citizenship, and to political communicability more generally. The question of *mediation* has some more general critical and philosophical dimensions, however, which are important to our task; it is to these we shall turn next.

1.3 Citizen media

Zeki Müren positioned himself at the forefront of new music media in Turkey: radio, 45 rpm, film, cassettes. All, in retrospect, shaped rather particular ideas about political belonging—and threats to it. At the time of the singer's early rise to fame, the state's radio station reached into the immediate hinterlands of Istanbul and Ankara, but not much farther. During these years many listened instead to Radio Cairo, which was easy to access if you had a radio set, and full of exciting sounds. The state's efforts to reform popular musical tastes inadvertently opened the door to the very sound worlds it was trying to keep out. Such sound worlds formed the substrate of Turkish films and cassette music in the 1970s, with the somewhat dismissive label 'arabesk' appended. It was not long before commentators started to discern an authoritarianism in the state's convulsive efforts to stamp it out, and coded democratic messages in arabesk itself—the music of "the people." The story is significantly more complicated, of course.[30] The state could easily enough have acted, particularly after the 1980 coup, when no detail of everyday life seemed to escape the punitive eyes and ears of the junta. Kurdish language music was ferociously targeted, for example.[31] But it seems that there was more to be gained from doing nothing about arabesk, a genre that the aging Zeki Müren, by then a kind of national treasure, was comfortably inhabiting. The state was thereby able, with little expenditure of energy or effort, to conjure with the idea of arabesk as a threat to the social order and, at the same time, to pose as a guardian of tolerance for these marginal voices. Arabesk seemed like dissent only because it suited the state, for a while, for things to appear that way.

The story chimes with a broad literature questioning the democratic potential of new media. The lines this literature draws have moved back and forth. The Frankfurt School's bleak diagnoses, which stressed the ways in which popular culture induced political obedience, were supplanted by a Gramscian line of thinking associated with the Birmingham School of Cultural Studies.[32] This shifted attention to what was at stake in the *use* and *consumption* of media, rather than its production. In the "ritual" practices of subcultural groups, defiantly democratic practices could be seen taking shape among postwar British youth, as they bought clothes and music and organized their leisure time. New thinking within the Frankfurtian tradition, in response, stressed the "material unconscious" of media systems—the unrecognized, if not repressed, reservoirs of sociality, labor, and pleasure—continually at play in their operation, unleashing, even as elements of such systems worked to suppress them, novel democratic imaginaries.[33] These fed a blurring of the boundaries between humans and technologies, and the embrace of "cyborg citizenship" alongside other posthuman philosophies of democratic activism.[34]

The new digital technologies bought such optimism to the boil. Established forms of authority suddenly seemed vulnerable to the powers of social media. The "Arab Spring" quickly demonstrated the limits of the "Facebook Revolutions," however. Celebrations of social media's capacity to mobilize have been quickly replaced by concerns about the opportunities it offers for the harvesting of data and surveillance. It is not surprising that authoritarian regimes (or distinctly authoritarian voices within liberal societies) seem more excited by the "democratic" potential of social media and AI than progressive liberals at the current moment. Many, at the time of writing, will continue to be perplexed by the spectacle of Saudi Arabia's offer of citizenship to "Sophia," a humanoid robot developed by Hanson Robotics in 2017. To put this in context, Human Rights Watch recently reported on the plight of some 10 million migrant laborers in Saudi Arabia, the poorest of whom, mostly refugees from neighboring countries, are kept in a state of extreme precarity beyond the protection of any citizenship regime. They also recently reported on the male guardianship system, which continues to treat women as permanent legal minors—even though they may, now, be permitted to drive their own cars.[35] One can only wonder what Sophia herself thinks about the matter.

From the point of view of media, the case of Zeki Müren in Turkey was not simply, as we have seen, a matter of a privileged relationship with one media system—with radio, 45 rpm discs, film, or cassettes. It is a story about his relationship with all of these over the course of many decades. The citizenship narrative associated with him would seem to have made a virtue of this. Zeki Müren was no entrepreneur. He exploited niches *within* emerging media technologies, rather than inventing new ones. He flitted around things, cleverly, moving not so much with the times as between them. He inhabited a space of mediation, rather than "a medium." He intimated that modern citizenship was a matter of dwelling within—an inhabitation of—such spaces of mediation. It was not a quest for a life of authenticity outside of it, in the face-to-face musical worlds of folk culture, or of the classical *meşk* learning system, or of traditional Sufism, for example.[36] If he "represented" anything, he represented mediation itself—a position underlined by his citational status in *Vizontele*, mentioned above.

Media theory, inflected by new currents of philosophical and critical thinking, has likewise moved away from the discussion of systems, formats, and new technologies. It has explored instead the broader domains of material and practice through which signs circulate. Nothing stands "outside" such a conception of mediation: signs have no independent existence, mediation no a priori confinement to the technologies habitually associated with it. Georgina Born's thinking on the subject has been particularly influential in music study. It has largely been conceived as a response to Latourian Actor Network Theory (ANT) and Deleuzian theorizations of the 'assemblage' (see, in particular, Born 2005, Born 2012, and Born and Barry 2018).

Music, she points out, raises an important question about ANT's inflexibly "symmetrical" understanding of the relationship of human to nonhuman network "actants." Music, in which the agency of nonmaterial, non-present actants (concepts, norms, rules) also needs to be conceptualized, demands for which we make distinctions about the nature of such agencies, rather than assume, a priori, that all are equal. It raises, too, important questions about the modeling of time, a point that Born makes by bringing a Husserlian language of "protensions" (the temporal "affordances," one might say, of particular tools) to bear on traditional Deleuzian conceptions of the assemblage. Such specificities give rise, for Born, to an integrated theory of music's "planes" of mediation (Born 2012).

Music study has been somewhat indifferent to this new wave of thinking about mediation. This indifference may have something to do with the habit of reducing questions about mediation to questions about specific media (radio, cinema, television, and so forth). This has limited musicology to the quasi-empirical field of reception studies, a needless narrowing of horizons in thinking about the political dimensions of new technologies. In ethnomusicology it may have to do with a long-standing preoccupation with groove and participation, as ethnomusicologist Matthew Rahaim has recently suggested (Rahaim 2017).[37] A "metaphysics of unity" has underpinned this preoccupation, he shows, one rather at odds with the kinds of philosophical and critical implications of a term like "mediation." The question of musical *citizenship* makes them inescapable, however. There are three critical spaces that deepen this connection.

The first might be labeled "neo-Gramscian." Half a century ago, the Birmingham school raised important questions about the relationship between media and democracy, a relationship understood—under the general rubric of "articulation"—in terms of the struggle over space and signs, and the fleeting counter-hegemonic alliances of popular culture (for instance, those that connected the punk movement with Black music in Britain; see in particular Clarke, Hall, Jefferson, and Roberts 1976). The struggle over space was made possible by emergent media and by an entertainment industry that increasingly addressed postwar youth. Space for resistance might be won, but just as quickly packaged by capitalism for consumption and lost. In stressing the activity of the bricoleur in a landmark book, Dick Hebdige emphasized the agency of both sign-makers and sign-readers (Hebdige 1979). The critical challenge for subcultural groups, according to neo-Gramscian theorists, was one of maintaining the energy and conviction required to keep the chains of signification open and their engagement with signs resistive.

Subcultural theory could be described as an incipient theory of citizenship and mediation. It concerned the significatory making and inhabiting of spaces we might label democratic—spaces of community, equality, and solidarity. It concerned the "ritual" practices that keep them energized and meaningful.[38] Popular music, we might note, played a particularly important role in it. It opened two productive lines of inquiry, even though the terms in which it did so now appear somewhat limited. One concerned what it was about "music" that enabled subcultural space making. The explanations subcultural theory offered were essentially historical (see, specifically, Clarke et al. 1976). With an end to postwar austerity, and a new era of consumption, "youth culture" flourished and small media technologies (transistor radios, cassettes) pushed music to the fore. The commodification of music for youth markets in postwar Britain may have been intense, but it was also an unruly matter. Listeners had unusually wide margins to hear as they willed, and to push fashions in unexpected directions, with lasting consequences, as with punk. Another concerned the ongoing *practices* that sustained the resistance of subcultural groups to capitalism and the parent culture. The subcultural "reading" and "resignification" of symbolic systems might appear to be evanescent, limited to moments of consumption. But these readings were underpinned by a combination of practice and performance (a combination evoked, if not systematically theorized, by the term "ritual") that entrenched their subcultural meanings and transmitted them to subsequent generations.[39]

A second might be labeled neo-Aristotelian. Its relationship with the question of mediation is related to a particular understanding of political emotions—and their mediation via art. Martha Nussbaum's extensive thinking on the subject is based on the idea of the emotions as *ethical*—as where and how we shape the questions of how we might live together and what is worth caring about (see, in particular, Nussbaum 2001 and Nussbaum 2013). The capacity of the arts to engage us ethically rests, for Nussbaum, on their "complexity," their ability to represent the multiplicity and layered temporalities of human emotion. In art, she argues, attentive, educated readers, viewers, and listeners come to recognize the forms of their emotional attachment to others, including the demands of reciprocity and compassion, the handling of negative emotions (such as grief and shame), and the cultivation of care. Without art, Martha Nussbaum states, "we will very likely have an obtuse and emotionally dead citizenship" (Nussbaum 2001, 426). Literature naturally plays an important role. Nussbaum's near neighbor in Hyde Park and former colleague at the University of Chicago, Barack Obama, had taken a leaf from her book when he stated in 2015 that novels had "taught him to be a citizen," to be "comfortable with the notion that the world is full of greys . . . [to understand] that it's possible to connect with somebody else even though they are very different to you" (Flood 2015). But music plays an important role in Nussbaum's thinking, too, sometimes "read" through literature, as in her discussion of the "little phrase" in the "Vinteuil Sonata" in Proust's *A la recherche du temps perdu*, sometimes interpreted from the sound world, as in her extensive discussions of Mahler.[40]

This is, of course, to take a somewhat lofty view of Art with a capital *A*. Nussbaum credits music with such powers based on what she considers to be its essentially nonrepresentational nature. She assumes educated, contemplative listeners, able to make these intricate interpretations and implement them in their lives. These are both questionable constructs today; some would say "elite." But that does not, in my view, invalidate the key insights of this line of thinking. An important book by David Hesmondhalgh shows how it might indeed be extended and deepened in popular music and mass-mediated listening (Hesmondhalgh 2013).[41] Music does its work, Hesmondhalgh shows, not only in the concert hall and opera house and other architectures of lofty feeling, but also in the "low intensity emotions . . . unmemorable, short-lived and multiple" (2013, 14) of everyday life. Music plays a vital role in the production and regulation of these emotions, particularly as they energize, synchronize, and intensify other tasks. We need to understand these scenes of listening, he argues, if we are to understand how music might contribute to *eudaimonia*, our "social flourishing." This Aristotelian concept, for Hesmondhalgh, supports practices of "commonality, community, solidarity" confronting neoliberalism's competitive individualism (Hesmondhalgh 2013, 84). But he understands that the values of commonality, community, and solidarity can push outsiders to the margins. The listening practices that interest him are built on the recognition of difference—of race, gender, and class—and their mediation. And this, for Hesmondhalgh, is central to their production of social flourishing.

A third, which we might label 'Burkean,' concerns a rather specific site of mediation—the mediation of the modern critic. It has some points in common with the previous two—with neo-Gramscian interest in how signs might enable the connection and mobilization of progressive social groups, and with neo-Aristotelian interest in art as a rhetorical practice constitutive of "social flourishing." But if art is to have civic dimensions—to contribute actively toward democracy in American society—the question of guidance and instruction becomes inescapable. Art does not speak for itself after all. Such questions preoccupied American critic and thinker Kenneth Burke, whose writings on jazz in the 1930s have been discussed by Gregory Clark (Clark 2015). Burke wrote about art in the 1930s, from a certain position of pessimism concerning mass media, and the destructive tendencies of American individualism. He placed a high value on art, and on aesthetic experience, which he understood in rhetorical terms. Art could, in his view, intervene powerfully in the central drama of political identification—the negotiation of self and other across fields of "difference and segregation," on one hand, and "sympathy and connection" on the other. He considered political identification—essentially nonverbal—to act all the more powerfully on "the inner self," all the more convincingly turning a political "ought" into an "is."

But it was jazz that particularly drew his attention. In part, this stemmed from his long correspondence with Ralph Ellison, which sharpened his sense of the racial issues jazz might be capable of addressing. And in part, it stemmed from his thinking about the necessary improvisations of political life, of democracy as something that requires a collective process of making things up as one goes along. In democracy the citizen must, in other words, react, and respond to others and to constantly changing circumstances. Constantly operating on the brink of incoherence and impossibility, jazz, for Burke, displayed faith in the possibility that something would always materialize, that things could always be wrestled back from the brink of chaos.

Burke—a critic, not a theorist, as Clark underlines—saw his role as one of educating the public, putting them in a position to recognize the rhetorical *potential* of art. It was not something he considered self-evident, or something that people could be relied on to automatically feel or "just know," even in jazz. We do not have to accept the implicitly patrician terms of Burke's position—that the public is dependent on the critic to "feel"—and translate—the civic rhetoric of jazz for them. In the wake of recent theorizing concerning Black structures of feeling, which suggest quite different ways of understanding it, this position now, of course, feels very problematic.[42] But they help underline an important line of thinking here. Signs of (musical) citizenship take shape in a complex environment of mediation, extending beyond the realm of technological media conventionally associated with sound reproduction. They involve human mediation, too.

Burkean criticism recognizes the mediatory powers and agencies of listeners, as people with a stake in the struggle over the signs of democracy and the power to intervene. The problem of White voices speaking for Black ones is an urgent one at the current moment. In the clamor of voices around modern citizenship, can we be sure we are listening to the right ones? And who, or what exactly, do we hear when we do? These are old questions, but they have been given a new lease of life in today's "vocal studies."

1.4 Citizen voice

Zeki Müren was living as a recluse in the 1990s. Turkish Radio and Television's (TRT) decision to honor him in 1996, after decades of neglect, would have come as something of surprise. A short ceremony was planned, taking account of the singer's extremely poor health. It was to revolve around the presentation of a microphone—apparently the one he used for his first broadcast with Turkish Radio Ankara in the 1950s. The singer seemed genuinely moved. Muttering a few nearly inaudible words ("I don't know whether to laugh or cry") he reached out to take it, but immediately seemed to struggle with its weight. His companion on the night, Hülya Aydın, took the strain. But it was still too much for the singer. Calling a short break, he retired to his dressing room, where he collapsed. By the time the ambulances arrived he was dead.[43]

The TRT saw the event as a circle closed. His remarkable journey had come to a sad end, but with a return "home." This view was to overlook, however, a decade and a half of systematic, ideologically driven neglect of the singer by the TRT. It was also to overlook the possibility that the heavy microphone itself had provoked his final heart attack—a possibility strongly hinted at in Hülya Aydın's later reflections. At whatever symbolic level one chooses to read the story, this was a (citizenly) voice that the state had, quite clearly, failed to find a home for. Objectified in the gifted microphone, it was a voice that, from the singer's point of view at least, may have quite literally become too heavy to bear.

'Having a voice' and democratic practice are more or less synonymous in many parts of the world. In some languages, Arabic for instance, the words for 'voice' and 'vote' are identical ("*sawt*"). The people "speak" at the ballot box, and in the deliberations of government via their representatives. But how we hear such voices, and what we hear in them are quite different matters. These questions are a significant preoccupation in today's vocal studies. And they have a significant bearing on what we might think we hear in a "citizenly voice," like Zeki Müren's. Lacanian theory has prompted a great deal of this thinking. The story of Zeki Müren's microphone would indeed seem to bear out some of its core claims.

Lacanian theory concerning the voice has been driven, in the first instance, by the idea of its uncanniness. This resides in the ways in which it mediates symbolic and real, inside and outside, language and sound, and thus constitutes an "object"—an unstable site of libidinal investments and identifications. Lacan called these "petits objets a," to indicate their ambiguous status as signs, located at "quilting points" in the symbolic order—where "symbolic" and "real" touch.[44] The voice, in this sense, is understood only partly as "belonging to" the speaker (or singer). Its ambiguity, and the resultant instability of the voice as a sign, or as a locus of utterances, is crucial. The "object voice" attracts, focuses, and absorbs an array of desires, fantasies, and projections.

These projections will not, of course, always be positive. Indeed, Lacanian theory would propose as a particular propensity of the voice its ability to stir memories of the maternal, of the auditory environment of the womb. With this ability comes a link to various processes of abjection, to the matter that needs to be rejected, and protected against, as the subject gradually assumes an identity (Silverman 1988, Chion 1999). In this way of thinking, the sound of the voice (indeed, sound in general) troubles its symbolic environment. Such "troubling" is often noticed in emergent media technologies and practices, such as sound in early cinema, or in the use of electronic microphones, or in today's voice recognition software. It prompts, to use Nina Sun Eidsheim's phrase, an "acousmatic question"—concerning the relationship between the voices we hear delivered to us by such technologies and the bodies and communities we infer from them. The first question we ask of voices, newly objectified, is, she points out, "whose voice is this?"

The inherently troubling nature of this question is, typically, noticed with the advent of new vocal technologies. Consider early microphones, for instance. The electronic microphones used in radio ushered in the age of the crooner, almost immediately a figure of suspicion and threat (see Taylor 2018). This was a voice that, in the view of critics, lacked the masculinity and vigor to fill a concert hall—as we have already seen, a heavily idealized space of "democratic" listening. But it had the power, nonetheless, to circulate like mist, in homes and hearts, in unsupervised sites of listening, potentially remote from the patriarchal eye.[45] Women seemed to hear something in it—a fact that disquieted the critics. Vallée, as is well known, used an acoustic megaphone on stage. The "objecthood" of his voice, and the threats associated with it, took shape around this highly visible, and strange, prosthetic.

But they would be normalized, as time went on, or routinized in new media pleasures. Voices in the earliest film "talkies" were considered by many to be a problem. Many were more preoccupied by what would be lost, in terms of the allure of the silent era's stars, than by what would be gained by the addition of sound.[46] Michel Chion showed how the acousmatic question at play here was quickly put to creative use by Hollywood (Chion 1999). Voices could, he showed, be moved on and off screen, added to and subtracted from the diegesis, not just for dramatic effect, but for the purposes of achieving a particular kind of viewing and listening pleasure. Such techniques would be absorbed into genre conventions. The "troubling" capacities of voice would become apparent again only through sophisticated historical and critical techniques.[47]

Lacanian theory helps us understand the terms and stakes of such struggles. They also help explain something of their repetitive and compulsive quality. Eidsheim's acousmatic question—"*Who is this?*"—is an unsettled one (Eidsheim 2019). Indeed, Lacan would suggest it is fundamentally unanswerable. Efforts to master it are not only doomed to failure; they also exacerbate the original condition of alienation and disconnect. Pleasure is involved, too, complicating these efforts. But the underlying struggles persist, and new vocal technologies often serve to intensify and focalize them. Lacanian theory is helpful in identifying these struggles—and pleasures. As many have pointed out, however, it is tied to its place and its time, making it a clumsy tool at best, when used to engage with specific historical, ethnographic, or political situations (Born 1998).

Its uptake in radical Black Aesthetics is, however, worth noting here. Critic Fred Moten's work has been central. Moten understands "voice" as a phonic eruption, originating in the screams of Frederick Douglass' Aunt Hester being beaten by her slave holder (Moten 2003). For Moten, this cry initiates what he calls "the break," understood as both a break*down* and a break for freedom, reverberant throughout Black history. Martha Feldman has explained the challenges Moten's work raises for traditional musicology (Feldman 2021).[48] But she also notes the kinship of Moten's writing with that of postsoul theorists like Francesca Royster, queer theorists like Freya Jarman, novelists like Nathaniel Mackey, and hauntology theorists like Avery Gordon, all of whom could be said to be preoccupied with, in Feldman's expression, 'fugitive voices.' "Fugitive" voice will always resist translation, transliteration, and transcription. In flight, they shape what Moten labels an 'undercommons,' a space that refuses "ever to fully sound in harmony, resting instead on a disordered space of often noisy sound" (Feldman 2021, 18).

The idea of vocal "fugitivity" is a provocative one in the context of citizenly voice. It might lead us toward radically different ideals of political collectivity and communication, grounded in the experience of those most violently marginalized and excluded by (White, male) democratic histories. As we will see later in Chapter 3, the relationship between something we might label 'fugitive voice' and political collectivity raises thorny questions. Can a fugitive voice stay still for long enough to establish "collectivity"? Who or what in that collectivity determine how it moves? What kinds of (deeply problematic) fantasies (of amplification, of redundancy) are in play when we claim to hear the one in many, the many in one (Middleton 2006, Connor 2016)?

A route around such questions is to be found in approaches to voice that draw on phenomenology, sociolinguistics, performance studies, and readings of Bakhtin. The principles underlying such approaches have been succinctly marshaled by Eidsheim: "Voice is not singular; it is collective. Voice is not innate; it is cultural. Voice's source is not the singer; it is the listener" (Eidsheim 2019, 9). Eidsheim shows how what she calls the 'thick event' of voice is subjected to 'thin listening,' compulsively assigning race and collectivity to voices in changing media and technological scenes. Efforts to master the acousmatic question fixate on those elusive vocal details we often label 'timbre.' Timbre would seem to offer the clues we need regarding gendered, sexual, or racial identity. More broadly, timbre seems to indicate the deictic dimensions of speech, which is to say the spatial and social relationships it shapes between speakers (who is where, and what is happening between them). Timbre is the key, too, to the "fundamentally social life of voice," as Feld, Fox, Porcello, and Samuels have remarked (Feld, Fox, Porcello and Samuels 2004, 341). "Speech and song entwine to produce," they go on to say, "timbral socialities" (Feld et al. 2004, 341).

'Timbral socialities' is an extremely useful concept, putting things on firmly ethnographic and historical terrain. But it raises some interesting questions. Speech and song "entwine" across a vast field of vocal and verbal performance, one that may defy mapping and involve porous border zones. 'Entwining' may be an elusive performative matter, in other words. Timbre, too, is an evasive concept, hard to disentangle, in practice, from melody, harmony, and rhythm in music, hard to distinguish from other parameters of spoken language.[49] How is it to be perceived, and who is doing the perceiving? The term 'socialities,' usefully in the plural, resists any simplistic reduction to 'public,' 'mass,' 'nation,' or 'community,' and points instead to what is emergent, felt, not yet quite settled in discourse. But one feels a need, already, to understand something about their limits, about the others such socialities both construct and exclude.

Orienting his approach to what he calls vocal 'qualia'—metapragmatic lexical, timbral, and other performative signs shaping the social interaction—Nicholas Harkness addresses such questions in his work on Korean church vocalizing (Harkness 2015b). The voices cultivated in Korean Protestant churches—a significant presence, it should be noted, on the international concert circuit—shape, as he shows, a distinctly modern kind of citizenly subjectivity within the country. They do so in part in opposition to another kind of voice, associated with genres like *pansori*—a voice understood as astringent, strained, and saturated with qualities of *han* (pain, sadness). A voice associated, in short, with the burdens of history and tradition, not progress and enlightenment. They do so also through the qualia readily attached to Protestant church vocal aesthetics—cleanness, civility, refinement. As Harkness remarks, such "perceived qualities of the voice become intimately linked to the narratives of Korea's Christian transformation from suffering to grace" (2015b, 319). The relationship of this "grace" to modern citizenship is a slightly complex phenomenon, given postwar Korea's long history of military rule. But it can be extrapolated, for the purposes of this argument, at least.

Harkness wants to explain how such vocal ideologies are produced. He wants, in other words, to be able to account for the struggles that take shape within them and around them, to give them sharper historical and ethnographic specificity. He does this by making a distinction between 'voice' and 'voicing.' Voice, for Harkness, is a "phonosonic" matter. It involves "bodily processes [including, but not restricted to] . . . the shaping of the physical surfaces of the mouth and the throat . . . real-time bodily manipulations of the larynx, pharynx, jaw, tongue and lips." "Voicing," by contrast, is a "tropic" matter, in Bakhtin's sense. It involves the ways in which "discursive forms index speakers—whether social types or individual speakers." It is instantiated in various forms of reported speech, all of which define changing ensemble relationships between narrating and narrated voice—a "discursive alignment to perspective" as Harkness puts it (Harkness 2015b, 323). Speech acts, in other words, always involve multiple voices. Politically speaking, Harkness remarks (citing Agha), "having a voice" "is to be engaged in forms of voicing . . . that are taken up in a wide 'social domain of recognition'" (Harkness 2015b, 323).

Korean Protestant church singing, he shows, is to be understood in the relationship between "voice" and "voicing." An example of this would be how Korean vocal students adjust their vocal behavior between conservatory and church. In the conservatory, the "*songak*" voice is construed perspectivally—a voice recognized and valued on the world stage, a sign of modernity as opposed to (pained) tradition, a "clean" as opposed to an "unclean" voice—in short, a process of voicing. But it also involves a kind of competitiveness and status consciousness that young Koreans consider inappropriate in church. They must engage and manipulate their voices accordingly. Church singing becomes the site of a rather complex citizenly struggle, taking place, in part, within the vocal apparatus of these young Koreans, in part in the kind of speech acts that they, their peers, and their directors employ to mediate them. Harkness shows how and where we might identify such conflicts in empirical terms and consider their outcomes in real historical time.

The new vocal studies prompt fresh questions for the study of citizenship and democracy-making. "Having a voice" is one matter; knowing who is speaking is a quite different one, as we have seen. Such questions gain focus, it would seem, the more they directly address questions of performativity. Thinking about the state-citizen relationships, and broader conceptualizations of sovereignty, have been moving in the same direction. What might the implications of this be for thinking about citizenship? And its relationship with music, sound, and voice?

1.5 Citizen performance

Artist and anthropologist Beyza Boyacıoğlu's "Zeki Müren hotline," connected with the Yapı Kredi Bank's Zeki Müren exhibition in 2014, invited listeners to leave a message for the dead singer. The Turkish daily *Milliyet* commented that the line was inundated with callers, "leaving voice messages, singing, and sharing their woes." One reportedly said, "To be honest, I don't believe you are dead. You are everywhere. You reach out to people and will continue to reach out to people. I'm going to carry on listening to you. Take care of yourself." Another mentioned the role Zeki Müren had come to play in Turkey's LGBTI movement. "Two years ago, I saw a billboard at a Pride rally which said 'I asked Zeki Müren and he said hang in there!' (*"diren dedi"*). I loved it and took a picture of it which I hang on to. Particularly at the present moment, when we are under so much pressure in this country, I look at that picture and feel better about things" (Yalçınkaya 2016).[50]

The Zeki Müren hotline participates in the kinds of intimate communication Esra Özyürek described between Turkish citizens and the long-departed Mustafa Kemal Atatürk in the early years of the AKP political hegemony—a hegemony interpreted by many as the end of Atatürk's secular, modernizing state (Özyürek 2006). It was manifested in Atatürk's miniaturization—statuettes and lapel pins seemed, to Özyürek, to be replacing the massive iconography that formerly dominated cities and landscapes. Another Yapı Kredi Bank exhibition—Özyürek underlines the prominent role banks had been playing in the process—presented images of Atatürk the father, the husband, relaxing at home. These were soon to be seen on the streets in neighborhoods that were resisting the AKP hegemony in one way or another. What did these invitations to (secular, modern) intimacy mean in the context of Turkey's violent neoliberal transformations, and its turn to religion? What kind of citizen did they imagine, and address?

Anthropologist Yael Navaro-Yashin explained the growingly fraught performances defining "citizen" and "state" in everyday political life in Turkey in terms of a pervasive climate of cynicism following the Susurluk incident in 1996 (Navaro-Yashin 2002). Findings in the aftermath of a car crash in the east of the country revealed hitherto unsuspected levels of complicity between government, mafia, and paramilitaries. As structures of belief about the state collapsed, they took compensatory and fantastic form in the everyday encounters Navaro-Yashin analyzed, usually involving material items of state, or religious, paraphernalia. The situation in question—the voiding of the state apparatus, its occupation by authoritarian and violent elements, the continual state of emergency, the entrenched cynicism of citizens—was by no means unique to Turkey. An emergent critical literature on sovereignty, in which Giorgio Agamben's and Michel Foucault's well-known work has been central, was shaping compelling new ways of thinking about the state and the citizen globally.[51]

Agamben showed how the antique state drew on a separation of *zoe* and *bios*, of the political life of the citizen and the "bare life" of the body, imagining subjects stripped of the former and reduced to the latter (Agamben 1998). This suggested that the state—the modern state, too—projects its sovereignty in the performances, sacrifices, and rituals gathering around such images of bare life, constructed in zones of exception to the law defined by the law itself. The emphasis on the state's capacity to govern through its sovereign power to define the conditions of life (and, thereby, death) was characterized by Foucault as biopower (Foucault 1979), by Mbembe as necropolitics (Mbembe 2019).[52] If Agamben's formulation, notoriously, allowed little or no space to imagine resistance or dissent or historical transformation, those of Foucault and Mbembe emphatically do. And Mbembe's shifted attention to the postcolonial peripheries, to the states of exceptions in which the contradictions at the heart of the state's performances are more starkly displayed, more obviously pressured by (globalization) migration and climate emergency, more violently played out in terms of security and terror, more blatantly farmed out to private corporations, more aggressively projected on bodies (terrorists, migrants, refugees) positioned beyond the law by the law.

Agamben's picture of the deep philological structures that underpin such (violent) performances of the state's sovereignty has been substantially reinforced by the global coronavirus pandemic of 2020. Bio-citizenship, the configuration of an entire—indeed, global—form of governmentality around public health, is by now a dully familiar concept, thanks to the coronavirus pandemic. The responsibilities of the state and the rights of citizens, now starkly opposed in debates polarizing "the economy" and "public health," take shape in the air we breathe and in the content of our bloodstreams.

Philosopher Paolo Preciado strikes a philological note suggesting that the virus not only defines community (those who pay the *munus*: i.e., tax or tribute) and immunity (those exempted from such responsibility), but also what he calls '*de*-munity' (those who might be "stripped from community privileges after having been declared a threat to the community"; Preciado 2020). The sequestering of the "demune"—old people in their care homes, university students in their dormitories—is secured by sovereign public performances of "immunity' that seem to come from another age. How closely we have learned to study the frailty of the new (and supposedly immune) sovereign bodies for signs of their struggles for breath, the clarity of their diction, the tone of their skin, the light in their eyes; how utterly precarious these performances are! But they are all that are needed, it would seem, to sustain an intensifying fantasy (or nightmare) of the state extending across the entirety of the political body and penetrating our own at ever-deepening levels. Agamben's rather static and ahistorical picture of sovereign power, arguably reproduced in Preciado's discussion of the virus, has been significantly complicated by the new populism. Those thinking through sovereignty, with Agamben, in the wake of the Iraq invasion and occupation tended to dwell on questions of war, terrorism, and states of exception. Following the financial crashes of the millennium, they increasingly focused on questions about the relationship between sovereignty and the economy. The rise of Donald Trump and Boris Johnson has suggested a new script for sovereignty, one of performative "enjoyment," as Mazzarella, Santner, and Schuster have recently argued (Mazzarella, Santner, and Schuster 2020). In part this has involved the representation of their opponents on the left as killjoys, elitists committed to negating popular pleasures, to "cancel culture." And in part it has involved a representation of the populist 'sovereign' as a carnivalesque and chaotic site of enjoyment, reveling in mistakes, contradictions, and non sequiturs; flouting basic norms of propriety and civility; engaged in extravagant displays of time-wasting self-indulgence, verbal and otherwise. Citizens are no longer enjoined to self-regulate, to maximize their economic capital. They are called instead to a kind of "jouissance," a participation in the pleasures of the figure of the sovereign, a threshold state between rational economic behavior and something else, something beyond. These give shape to the "fundamental fantasies that make multitudes governable," Mazzarella, Santner, and Schuster observe (2020, 5).

The picture Mazzarella, Santner, and Schuster present may not on the surface appear an optimistic one concerning citizenship. But the new forms of governmentality they identify are, in the first instance, risky and unstable (as the chaotic end of Trump's presidency was later to reveal).[53] They are, in the final analysis, performative; performativity admits the intrusion of extraneous elements into the flow of events. And, in the second, they render such forms of governmentality recognizable to the citizen. If they shape the "fundamental fantasies" of citizenship, they also shape how citizens themselves might hold their governments to account, or at least, find them wanting. This is still, of course, hardly an "optimistic" picture of things. But it prompts recognition of some of the longer-term historical processes that shape democratic culture. The late-liberal nation-state in the Global North may have changed beyond recognition, and its citizenship narratives, already "shambling and incomplete" (Kidron 2020) may now be in a state of crisis. But something is always emergent in such situations.

The new literature on sovereignty, with its emphasis on performativity, has shown us where we might look—and where to listen, too. Sound, after all, seems close to the surface of these performativities. They are hard to imagine, for instance, without summoning to mind the timbral qualities of Trump's (or Orban's, or Erdoğan's, or Bolsinaro's) political oratory, the populist values associated with them, and the ears that have become receptive to them—indeed, yearn for them. Mazzarella, Santner, and Schuster's observations about sovereign jouissance point to a kind of conviviality that may, too, have significant sonic or musical components. Maria Sonevytsky (whose work I will discuss in more detail in Chapter 2) makes a related point regarding the "wildness" cultivated by today's popular musicians in Ukraine (Sonevytsky 2019). Sovereign power might exploit that wildness. But today's musicians might also use it to imagine new spaces of dissent. Because wildness, in Ukraine, involves a radical state of openness and receptivity to not just human but non-human "others." It has, as Sonevytsky shows, proved fertile ground for the imagination of new citizenship practices in unpromising circumstances.

1.6 Conclusion

The current interest in citizenship in ethnomusicology takes shape, then, against a rich and still-evolving background of thinking about listening, mediation, voice, and sovereignty. The reference points in this discussion have been anthropology, sociology, cultural studies, literary theory, film theory, and analytic and continental philosophy, as well as more recent interdisciplinary field like sound studies and vocal studies. This discussion establishes, clearly enough, then, that ethnomusicologists are not asking the questions they do about citizenship in a vacuum, or in a relationship of dependence upon anthropology. It also suggests that the question "what does music (or ethnomusicology) *add*" is somewhat misdirected. Music, if we start with Rousseau, has been central to these currents of thought from the outset, not a supplement. And what we might now call "ethnomusicological" questions about citizenship can trace at least some of their origins to Rousseau's questions about "Ranz des Vaches." It is not simply the case, then, that ethnomusicologists have turned up late to the party. They were there at the very beginning—before they even knew they were ethnomusicologists.

The more pressing question is what ethnomusicologists might do to keep these long-standing conversations about citizenship open and productive. The metaphor that comes to mind is that of a delta. In a delta, waterways merge and diverge because of alluvial flows. They slow down because of silting, forcing unpredictable sideways movements and connections with neighboring channels ('avulsion'), whose waterflow it momentarily strengthens before succumbing to the same inevitable process. The landscape appears, from certain angles, chaotic and unmappable. But it has its own logic, and is a scene of fertility, too. Things spring to life in it. I am suddenly thinking about flying north out of Cairo airport and the vision of dazzling green after the city's ochre dust. The view from the air is breathtaking.

Two questions spring to mind, if I might extend the delta metaphor further. One, if we picture ourselves navigating it, is how we might do so with a bit of freedom—freedom to hurry along or dawdle and admire the view, freedom to hail others or to find a solitary spot. The other, if we picture ourselves as the temporary guardians of a patch of land and its waterways, is what we might do—as we navigate—to sustain the broader ecosystem, to keep it open for those who might follow. The question is not one of destinations, or the speed with which we attain them. What destination, after all? Deltas end in mud. But if we think of the intellectual and critical terrain discussed in this chapter in these terms, we might see that ethnomusicologists are moving along more quickly, and in fresher water, than they perhaps realize. I will explore this contention in the next chapter, a review of recent ethnomusicological literature on citizenship.

I also want to connect it to the rather specific ecologies of music study. I attempt to do so in the final chapter, Chapter 3, with the aid of three case studies, "the citizen on his bike," "the citizen in the crowd," and "the citizen in the square." They are drawn mainly from my own ethnographic work, reading, and reflection. I delve into them to show how questions about music and citizenship might connect with current thinking in our field about mobility and disability, about multitudes and the collective political subject, about protest and activism today. This agenda does not exhaust the field of inquiry, obviously, or offer a comprehensive map of it. Other topics—sexuality, race, and environment, for instance—while certainly not neglected here, might well have been thematized more explicitly. The intention is, though, to push some rather specific understandings of the relationship between music and democratic practice back toward more general questions.

Two of these three case studies (the citizen on his bike and the citizen in the square) reflect a long-standing focus in my own longstanding interest in the Middle East and North Africa (henceforth MENA) region. This area studies bias is not at all irrelevant to my topic. The question of citizenship is a sharp and uncomfortable one in MENA, not least the question of how we look at it from afar, in the wake of recent neocolonial military ventures in Iraq, Libya, and Afghanistan; the ongoing civil wars in Syria and Yemen; the seemingly unsolvable Israel/Palestine and Armenia/Azerbaijan conflicts; the Arab Spring and the entrenchment of (Western-backed) authoritarianism across the region; the "migrant crisis" and the rise of Islamophobia in Western Europe. Some of these questions have been signaled already, if a little obliquely, through the figure of Zeki Müren. I will return to them more directly in the concluding chapter of this book. Suffice it to say here that I consider this vantage point important as we wrestle with question of citizenship today, and not, as we often seem happy to believe, a zone of exception to rules established elsewhere. This view will make more sense in broader perspective, in discussions of music and citizenship located in Latin America, South and East Asia, Europe and sub-Saharan Africa. It is to them I now turn.

Notes

1. The North Circular Road, planned in 1910, completed in the 1930s, upgraded in the 1960s, and still an object of complaint and protest today, constitutes a 45-mile ring around Central London, along with its poor (though undoubtedly nicer) sister, the South Circular Road. In popular parlance it is known as the "North Circular."
2. For a short history of Citizens Assemblies, see, particularly, O'Leary 2019. Her account is mainly focused on their role in the Irish "Same-Sex Marriage" and "Abortion" Referendums in 2015 and 2017 respectively, which prompted major changes in legislation in favor of both. Gerwin 2018 is a statement of political advocacy, based on the author's own involvement in the first Citizens' Assembly in Sopot, Poland. It concentrates largely on formal matters, but devotes some space to the question of attentive listening. The Citizens' Assembly website tells the English side of the story from the perspective of the Sheffield academics who had initiated the 2012 and 2015 assemblies in that city. This, too, is in advocacy mode, but informative on the debates about pressing devolution issues in the United Kingdom (https://citizensassembly.co.uk/democracy-matters/sheffield/).
3. O'Leary primarily wanted to suggest that Citizens' Assemblies were unlikely to have supplied an answer to the (ongoing) Brexit crisis. This stance acknowledges that Brexit might be understood, still, as a crisis of national listening.
4. We have been satirizing our belief in the civic powers of that "cup of tea" on these islands since the time of Alexander Pope, after all. Pope's *The Rape of the Lock* of 1712 wryly documents its protagonist, Belinda's, tea, coffee, and chocolate habits, and his age's assumptions about their civilizing properties. See Canto IV: "Oh had I rather unadmir'd remain'd / In some lone isle, or distant northern land; / Where the gilt chariot never marks the way / Where none learn ombre, none e'er taste bohea!"
5. I refer to Boris Johnson's Conservative Party's landslide election victory in December 2017. Its winning slogan was "Get Brexit Done." Labour, the main opposition party, had failed to connect with the Brexit issue from the outset, and proved unable to counter it.
6. Scott Burnham's *Beethoven Hero* (Burnham 1995), contextualized in debates in music analysis going back to the nineteenth century, established significant new terms for critique of the myths of Beethoven heroic style. Laura Tunbridge's anniversary year *Beethoven: A Life in Nine Pieces* (Tunbridge 2020) explores the checkered history of these myths in

a subtle narrative woven around key compositions, which all tell unexpected stories.
7. "Any biography of Beethoven is in fact a portrait of the universal artist, and demonstrates that the most fascinating careers are never straightforward. Granted, the young Beethoven was incredibly talented, but his genius was the result of the determination and imagination with which he responded to the obstacles in his path. In this sense, he is the prototypical modern citizen who, regardless of background or origin, can take control of their life in order to achieve greatness." For an example of the promotional literature in Bonn's festivities, see *Beethoven: World, Citizen, Music* (https://www.bundeskunsthalle.de/en/beethoven.html). Hörl's Beethoven sculpture project—"inviting [the public] to form a new idea of Beethoven"—is perhaps best introduced to those who do not know it via his own website, https://www.ottmar-hoerl.de/en/projects/2019/Mai/Ludwig_van_Beethoven_engl.php.
8. I am very grateful to Michael Fend, for sharing a draft of this chapter some years ago, early in the process of writing this book, and to Giuliano Danieli for conversations and some Italian press clippings on the subject.
9. Twelve do (see bibliography). By my reckoning, a further thirty-one in this bibliography, located squarely within recent ethnomusicology, reference the term in chapter or section headings, footnotes, index entries, or comments extensive enough to indicate a more than casual engagement with the concept.
10. Robert Adlington's project in Huddersfield, focusing on the Western tradition and its key musical institutions, is the significant exception in recent years. See Adlington and Buch 2020.
11. The key names in the modern "civic" republican tradition, as reflected in that volume, are those of Jean Jacques Rousseau (1762/1968), John Locke (Locke 1689/1988), T.H Marshall (Marshall 1950/1983), and Hannah Arendt (Arendt 1951).
12. The work of the Manchester School, revolving around Max Gluckmann, was central to this concept, extending the preoccupations of Edward Evans-Pritchard's "political anthropology" into the sub-Saharan African "Copper Belt" cities. A key point of reference in this tradition is Clyde Mitchell's *The Kalela Dance* (Mitchell 1959), especially worth mentioning here because of its focus on music and dance.
13. Naila Kabeer's edited volume, *Inclusive Citizenship: Meanings and Expressions*, is perhaps the most systematic effort to theorize citizenship from the bottom-up perspectives of everyday language, a language that, she underlines, is "horizontal" (concerned with citizen-citizen

relationship, not citizen-state relations), and which engages with supranational solidarities organically (Kabeer 2005).
14. On the senses and citizenship see in particular Trnka, Dureau, and Park 2013, which was the first edited collection to bring affect theory systematically to bear on the emergent anthropology of citizenship.
15. I chose the expression "music study" to indicate today's gestures toward a more inclusive, less hierarchical conception of 'musicology.' There are strong—and good—arguments against Nicholas Cook's proposition that "we are all (ethno)musicologists now" (Cook 2008), however. See, among others, Nooshin 2016.
16. I worked through the connections between these singers, across different historical periods, and different popular cultural regimes, devoting a chapter to each, in *The Republic of Love: Cultural Intimacy in Turkish Popular Music* (Stokes 2010b).
17. I refer to author Edip Özışık, whose positive interest was, no doubt, motivated by his efforts to promote the work of his brother, who composed for Zeki Müren. The sustained terms of this discussion are of interest, though. For those who can read Turkish, see Özışık 1963; alternatively, see Chapter 3 of Stokes 2010.
18. Mauss developed the concept of the 'total social fact' in his classic study of the gift, embracing "legal, economic, religious, aesthetic, morphological and so on" elements that weave an entire society together (Mauss 1966, 76).
19. On rebetika in Greece see Tragaki 2007; on sevdalinka in Bosnia see Pennanen 2010; on enka in Japan see Yano 2003; on fado in Portugal, see Gray 2013; on dangdut in Indonesia see Weintraub 2010; on sertaneja in Brazil see Reily 1992, among others.
20. A number of studies focus on the role of small media in the construction of these "civil" transnational imaginaries, and music—embedded in sentimental literature and film—is often central to these discussions. For a wide-ranging analysis focusing on Chinese transnationalisms beyond China, and a discussion of popular icon Grace Chang extremely relevant to this discussion, see Jones 2020.
21. See note 17.
22. He made over his entire estate to the Mehmetçik Vakfı, a military foundation in Turkey, on his death.
23. The compensatory and "symptomatic" dimensions of the microperformative are a vital theme in Navaro-Yashin's analysis of a slightly later moment in Turkey's pre-Erdoğan history, to be discussed in more detail below. See Navaro-Yashin 2002.

24. I encountered it in written form in Bülent Aksoy's liner notes for the double CD of Müren's early TRT recordings (Aksoy 2002).
25. The passage in question is this: "*Chez les anciens on se faisait entendre aisément au peuple sur la place publique; on y parlait tout un jour sans s'incommoder. Les généraux haranguaient leurs troupes; on les entendait, et ils ne s'épuisaient point. Les historiens modernes qui ont voulu mettre des harangues dans leurs histoires se sont fait moquer d'eux. Qu'on suppose un homme haranguant en français le peuple de Paris dans la place de Vendôme: qu'il crie à pleine tête, on entendra qu'il crie, on ne distinguera pas un mot. Hérodote lisait son histoire aux peuples de la Grèce assemblés en plein air, et tout retentissait d'applaudissements. Aujourd'hui, l'académicien qui lit un mémoire, un jour d'assemblée publique, est à peine entendu au bout de la salle. Si les charlatans des places abondent moins en France qu'en Italie, ce n'est pas qu'en France ils soient moins écoutés, c'est seulement qu'on ne les entend pas si bien. M. d'Alembert croit qu'on pourrait débiter le récitatif français à l'italienne; il faudrait donc le débiter à l'oreille, autrement on n'entendrait rien du tout. Or, je dis que toute langue avec laquelle on ne peut pas se faire entendre au peuple assemblé est une langue servile; il est impossible qu'un peuple demeure libre et qu'il parle cette langue-là*" (Rousseau 1762/1993, 125–126). I draw here (though I came across it only late in the day) on Mondelli's thought-provoking account of French Revolutionary singing practices (Mondelli 2016) as well as on Rouget's interpretation of the "Ranz des Vaches" episode in the *Essai* (Rouget 2015).
26. Such as the Federalist Theater in Boston, founded in the 1790s, rivaled by the Republican Haymarket Theater. See Butsch for further discussion (Butsch 2008, 25).
27. Butsch cites the *Spirit of the Times*, a "news paper of leisure for affluent sporting men," to give a flavor of the mood in 1847. "The pit is a vast sea of upturned faces and . . . red flannel shirts, extending its roard and turbid waves close up to the footlights on either side, clipping the orchestra and dashing furiously against the boxes—while a row of lucking and stronger shouldered amateurs have pushed, pulled and trampled their way far in advance of the rest, and actually stand with their chins resting on the stage. And now Mr. Jack Scott makes his appearance in one of his favorite characters and is greeted with a pandemoniac yell as he rushes with gigantic strides down to the front . . . at length, after executing a series of the most diabolical grimaces, during which the sympathies of the audience have been working themselves up to a pitch of intense excitement . . . At this thrilling spectacle the enthusiasm of the audience finds vent in a perfect

tornado and maelstrom united of 'hi hi's,' cat-calls, screamings, whistlings and stampings. 'That's it Jack,' 'Give him thunder you old buster,' 'hurrah for Scott!,' 'Oh, get of[f] my toes,' 'Put your toes in your hat!' 'I say you Jo Jackson up in the third tier! Come down here and I'll kick yer into fits!'" (Butsch 2008, 28).

28. Central coordinates in this by now very well-established discussion include, in addition to Cavicchi 2011, Thompson 2002, and Erlmann 2010. Film theory has played a particularly important role, so Hansen 1991 must be mentioned as well, among others who have brought the question of the viewing and listening subject together. All are dialectically sensitive to the question of turning points and the "litanies" (Sterne 2003) that are routinely used to oppose hearing (and viewing) before and after "modernity," however defined.

29. As Butsch observes (Butsch 2008, 117–125), American media theorists tended to be more interested in what "mass audiences" were *not* doing, rather than what they were, always assuming mass media meant isolation and alienation. It was only the work of Paul Lazarsfield at Princeton and then Columbia in the 1940s that would turn this around, focusing on how media audiences interacted, and watched and listened as groups. Solitude in the crowd could perhaps be described as *the* fundamental trope of American cultural critique (see Putnam 2000). Regarding the threats a non-regulated radio might pose, Representative Luther Johnson put the matter this way in 1927: "It will only be a few years before these broadcasting stations, if operated by chain stations (networks), will simultaneously reach an audience of over half our entire citizenship . . . American thought and American politics will largely be at the mercy of those who operate these stations . . . then woe to those who differ with them" (cited in Butsch 2008, 85). The language might stay the same, with each successive new media "revolution," but the anxieties—and backward-projected fantasies about truly "democratic" media—would seem only to grow, as the current Facebook debates suggest.

30. See Stokes 2020a, an effort to see these complications within the Turkish national context in the 1980s.

31. The Turkish part of the story is only just beginning to be told (see, for instance, Aksoy 2019), but most of the evidence is still anecdotal. A generation of Kurdish singers, like Şiwan Perwer, were obliged to leave the country. The mere possession of his cassettes, listened to across Kurdish Turkey, put those who owned them in serious trouble. Şiwan Perwer joined a long line of Kurdish-speaking musicians born in Turkey or on its borderlands who have made their living elsewhere, such as Mehmet

Şexo, Eyşe Şan, and Aram Tigran, typical of musicians from an earlier generation who managed to make some kind of career for themselves in Baghdad, Yerevan, or Athens.

32. On the Frankfurt school and popular culture, there is, of course a vast literature. Richard Leppert's edition and Susan Gillespie's translation of Theodor Adorno's writings on music continues to be indispensable (Adorno 2002). On the broader historical and political contexts in which Gramsci's writing was absorbed by the British New Left (and thence into "Birmingham School" cultural studies), see Kenny 1995.
33. In film studies see in particular Hansen 1991. For a more theoretically explicit statement in anthropology, see Mazzarella 2004.
34. The key philosophical statement on posthumanism and democracy is Braidotti 2013. On cyborg citizenship, see Gray 2001.
35. On "Sophia," see Emily Reynold's sobering reminder of what citizenship in Saudi Arabia actually means for those (human beings) who live there (Reynolds 2018). On Saudi Arabia's driving-law changes, and what they conceal, see Begum 2018, and on the status of migrants in Saudi Arabia, see Human Rights Watch 2020.
36. Meşk is the common term used in Turkey to describe face-to-face learning in the arts and music from a recognized authority, with greater or lesser degrees of formality.
37. The key (indeed, classic) ethnomusicological texts in what we might call "groove and participation theory" are Keil and Feld 1994, and Turino 2008.
38. The anthropologist in me cannot quite resist putting scare quotes around the word. The subculture theorists were not at all invested in theorizing ritual and seemed to have little interest in what anthropologists had to say on the matter.
39. Subcultural theory had little to say about the prospects for democracy and citizenship in the world of the "parent culture"—the "grown-up" world of voting, party politics, and political representation. In a recent book about democracy in the European Union, Perry Anderson wonders whether political representation in liberal democracy is "an act of a basically aesthetic nature . . . an effect of style, beyond fact or value" (Anderson 2021). The European Union, he remarks, currently faces a question about representation that has "haunted Western politics since the Enlightenment." Its dominant political philosophy, associated with the Amsterdam School, understands representation in "basically aesthetic" terms. Such a concept pictures the representative as capable of winning the assent of those represented, but also as being capable of pursuing the creative compromises and alliances required by democratic politics. Populists

across the continent, meanwhile, stress the "biometric," and attack the ("European") alternatives as elitist and inauthentic. This is a precarious situation, and the (European) citizen has hard choices to make. The two alternatives are, clearly, open to abuse, both capable of obscuring the machinations of power, and, indeed, corruption. The crisis is only partly to do with the ever-growing plausibility of the "biometric" sign, and the concomitant rejection of mediation, negotiation, and compromise (residually at play, Anderson implies, in the "aesthetic"). It is also one of the citizenry's depleted skills in imagining the signs of democracy in any other terms.

40. Proust and Mahler are discussed throughout Nussbaum 2001.
41. Though it takes a very different route, so, too, does Ariana Phillips-Hutton's important critique of empathy in the use of music in conflict resolution; see Phillips-Hutton 2020. The broader critical configurations of ethnomusicology's "emotional turn" are explained and outlined in Garcia 2015, particularly relevant here for its location of the question of "affective citizenship" within it.
42. Moten 2003 is central to this problem. Feldman's thinking about the relevance of Black radical aesthetics to musicology are worth mentioning in passing at this point (Feldman 2021); see also note 48.
43. I discussed this incident at the beginning of my *Republic of Love* (Stokes 2010b), though I did so without the benefit of some TRT and backstage mobile phone footage that I only recently discovered, showing the sad aftermath of the interview in graphic detail. Readers who really want to see this for themselves can find it, at the time of writing, with a quick search online in Turkish.
44. The principal points of reference in the critical discussion of voices and sounds as "objects" in search of "subjects"—in other words, within or adjacent to the framework of "acousmatic" theory—are Dolar 1996, Eidsheim 2019, Feldman and Zeitlin 2019, Kane 2014, Middleton 2006, Steintrager with Chow 2019, and Žižek 1996.
45. As Martha Gellhorn put it concerning Vallée in 1929 in the *New Republic*: "He is their darling, 'their song lover.' He is the best yet. Rudy Valentino wasn't in it. The dead are forgotten anyhow. Nobody's in it. Give us Rudy Vallée. Give us this tall, slender, simple boy, with his blond, wavy hair, his tanned face, his blue eyes, and his gentle voice that makes love so democratically to everyone. He is, indeed, the best yet" (Gellhorn 1929/2012, 318).
46. The literature on the anxieties about voice in the early talkies era has been conveniently gathered in Taylor, Katz, and Grajeda's anthology

(Taylor, Katz, and Grajeda 2018). See, for an overview, Taylor's 'General Introduction' (Taylor 2012).
47. Kaja Silverman's work has been central here, bringing gender theory to bear on the question as a means of pushing Chion's acousmatic question against the grain. See, in particular, Silverman 1988.
48. The elusive and highly complex relationship he maps between "sound" and "voice" being one of them (Feldman 2021, 12–13).
49. The complexity and richness of the challenge of timbre to musicology is explored systematically in Dolan and Rehding 2021. From the time of Adler, they note, it has either been "other" to musicology's central projects, or a "wastebasket category" (2021, 22), into which all sorts of things that do not fit elsewhere and make themselves readily available as musicological or music theoretical "facts" get chucked. An alternative (Western) music history might be written, stretching between Rousseau and Schonberg, and engaging with various moments of self-conscious musical renewal in between. Anthropologists arguably have less at stake, less "history" as far as the term 'timbre' is concerned. Harkness (2015a) points to its slipperiness in relation to anthropological theorizations of voice, subsuming it under the broader semiotic category of qualia—an array of metapragmatic sign-making activities that organize spatial and social (i.e., deictic) relationships in the act of speech, drawing speakers' and listeners' attention to the (social, political, moral) dimensions of the interaction itself.
50. I am grateful to Beyza Boyacıoğlu, who has kept me in touch with this fascinating project from the outset.
51. An important anthropological agenda regarding sovereignty was established by Begona Aretxaga (Aretxaga 2003).
52. Foucault's thinking can be evoked with his statement, in the *History of Sexuality*, that biopolitical power is "a right of seizure: of things, time, bodies and ultimately life itself; it culminated in the privilege to seize hold of life in order to supress it" (Foucault 1979, 137). Mbembe's conception of biopolitics can be succinctly summarized in his observation, in *Necropolitics*, that "nearly everywhere the political order is reconstituting itself as a form of organization for death. Little by little, a terror that is molecular in essence and allegedly defensive is seeking legitimation by blurring the relations between violence, murder, and the law, faith, commandment, and obedience, the norm and the exception, and even freedom, tracking, and security. No longer is the concern to eliminate, via the law and justice, murder from the books of life in common. Every occasion is now one in which the supreme stake is to be risked. Neither the

human-of-terror, nor the terrorized human—both of them new substitutes for the citizen—foreswear murder" (Mbembe 2019, 7).

53. I refer to the storming of the Capitol building in Washington, DC, incited by Donald Trump on 6 January 2021 when it became clear he was going to lose the elections to (current) President Joe Biden. At the time of writing, it continues to be very hard to know what the long-term consequences of this will be.

2
Ethnomusicology of Citizenship, Ethnomusicology as Citizenship

Ethnomusicology's engagement with the term started under the rubric of 'sonic citizenship' (Stoever-Ackermann 2011, O'Toole 2014, and Adrisani 2015).[1] The qualifier 'sonic' soon disappeared. The word 'citizenship' shifted to the right of the colon in book and article titles, merging with a string of others. Later, it would filter down into chapter headings, conclusions, footnotes, and index entries. This might look like a burst of energy followed by a dilution. But my contention in this chapter is more or less the opposite. It suggests to me, rather, that the term has been absorbed at deeper and deeper levels, and in ever-widening circles. This makes it a somewhat difficult field to parse. I will explore three trajectories of the term here, labeling them, in turn, 'identity,' 'technocracy,' and 'intimacy.'

These are provisional labels at best. Some of the texts I discuss under one heading might equally be considered under another. Discussions about identity politics and intimacy are closely related, for instance. The level of absorption in each differs, so the term "citizenship" might be relatively close to the surface of one, distant from it in another. The temporal frameworks of each do not align particularly well, either. In some I range further in time than in others. They will, however, help me construct a wide-angled picture of how ethnomusicology has engaged with the idea of citizenship in recent years—an exercise in parallel play, I argue, rather than concerted theorizing. The conclusion to the chapter is a brief attempt to evaluate the ethnomusicological field and to see where it might go.

Music and Citizenship. Martin Stokes, Oxford University Press. © Oxford University Press 2023.
DOI: 10.1093/oso/9780197555187.003.0002

2.1 Identity

Citizenship has been defined as a "fantasy of political belonging without Others."[2] Another way of putting this might be "a fantasy of political belonging without 'identity.'" This is both a provocative and an ambiguous formulation. Does the word 'fantasy' suggest forms of displacement or substitution that pull, nonetheless, toward the inclusive political community? Or does it suggest the very opposite—a masking of structural exclusions and social injustices that ensures it will never be reached?

We could approach music, similarly, as a "fantasy of cultural belonging without Others"—at least, in the West. Those who insist on understanding it with other eyes and ears risk censure. Inquiries into Beethoven's Whiteness or Bach's masculinity continue to rattle those committed to the idea that their music is "universal," and that discussion of them is somehow exempt from such lines of inquiry.[3] Both of these terms—citizenship and music—seem particularly resistant to thinking in terms of identity. Identity has, consequently, been indispensable to critical thinking in both areas over the last two or three decades.

But reaction has set in. In ethnomusicology, "identity" is now regarded with a measure of suspicion. To explore things in identity terms is to invite the charge, by some, of complicity with the ethnic logic of the nation-state, with violent difference-making, with the negation of histories of cosmopolitanism and musical exchange with neighbors.[4] The multicultural state, in which "identity" takes administrative and bureaucratic shape, only compounds the problem.[5] The critiques are, necessarily, cautious, however. Ongoing racial-justice issues reframe and reanimate the debates over identity politics; "multiculturalism," under sustained attack by the political right, continues to have thoughtful defenders. Arguments against identity could now be said to have the floor, but it has not, it would seem, been entirely banished.

The question of citizenship offers an opportunity for ethnomusicologists to engage with the critiques of identity, while attending to longer-standing issues of race and ethnicity. Citizenship has, after all, historically been construed as the only possible alternative to nation-state belonging defined in ethnic and racial terms. The latter have, however, never been far from the surface. The contradictions and confusions are, as often as not, quickly noticeable in music. Early efforts to think this through have, unsurprisingly, been cautious in their claims about citizenship. Avelar and Dunn's *Brazilian Popular Music and Citizenship* of 2011, for example, describes musical practice as both "agent and image of citizenship"—a pithy and useful formulation (Avelar and Dunn 2011, 1). They propose a postcolonial concept of 'cultural' citizenship extending Marshall's influential definition of 'civic,' 'political,' and 'social,' citizenship sequentially (Marshall 1950/1983). Marshall had shown how "social" citizenship in the post–Second World War social-democratic West was inflected by the hegemony of a technocratic middle class, who saw political participation in terms of self-management and studious interiority. In the postcolonial states of Latin America, and in Brazil in particular, however, Avelar and Dunn argue that 'cultural citizenship' meant something rather different.

Here it was, to a great extent, a top-down way of managing difference. Brazilian nation-building had to reconcile the very different experiences of former slaves, indigenous people, and immigrants, and vast differences of wealth and opportunity. Music provided a particularly effective means of doing so (Reily 1994). It took on authoritarian meanings quickly. Vargas's samba cult lay at the heart of his Estado Novo, as David Treece shows (Treece 2013). Brazilians could thereby be invited to dance, party, and enjoy themselves, and, most importantly perhaps, occupy themselves in huge numbers in the organization of its major festivals. If it was a celebration of Blackness, it was one choreographed by the state to make something specifically "Brazilian" of it. "Cultural citizenship" stems in part from the instrumental use of culture to discipline and instruct the masses, according to a certain vision of racial cooperation cultivated by Brazil's ruling cliques and technocratic elites. Such instrumental (and instrumentalizing) views of culture and citizenship survived the transition from authoritarianism to neoliberalism more or less intact (Moehn 2011)—a familiar story elsewhere.[6]

The refusal to romanticize citizenship in Avelar and Dunn's book is helpful. So, too, is the idea of music as "agent and image of citizenship," a formulation I will come back to repeatedly. The questions it leaves, however, are "to whom, to what groups of people, does such agency attach?" and "whose image?" Avelar and Dunn tend to see things in top-down terms—musical signs of ethnicity and race "tamed" to validate authoritarian and neoliberal citizenship cultures. Such agencies and images might well be experienced "from below" differently. Two recent studies bearing the word "citizenship" prominently in their titles start from exactly this premise.

The first of these is Ilana Webster-Kogen's *Citizen Amari: Making Ethiopian Music in Tel Aviv*, a complex and revealing case of the conflicting pulls between race and citizenship (Webster-Kogen 2018). "Ethiopianess" in Israel is an extremely fraught category with regard to both. Those who claimed Jewish roots in Ethiopia ("Beta Israel") once lived mainly as smiths, potters, and ironworkers. A major wave of immigration to Israel took place in the mid-1980s, following the dramatic airlifting of refugees from the Sudanese border by the Israeli Air Force. In Israel, the "Etyopim" immediately provoked broad debate about whether they really were Jews or not, and they have continued to be marginalized. Webster-Kogen attributes this marginalization to inflexible top-down conceptions of integration, to the decline of traditional routes to Israeli citizenship (primarily military and labor), and to diminishing state support for groups pushed to the social and economic margins. There is a significant measure of racism in this situation, too, as she notes.

These factors have stimulated a variety of more or less strategic musical engagements with Blackness and Africanicity among Ethiopian-Israelis, which she distinguishes as Ethiopianist, Afrodiasporic, and Zionist. The first is exemplified by nostalgic repackagings of Ethiopian culture in bars and restaurants, involving traditional instruments such as *krar*, traditional dances such as *eskesta*, and the use of the Ethiopian musical modes (*qingit*). The second, exemplified by singer Ester Rada, is "a composite Afrodiasporic style comprising soul, reggae, jazz, gospel, and Ethio-jazz" (Webster-Kogen 2018, 19), sung in English, enabling a degree of mobility on the World Music stage.[7] The third, exemplified by the Idan Rachel Project, locates Ethiopian sounds within an Israeli melting-pot ideology, reaching out and integrating musicians from various different immigrant backgrounds within Israel, and beyond.

Weaving between, and strategically blending these options, Ethiopian musicians "navigate their uncertain status in Israeli society through sound with an effectiveness notably lacking in political organization and community work" (Webster-Kogen 2018, 8). This evaluation depends, to a certain extent, on exactly what is meant by the word 'effective' and how it might be measured. But what is intended, clearly, is an acknowledgment of the aesthetic domain. This is encapsulated by the Ethiopian expression 'wax and gold' (*sem-enna-werq*), which refers, specifically to the poetics of the Azmari, the traditional Ethiopian bards. It is associated with praise singing and "naming": in other words, the maintenance of political hierarchies. But it is also understood by Azmari to be set apart from these hierarchies. From our perspective, we might say that the one cannot entirely be reduced to the other.

At root, "wax and gold" is a sensibility to the relationship between meaning and sound specific to the Semitic languages. Here, typically, clusters of meaning adhere to three-consonant verbal roots. Inflections of these roots ('voweling') add not only syntactic structure but also bring adjacent fields of metaphor into play. Skilled vocal performance among experienced and intelligent listeners navigates these metaphorical and syntactical fields, playing on ambiguities, evoking multiple and sometimes contradictory meanings. The meanings (and ambiguities) of words depend on their placing in the song, and on the skill of the vocalist to place them well. In the Amharic context, it means poets can praise and taunt at the same time. Those praised have good reason to fear (and court) these poets' powers. In the Israeli context, it means vocalists can signal seriousness and moral purpose as they use their music to negotiate a minoritized status there.

The second is Siv B. Lie's *Django Generations: Hearing, Ethnorace, Citizenship and Jazz Manouche in France* (Lie 2021). This explores the heritage of France's "Manouche," a community of Roma long resident in France, particularly concentrated in the Alsace region. Their association with jazz goes back to Django Reinhardt and the Quintette du Hot Club du Paris (founded by Reinhardt, himself Manouche, in 1934). But the emergence of "Jazz Manouche" is a significantly later phenomenon. In the latter decades of the twentieth century, French Manouche began to share their interests in jazz and folk music with

German Sinti (the predominant Roma community there), then enjoying some attention in Germany's nascent World Music scene. A repertory of Hungarian and Romanian folk music (particularly the *czardas*) began to inflect the genre in France and underline its Roma identity. Meanwhile, Roma activist groups such as APPONA ("L'Association pour la Promotion des Populations d'Origine Nomade d'Alsace") were looking for expressions of Roma identity that might further their advocacy for Manouche rights.

French citizenship resolutely refuses to acknowledge race or ethnicity as the basis of special claims or differential treatment. Manouche have always, nonetheless, been racially and ethnically marked by the French state. In 1912, Manouche were required by a new law to carry *carnets anthropométriques*, which labeled them 'nomade' and obliged them to check in with the police every three months. Under the Vichy regime they were interned; many were sent to concentration camps. Aggressive sedentarization policies continued after the war, pushing many Manouche into slums. In 1969 the term nomade was officially replaced by supposedly less discriminatory '*Gens du Voyage*.' Though not an explicitly ethnicized term (since it also applied to non-Manouche), sedentarized Manouche, by now the large majority, were labeled "sedentarized *Gens du Voyage*" (Lie 2021, 14). Manouche continue, in other words, to constitute a zone of ambiguity as far as French citizenship is concerned—their identity partially acknowledged, partially obscured, and thereby a significant diagnostic of the problems of France's "color-blind racism" (Eduardo Bonilla-Silva's expression; Lie 2021, 34).

Lie's take on "citizenship" is more explicitly theorized than Webster-Koegen's, but it shares some of the same premises and points of departure. Music, in both cases, is portrayed as how and where a minoritized group redresses the imbalances of *cultural* citizenship, understood broadly as *participation*. Music is a space of public participation, but one that enables the simultaneous address of the minoritized group and the broader society. It serves as a convenient focus for nongovernmental organizations (NGOs) and activists. It is sufficiently unthreatening to the broader society (who have learned to value the entertainment such minoritized groups provide), but sufficiently broad in scope to permit broader citizenship projects (the promotion of health, literacy, education, women's welfare) to take place under its general umbrella. Regional festivals draw attention to the (in)visibility of minoritized groups in historic cities. Music is also, in Lie's view, a zone of creative ambiguity, where the difficulties of reconciling ethnoracial and citizenly belonging can be left strategically unresolved. This gives musicians and their audiences scope to inflect a given musical situation one way or another, according to shifting and situational calculations. Sometimes, as Lie shows, this involves deciding when, and how, and among whom the "jazz" dimension might be emphasized, and when the "Manouche." Sometimes, conversely, it is a matter of stressing Jazz Manouche's "ineffability," the difficulty of putting its Manouche-ness into words. "To say that a sound is ineffable," Lie says neatly, "is to manage ambivalence about the claim one wishes to make" (Lie 2021, 153)—about Manouche citizenship in France, among other things. This ambivalence is a way of keeping the parameters of the discussion open, capable of evolving strategically in the face of ethnonationalist backlash, and the ever-intensifying pressures of neoliberal capitalism.

Both share a certain caution, too. It is not just that it will clearly take more than a few successful festivals or declarations of "heritage" to right historical wrongs dating back centuries (in the case of the Manouche, at least). It is that music is too easily pressed into the service of problematic kinds of ethnic entrepreneuialism. Many of Lie's Manouche interlocutors, for instance, align readily with the French state's desire to see minorities proving their citizenly worth by starting up businesses and becoming successful entrepreneurs. Their citizenship claims become legible to the state, in other words, only within the terms neoliberal capitalism allows. The festivals and sites of activism she describes are complex spaces, then, their music pulled in different directions—by those who see it as a platform from which to promote Manouche citizenship, by those who see music performance itself as a kind of "imaginative labor" toward a more inclusive citizenship (Lie 2021, 187), by those who see it as an opportunity to make money for themselves or hone their artistic reputations. The complexity that both authors stress—seeing musical citizenship *both* from above and below—underlines the impossibility of discerning an ideal citizen, or pure citizenship in such scenes. The focus in both, rather, is on the ways in which ethnographic engagement with a minoritized music might reveal the broader dilemmas of contemporary citizenship.

Webster-Kogen and Lie's approaches resonate in important regards with recent developments in the ethnomusicology of migrants and refugees.[8] The question of citizenship hovers on the edges of this, too. This literature has long been engaged with the problematic legacy of social scientific models of migrancy preoccupied with questions of social change and integration.[9] The Global North's "migrant crisis" of 2015, a confected and aggressively manipulated response to mass flight from the wars in the Middle East and Central America's disintegrating "Northern Triangle" (Guatemala, Honduras, and El Salvador), significantly sharpened ethnomusicological discomfort.[10] An objectivizing social-scientific language—a "map" of the problem of migrancy, as Ozan Aksoy put it (in Rasmussen et al. 2019, 299)—began to seem not only theoretically unattainable but also ethically questionable. The difficulties of fieldwork in refugee camps—difficulties not only of access but also of communication with hard-pressed camp administrators and aid workers—prompted alternative conceptions of what research in such contexts might look like, and what its purpose might be.

Evocations of citizenship in these or related contexts (see, for instance, Wilford 2017 on Algerians in London and Western 2020 on Syrians in Athens) have drawn attention to convergences between researchers and activists, similarly invested in music as a way of sonicizing refugee presence and claims, as means of strengthening solidarity within and between groups of refugees, as a cultivation of the "receptivity, respect, empathy and awareness" (Impey in Rasmussen et al. 2019: 288) essential to democratic and peaceful coexistence, and as an opportunity for pleasure and playfulness, irreducible to other goals. The term citizenship invites reflection on the values researchers and migrant or refugee activists might share, the projects they might set in motion together, the writing, performances, exhibitions, recordings, and other musical happenings they might craft together.[11] It invites reflection, too, on the practices (and distribution) of critical thinking within such scenes, and the manner of its communication. The academic researcher may feel a stronger obligation to reflect, historicize, and contemplate unintended or undesirable consequences. But the researcher is unlikely to be the only one reflecting, historicizing, and contemplating, or indeed writing.[12] It invites reflection, finally, on the prospects and challenges of ethnomusicology *as* citizenship, and not simply an ethnomusicology *of* citizenship. I will return to this distinction at the conclusion of this chapter.

The next section concerns the ethnomusicological literature on what I might label the 'technocratic citizen'—in other words, music and musicians in the cultural bureaucracies of new nation-states. It will develop the idea of music as the "agent and image" of citizenship. It will be concerned, too, with the relationship of the ethnomusicologist to the scenes of citizenship-making they encounter. But it does so in contexts that, quite often, challenge conventional understandings of the relationship of art and music to democratic progress.

A phrase uttered by Mustafa Kemal Atatürk, inscribed in gold lettering above the main concert salon of the national radio station in Istanbul, seems a good place to begin. "The capacity of a nation to embrace change in music is a measure of its capacity to embrace change elsewhere," he opined.[13] I spent many hours of my life in sitting underneath this sign and had committed it to memory long before I could conceptualize its convoluted grammar. It positions music and musicians at the forefront of the secular Turkish state's early twentieth-century efforts to forge new citizens. It is a technocratic image of music modernized by choirs and orchestras, archives, media, and conservatories. It has been an enduring—and dynamic—one. Music's promise to "measure" a citizenry's progress is alluring, but also potentially troubling. Music may not, after all, furnish the evidence technocrats are hoping to find. Where other measures of citizenship are elusive, or not readily available for public discussion, such matters can assume disproportionate importance.[14] Will discussions of "musical citizenship" always be compromised, in such situations? Are they necessarily indicative of authoritarian political cultures, of incomplete "transitions" to democracy?

2.2 Technocracy

The ethnomusicological response to such questions has been ambivalent and betrays a certain anxiety. In context, it is not hard to see why. It was not until the late 1980s that ethnomusicologists in Western Europe and North America began to look with confidence at "traditional" music in state cultural bureaucracies, conservatories, and media systems. Ideals of authenticity had made them an unattractive prospect for an earlier generation. Such institutions were to be regarded, at best, as a natural hazard, to be negotiated like mountain ridges or boggy terrain on the way to one's proper destination. At worst, they were to be seen as a political interference, a censoring force deforming traditional culture to serve a non-democratic agenda. Little was thought to be gained by partnering up, either, with researchers or students associated with these institutions. Attitudes of (polite) mutual suspicion usually prevailed.[15]

Ethnomusicology was changing in the 1980s, however. It was learning to debate its colonial roots and question the veiled politics motivating its research practices and the construction of its objects. The cultural bureaucracies of the new, postcolonial nation-states, with their unapologetic attitude toward the manufacturing of "tradition," no longer seemed quite so "other."[16] Different things were at play. With the political collapse of the Soviet order in 1989, ethnomusicologists with long-standing research interests in Eastern Europe and Central Asia found themselves in a rapidly changing environment. They were now observing their old interlocutors ducking and weaving on the fringes of officialdom, negotiating a bewildering proliferation of agencies and markets both within and beyond the state.[17] The "transition" to a market economy was clearly going to be a very messy business, the term itself already a doubtful one. Musicians, like many others, had very little to guide them. What did their new freedoms actually *mean*, economically and politically?

In 1989 these were unsettling questions for ethnomusicologists, too. The Soviet order ensured that a certain ambivalence among liberal Western scholars about "actually existing socialism" had remained buried. The new orthodoxies of "transition" and an emerging "transitology" laid it bare. Where, in the competing soundscapes of Central and Eastern Europe at that time, was democracy to be *heard*? To take the well-documented case of Bulgaria, for instance, was it to be heard in the music of the Roma—minority professionals, now free to make money, whose music suddenly seemed to capture the energy and optimism of the moment (Rice 1994)? Or in the continuation of the state's folk music tradition there, suddenly forced to justify itself and orient itself to outside markets (Buchanan 2005)? Or in the new freedom to consume—and play—Western rock, pop, or jazz (Levy 2007)? Or in nostalgia for the musical cosmopolitanism of the once disavowed Ottoman past (Buchanan 2007)?

With the passing of time, the issues have become a bit clearer. I would like to discuss two recent ethnographies, Kerstin Klenke's *The Sound State of Uzbekistan: Popular Music and Politics in the Karimov Era* (Klenke 2019) and Nomi Dave's *The Revolutions' Echoes: Music, Politics, and Pleasure in Guinea* (Dave 2019), that lay them out admirably. Turning to the first, Klenke observes at the outset that *estrada*—the popular music with which she is concerned—in Uzbekistan is a topic that might seem uniquely unattractive to ethnomusicologists. It is a cosmopolitan popular music associated with the Soviet imperium. It is produced by a cultural institution of enormous power, the O'zbeknavo Conservatory, which enjoys a palace-like prominence on Tashkent's main square. Its musicians and administrators take pride in their service to the state "in perfecting the people's moral qualities and in educating and raising their aesthetic tastes" (Klenke 2019, 254). In their eyes, this involves the forging of a musical modernity with the judicious incorporation of "national" ("*milli*") elements.[18] "National" estrada thus saturates the airwaves in Uzbekistan with—to outside eyes—saccharine images of touristic beauty spots, of modestly clad women, of cloying expressions of love for the nation and its virtues. It also constitutes—again, to outside eyes—a vast economy, employing thousands, but suffocating them in a punishing, and pointless, round of festivals, competitions, and regional tours.

Musicians in Uzbekistan participate in this system, it would seem, not only willingly, but with a palpable degree of pleasure as well.[19] Klenke points out that this only seems like a problem from the point of view of somebody brought up to believe art and bureaucracy do not mix—somebody who has inherited, in other words, and with whatever degree of acknowledgment and self-awareness, the bourgeoise aesthetic romanticism of the West. The questions we should probably ask, she suggests, are questions about bureaucracy itself. Why does it grow, when common wisdom—in a world of deregulation and supposed market freedoms—suggests it should be in retreat?[20] And how do people accommodate themselves to its growing demands? One explanation for the continued vigor of this mighty cultural bureaucracy in Uzbekistan lies in the continuity of Soviet-era cultural structures, structures of the mind every bit as much as of structures of concrete and steel. It also grows, Klenke suggests, because of the competing claims of NGOs, chief among which, at the time of Klenke's research, was an arts organization (the Fund Forum Uz, or "FFUz") run by the daughter of the President, Gulnora Karimova. What remains of the state system considers itself to be under threat. It has reacted by tightening its grip on the systems that regulate public performance, specifically its monopoly on the distribution (and revoking) of licenses. This monopoly is crucial in pushing up, or down, the '*reyting*' of musicians, ensuring airtime on state media, creating visibility at national festivals and on official tours, and enhancing their standing in the market for wedding music. It is, necessarily, a constant preoccupation for the musicians themselves.

The bureaucratic systems that musicians negotiate in this way requires their active complicity. The word 'complicity' suggests cynicism, strategizing, and general career-mongering. This certainly exists, as Klenke's ethnography amply demonstrates. But so too does belief and pride in what the estrada system has wrought. The one clearly does not necessarily exclude the others.[21] The question is one of how belief in, and commitment to, this all-embracing but extremely rickety system is both generated and managed. Klenke suggests that one answer lies in the ambiguities inherent in bureaucratic language—for example, in the extremely vague ways O'zbeknavo committees and audition juries verbally formulate the "national" and "spiritual" elements they would like to see in estrada. Definitions tend to be drawn in a negative fashion. Sounds and instruments too reminiscent of specific ethnicities (notably Tajik) are proscribed, leaving plenty of room to maneuver with the "traditional" instruments in the ethnic mainstream. Specific references to Islam, in lyrics, in dress, in visual iconography, or in sonic texture, are proscribed, leaving plenty of room for more generalized exhortations to good moral behavior. What is *not* wanted is stated; what *is* wanted is constantly unclear. There is then, on closer inspection, a surprising amount of space in which to innovate and experiment.[22]

The reyting system, too, plays a role in mediating the ambiguities of these proliferating bureaucratic demands. This is an informal system, a way of talking about prestige and symbolic capital among performing artists in Uzbekistan. Movement up the administrative hierarchy, evident in the pecking orders established for national festivals, involves an increase in a singer's perceived reyting. But so, too, does one's status on the wedding and media circuit. Reyting allows musicians to reconcile the conflicting demands of the state and the market, to experience them as a single domain of professional endeavor. It does not always work, as Klenke shows. Musicians are prey to scandals, resulting in lost licenses, or the allocation of punitive administrative loads. As in any sphere of professional life, they get exhausted, disillusioned, or burned out. But, as Klenke emphasizes, it is rarely "the system" itself that is considered the problem. The blame falls, rather, on corrupt or incompetent individuals within it.

The pleasures of citizenly participation in this world would seem, from Klenke's detailed account, to lie mainly in the sociability, stability, and sense of purpose it offers. The music must be a motivating factor, too. It would be hard to imagine otherwise. "National" estrada in Uzbekistan is a complex mix of styles and genres, an amalgam of musical signs, attached to other—non-Uzbek—histories. Listening would seem to be a matter of negotiating a domain of ambiguity, of partially avowed, partially disavowed musical meanings. Tact, judgment, the appropriate choice of words and gestures, and steering ambiguous pleasures in the right direction are presumably valued. But, in such worlds, who listens, with whom and how? And what exactly are these pleasures—and associated social competencies?

Nomi Dave's recent study of the afterlife of revolutionary music in Guinea explores similar questions in a quite different environment. Her research took place among long-standing communities of state-sponsored professionals and the descendants of hereditary praise singers ("*jeliya*") (Dave 2019). The latter, who specialize in the art of "naming," play a central role in music's politics—and pleasures, as Dave consistently stresses—across West Africa. These are very deeply rooted in Guinean society. They are what made Sekou Touré, the country's authoritarian leader, embrace music and musicians in the first place. This embrace ensured livelihoods and a prominent place for musicians in the postcolonial state's imaginary. Musicians reciprocated, for the very large part, with a display of loyalty that lasted generations. Indeed, they lasted long after Touré's death in 1984, as Dave's research a quarter of a century later shows.

Their support was not, of course, unconditional. Even though jeliya families supplied the professional expertise the postcolonial state required, they found themselves treated with a degree of suspicion. They were associated, after all, with praise singing for the ancien régime, and with the minority Mande-speaking population, too. Their tricky way with words and their prodigious memories meant the new state could not make enemies of them, either. Its cultural administration devised an alternative: the twelve-piece ensembles that harnessed the cosmopolitan guitar sounds, the Latin American rhythms, and the Congolese rumba, circulating around much of Central and West Africa. Guinea's postcolonial musical experiment was a familiar one in the African context, even if the postcolonial rhetoric Touré attached to it was idiosyncratic and ideologically opposed to that of his Senegalese neighbor, Léopold Senghor.[23] Jeliya were, as a consequence, part in and part out. They were "in" to the extent that their praise singing could be incorporated into these ensembles and that the praise singing itself might be directed at the regime. They were "out" to the extent that the older jeliya style, solo praise singing accompanied by a *kora*, responding to whoever was showering them with money, had been consigned to the past.

As in many other parts of the world, the restructuring following Touré's death was pressured by debt and international markets. It was facilitated, too, by a series of military coups. Emergent new agencies within the state looked for support from musicians who might "name" them. A significant element of this support was to come from female praise singers, '*jelimuso*.' They swiftly proved capable of adapting the art of the jeliya to new circumstances, Dave shows. Her analysis suggests that the rise of women praise singers accompanied, in part, the growth of female political and trading networks, and, in part, demands in the new music market for spectacle and glamor. But these performances still bore, as she shows, the marks of Touré's musical politics. They emerged organizationally from a world of musical officialdom instigated by Touré, and they continued to be wrapped in the kind of progressive postcolonial rhetoric he attached to it. Jeliya had managed to attach their own project—a project of naming and thus shaping the power and agency of powerful individuals—both to that of Touré's state, and to its successor. Their musical knowledge and skills, transmitted from generation to generation, maintained both the political salience, and the deep pleasures, associated with that naming.

Naming, Dave argues, enables the continuity of political subjectivities over a period of transition. It also involves a precarious and highly performative bargain with power. During the period of authoritarian rule, jeliya, albeit a diminished presence in state ensembles, maintained a historical memory of the contract between patrons and their clients. That continuity was to be felt, Dave shows, in jeliya melodic contours, which permeate the broader musical environment, and in a long-standing vocal ideology valuing words that come "from the stomach" (i.e., honestly), rather than "the mouth" (i.e., glibly). Listeners, too, needed to be sufficiently smart to know which was which, and might take pleasure in assuming such responsibilities. Somewhere in the performative interactions of named, namer, and listener, power might be held to account. After Touré's death, jelimuso, freed from his cult and its ensembles, began to ply their trade with Guinea's new power brokers. No longer half-hidden, and stripped to the essentials (specifically, a kora ensemble) and accompanied by more and more flamboyant showers of money, the jelimuso's "naming" was, at the time of Dave's research, shaping a new image of citizenship in the postcolonial state.

The picture of national traditions and their afterlife is considerably complicated, as both Klenke and Dave indicate, by another powerful institutional presence in the field of culture-making: NGOs. In new nation-states, these often present themselves in terms of cosmopolitan-sounding agendas of regional democracy, minority rights, peace, education and development. They also often claim to be an alternative to state cultural institutions, institutions tied to bureaucratic and outdated cultural policy-making. But the reality, as Klenke notes of FFUz in Uzbekistan, is considerably more complicated. FFUz, for instance, posed as an alternative to Uzbek state cultural institutions, offering "real artists" an opportunity to free themselves from the shackles of the state and carve out international careers for themselves. It enjoyed some success, attracting a handful of stars in the state system. In practice, however, its main purpose was to enable Gulnora Karimov, President Islom Karimov's daughter, to build a media power base for herself during a period of political rehabilitation, out of the public eye. It could be considered, in other words, as a network extension of the state's ruling clique. As Klenke shows in Uzbekistan, musicians are left with the immensely tricky task of negotiating not just one but two ambiguously separated systems of state patronage.

The role of NGOs in the administration and curation of "traditional" or "national" music has, on the whole, been treated cautiously by ethnomusicologists. The place of music in UNESCO's Intangible Cultural Heritage (ICH) scheme, introduced in 2003, is a—much discussed—case in point. The scheme can justly be celebrated for its record in improving the international visibility of traditional cultural practices, cultivating awareness of sustainability issues, strengthening the hands of practitioners when their livelihoods are threatened, and creating possibilities for cultural interactions in the Global South not routed through the Northern metropole.[24] It has also, gratifyingly, embraced the work of practicing ethnomusicologists, rather than talking over their heads. Criticism has hovered, however, over the way it supports the soft-power strategies of authoritarian states, for its commodification and bureaucratization of traditional culture, and for its unintended consequences on the ground.[25] Where nonstate actors make applications for ICH status for practices that cannot easily be claimed, or are regarded with suspicion, by one or another of the various states involved, such unintended—and usually negative—consequences multiply (see Kutmaa 2018 on just such an Estonian case).[26] But such criticisms have, for the most part, been veiled.

When it comes to the question of how NGOs promote Western art music ("WAM") in the global South, or among communities of migrants and refugees in the global North, views harden, however. The El Sistema program in Venezuela, for instance, captured the attention of many in its early years for its claims to be taking children off the streets, and providing them with a first-class musical education and concert careers. Geoffrey Baker argued, however, that it has operated on undemocratic—indeed, authoritarian—principles, and that it does little for the poverty or diminished life chances it purports to address.

Its only demonstrable success, he suggests, is in satisfying the dubious urges of its wealthy Northern backers to show art and music doing good among the poor and needy (Baker 2015).[27]

A study of the music NGOs that have sprung up on the West Bank in Palestine advances this discussion considerably (El-Ghadban and Strohm 2013). On the face of it, these NGOs resource institutions creating a precious opportunity for Palestinian children and young adults to learn WAM (alongside a certain amount of their Palestinian and other Arab music). The stranglehold exercised by the Israeli authorities has, however, meant a chronic lack of facilities and public services across the West Bank. Cultural provisioning, greatly facilitated by UNESCO's recognition of Palestine on 23 November 2011, has been something of an exception. The Palestinian state, lacking a properly functioning health system, nonetheless boasts a national conservatory capable of fielding no fewer than (at the time of writing) five symphony orchestras, and a number of organizations like Kamandjati in Ramallah providing an impressively high level of both Western and Arab music training.[28] They are supported by an equally impressive array of funding agencies.[29] As El-Ghadban and Strohm point out, the common terms of this funding are emphatic. "Culture" is routinely portrayed as a "basic need" (189), a "manifestation of humanity" (192), vital to the building of a society on principles of "co-existence, evolution and dynamism" (188), and thus contributing toward peace. Some of the funding is tied explicitly to bringing Palestinian and Israeli children together. Most of it puts a high premium on ideas of exchange, collaboration, and dialogue.

El-Ghadban and Strohm underline the instrumentalization of the idea of "culture" in this context, its explicit conceptualization as a resource in the building of civil society and the pursuit of peace. Its claims are, typically, framed in terms of the rights of the individual citizen rather than the affirmation of collective identities. Musicians on the West Bank today are obliged to acknowledge these terms if they are to find jobs as teachers, find funding for their own projects, and have their voice heard on the international stage. The political and musical consequences of this requirement are not easy to determine, as El-Ghadban and Strohm stress. They observe, however, that the terms of this funding share much with broader reframings and instrumentalizations of culture in neoliberalism and are thus hardly value neutral. They note the ongoing collapse of the Palestinian Authorities patronage and pedagogy system built up during the first *intifadha*, the turning away from song and the embrace of instrumental music. In consequence of learning in institutional environments saturated with this kind of language, young Palestinians now tend to understand music-making as a contribution toward "peace" rather than "resistance."

The framing of a music education focused exclusively on instrumental music on the West Bank in terms of "shared humanity" and "universal citizenship" has undermined the capacity of song to shape collective memories, identities, and claims. Without this capacity, El-Ghadban and Strohm aver, a broader social justice in the region, and realistic prospects of peace, will constantly be deferred. This is instructive as a case study, showing how, worldwide, NGOs occupy more and more prominent positions in states dealing with the legacy of authoritarianism, or bankruptcy, or occupation. Their role in the instrumentalization of culture grows, explicitly subordinating it to the norms of global governance—peace, democracy, the eradication of poverty, and so forth. Despite these lofty aims, funding and political patronage often link them materially, and far from neutrally, in more localized struggles. And despite the language of citizenly inclusion, terms of access can on the ground be highly uneven and heavily qualified. Similarly, entire musical fields (like Palestinian song) can find themselves marginalized, with political consequences that become clear only over time.

The question of where, and how, and by whom democracy is to be *heard* in these highly administered, highly institutionalized scenes of postcolonial culture-making involves some important shifts of critical emphasis. No longer are we leaping to conclusions about the role of art and music in authoritarianism in generating "snoozy conformity," as philosopher Martha Nussbaum once put it (Nussbaum, quoted in Dave 2019, 8). Authors such as Klenke and Dave suggest how the manufacture of national musics by the state in Uzbekistan and Guinea may, over time, have shaped alert and thoughtful citizens, not merely obedient or cynical ones. ('Over time' is, perhaps, the important term here—ethnomusicologists tied to the shorter schedules necessitated by fieldwork funding may miss this.) Work on NGOs, such as that discussed above, has, meanwhile, put a serious question mark over the democratic rescue narrative associated in such contexts with WAM.

To speak of "pride" in the Uzbek estrada context, as Klenke does, or "pleasure" in the Guinean context, as Dave does, is to shift the discussion of citizenly musical participation firmly in the direction of emotions, affects, and embodiments. The sensibilities we encounter here are a complex historical and political proposition. They attach to sexuality and desire as much as to the orderly social narratives of conjugality and reproduction. They attach to neighborhood and city as much as to the map of the nation-state. They attach to mixing and conviviality as much as to the racial and ethnic hierarchies of national belonging. They have lent themselves to manipulation by emergent practices of governmentality, notably those associated across the world with neoliberalism and the "shrinking" of the state. They have also given rise to new forms of political critique, associated with what some describe as "intimate" imaginings of the citizen. "Intimate" citizenship has been something of an ethnomusicological preoccupation during the 2010s, which my next section will attempt to review.

2.3 Intimacy

Political theorist Ken Plummer succinctly defined 'intimate politics' as "the decisions people have to make over the control (or not) over one's body, feelings, relationship; access (or not) to representations, relationships, public spaces ... ; and socially-grounded choices (or not) about identities, gender experiences, erotic experiences." (Plummer 2003, 13). Plummer saw its roots in the radical sexual politics, the deregulation and dismantlement of the state's redistributive functions, and the information age of the 1970s. These developments, he showed, put the language of citizenship as defined by liberal historians and theorists such as T.H. Marshall under considerable pressure (see Marshall 1950/1983). The private sphere was no longer one defined by the conjugal couple and the nuclear family, or the public sphere by a middle class oriented toward high culture. New media and digitization meant a proliferation of publics beyond the state, and dramatic new possibilities for political self-actualization. 'Intimate citizenship,' as concept and practice, took shape then in reactive terms. Inevitably, as Plummer implied, it is a contradictory matter—emancipatory, but easily enough captured by state and capital. Like Marshall, Plummer continued to see citizenship in terms of an evolving repertoire of signs and symbols, over which more or less powerful social groups compete in moments of historical transformation.

Like Marshall's sociological account, however, Plummer's view was limited by its assumption that the West has set the terms, and tempo, of this evolution. Anthropologist Michael Herzfeld raised the question of intimate citizenship in Greece, throwing that assumption into question in a well-known study (Herzfeld 1997). Herzfeld showed that from a certain European point of view, Greece is simultaneously political "self" and "other." It may be the birthplace of European democracy, but it stands, nonetheless, in continual need of being taught lessons in democracy by Europe. From a certain Greek point of view, the matter is mediated through a conception of modern Greece's irreconcilable "Hellenic" and "Byzantine" elements. "The West," Herzfeld thereby shows, is made both on and with its peripheries, the non-Western other always already at play in that making. Herzfeld shows how Greek citizens become active participants in this *disemia*, this conception of Greece as simultaneously self and other. He shows how they recognize the gap between claims and realities, the latter a zone of "embarrassment" and "rueful self-recognition" (Herzfeld 1997, 6). He also shows how "assurances of a common sociality" both temper their expectations on the state and enable them to make claims on it when the situation demands. If the state represents itself as family, for instance, implying citizens should be obedient, respectful, and responsible bearers of its honor, citizens might couch their own claims and demands of the state in exactly these terms.

Herzfeld's writing about the intimate citizen assumed importance for ethnomusicologists at a particular historical moment, in the aftermath of seismic changes in Eastern Europe in the 1980s. These saw the Yugoslav wars, the collapse of the Soviet-backed socialist states, and the emergence of Turkey's regional hegemony. They also witnessed an academic, as well as political, preoccupation with the question of the "transition" to market society, democratic citizenship, and European

Union membership. The issue of EU expansion was forced, according to many commentators, by Britain's strong voice in the EU at the time, its desire to create a counterweight to France and Germany, and the need to repay the Central and Eastern European states for their participation in the Gulf War. This expansion accentuated the question of democratic culture—or the perceived lack of it—in these transitioning states. For Britain's (many) critics, these countries were simply not "ready."

The question hovered over the Eurovision Song Contest in these years, which the "transitioning" nations clearly took seriously as an international stage on which they might project their democratic aspirations (Tragaki 2013). The Eastern European entries in these years borrowed winning strategies off one another, making much of their audibly and visibly shared Ottoman heritage. Eastern European nationalisms have been based on a systematic repudiation of their shared Ottoman past. In the years of Soviet-backed state socialism, Eastern European citizens began to imagine their (unpopular) states' failings in terms of this past's persistence, and to project their ambivalent feelings about it onto music and professional musicians in particular.[30] The exuberance and transgressive energies of these professional musicians found their way into Eastern European Eurovision performances in these years, blending seamlessly with the competition's freshly asserted queer identity. These were, as many ethnomusicological commentators underline, classic displays of intimate citizenship in Herzfeld's terms. They showed how "rueful self-recognition" and "embarrassment" might be mastered, enjoyed, and imagined as a kind of democratic energy, as a will to lively citizenship.[31]

If Herzfeld's thinking about cultural intimacy—and ethnomusicological engagements with it—displace the centrality of the "West" that is assumed, rather normatively, in Plummer's otherwise useful definition of intimate citizenship, other traditions of thinking help us extend its time frame. For Plummer, intimate politics are tied to globalization, new communication technologies, and the social movements of the 1970s. But this "moment" can be extended backward considerably. In *The Sentimental Citizen*, for instance, political theorist George Marcus connects today's politics of emotion, and the cognitive theory that might, in his view, help us master it democratically, with those of the eighteenth century—with Rousseau's fascination with *pitié*, with the sentimental theory of Smith and Hume, and with the American and European revolutions (Marcus 2002). Lauren Berlant, already mentioned, addressed "sentimentalism's unfinished business" in a trilogy (Berlant 1997, 2008, and 2011) in quite different terms, exploring the "cruel optimism" of democratic yearnings shaped over some three centuries of literature, political writing, melodrama, and film. These all bear, she shows, on today's citizenly "counterpublics," made up of social and political struggles over love, sex, and care.

Her idea of 'diva citizenship'—adult and "live," as opposed to infantile and scripted—suggests obvious ethnomusicological applications. The idea of stars "representing their nation," vocally, is an old and well-documented one—Egypt's Umm Kulthum, Portugal's Amalia Rodrigues, and Argentina's Carlos Gardel spring to mind (see, respectively, Danielson 1997, Ellen Gray 2013, and Collier 1986). As with Zeki Müren, we might ask which nation, exactly, they represented, and how reliably they did so. With Nasser's pan-Arabism, Umm Kulthum stood in the minds of many for the entire Arab nation, but where and what was that, exactly, especially after the union of Egypt and Syria failed, and Egypt was defeated by Israel in 1967? Amalia Rodrigues may stand for Portugal, but her memory must be wrested back from Salazar and the broader legacy of Portuguese fascism, which laid claim to her in the 1970s. Hollywood turned Carlos Gardel into an icon of Argentina, but this is significantly complicated by his Uruguayan birth and upbringing.

Star vocalists have often found themselves entangled, in one way or another, in difficult moments of political transformation, in ambiguous exits from periods of authoritarianism, or in violent postcolonial struggle.[32] Berlant's insistence on the ambivalence of attachment—erotic, political—suggests a route into these questions, and the complex symbolic valences of the "diva citizen." Two ethnomusicological ethnographies engage directly with Herzfeld and Berlant's rather different, but overlapping, approaches to "intimacy": my own *The Republic of Love: Cultural Intimacy in Turkish Popular Music* (Stokes 2010b) and Maria Sonevytsky's more recent *Wild Music: Sound and Sovereignty in Ukraine* (Sonevytsky 2019).[33] Both, like Herzfeld, engage with the fraught questions of citizenship on Europe's margin.

Both, like Berlant, engage with "diva citizens," with complex "star" bodies and voices pressed into citizenly signification.[34]

Following the pattern of the previous two sections, I might at this point have presented both as contrasting case studies as a means of drawing the reader's attention to the questions they share. But there is little need to summarize *The Republic of Love*, since I have reprised so much of one of its case studies (Zeki Müren) in Chapter 1. Instead, I will discuss two earlier books that make for a productive point of comparison with Sonevytsky's, Marie Virolle's *La chanson raï: De l'Algérie profonde à la scène internationale* (Virolle 2000) and Andrew Weintraub's *Dangdut Stories: A Social and Musical History of Indonesia's Most Popular Music* (Weintraub 2010), before turning to Sonevytsky's in a bit of detail. Something about the "diva citizen" will emerge from this broad postcolonial perspective, and with it, I believe, something about how ethnomusicologists have construed the question of "cultural intimacy."

Algerian rai, as described by Marie Virolle (Virolle 2000), sprang from the folklore of Sidi Bel-Abbes in the west of the country in the early decades of the twentieth century. This folklore bought together the musical cultures of shepherding and wedding celebrations and it was dominated by female praise singers ("*medahhate-s*"). Urbanization, colonialism, and the anti-colonial struggle pushed villagers into the port districts of Oran and Algiers. This migration mixed village music with that of poor Europeans immigrants, and the local classical music, whose performers and patrons prominently included members of Oran and Algiers's Jewish community. It found a home in the cabarets and recording studios of Oran, and a corresponding intensification of its poetics of *mihna* ("pain," seen, in Virolle's view, from a specifically female angle). Local stars emerged, notably Cheikha Rimitti, whose nickname apparently derived from her formidable presence in bars (and her catchphrase "*remettez un autre!*", "pour me another!"). The newly independent Algerian state had no time for rai, however, which it deemed too feminine, too whiny, too hybrid to be taken seriously.

Two developments changed this. An Algerian army colonel, Hosni Snoussi, pushed for the establishment of a rai festival in 1985. His motives are unclear, but they coincided with a moment of economic liberalization, and the Benjadid regime's recognition that a serious problem was brewing among Algeria's youth. The second was the emergence of "Cheb" Khaled as a pioneering figure in French World Music circles.[35] As Algeria slid toward civil war, production shifted to France and the Khaled-dominated "World Music" sound. Islamist forces turned on the rai singers who remained in Algeria with grim ferocity. Its appropriation by the state weakened it as a vehicle of protest but made it a target for its opponents.[36] In Virolle's view, writing soon after the end of this brutal war, there was to be no return to a poetics of mihna. But the memory of Cheikha Rimitti, celebrated for her sly wit as well as her piercing voice, served as a touchstone of a kind of postcolonial national authenticity.

A second instance, emerging from the world of Indonesian dangdut, figures in Andrew Weintraub's study of the genre (Weintraub 2010). Dangdut brought together elements of Hindi and Egyptian film music, "*orkes melayu*" urban classical music and Portuguese-derived kroncong. In the 1950s, orkes melayu was dominated by musicians of Arab descent (Said Effendi, Ellya Khadam), singers with "soft, sweet, and smooth" voices, of which it would be said that "those feeling sad would feel even sadder, whereas those in love would feel even more deeply in love" (Weintraub 2010, 48). Said Effendi and Ellya Khadam led the developments in orkes melayu that would turn it into dangdut.[37] The ensemble expanded, the sound of the flute predominated, and the *chalte* dance meter became more accentuated. But the major transformation took place in the 1970s with a figure who was to dominate the genre for at least two decades: Rhoma Irama. The entertainment industry grew dramatically under Suharto's New Order. Rhoma Irama's films (the main vehicle for dangdut stardom) directly addressed the struggles of the *rakyat*, Indonesia's working class, and he cultivated a huge audience. His dangdut innovated with Western rock and pop elements. Critics, however, found its *cengceng* (weepiness) embarrassing, its political messages contradictory.

But state interest grew in the 1990s, fueled by the rather public power struggle between Secretary of State, Moerdiono, and Minister of Education, Harmoko. Moerdiono made much of his love, Harmoko his dislike, of dangdut. Moerdiono's populism won the day, in the event. Dangdut was embraced by the newly privatized media channels and new state-sponsored cultural organizations. Interest in the genre grew in Malaysia and Japan. A middle-class audience in Indonesia, previously contemptuous of dangdut, now began to find it charming and nostalgic. Indonesian academics jumped on the bandwagon. Dangdut divided into two, an "upgraded contained kind that articulated with state-supported culture, and the downgraded excessive kind that did not belong" (Weintraub 2010, 150). Rhoma Irama held the tensions and contradictions of the field together, but his grip on it waned with age. It eventually fragmented, falling prey to economic crisis, pious backlash, and regionalization, though Irama himself has continued to be a potent figure of nostalgia.

We turn now to Ukraine. Ukraine's fraught identity shift from Soviet bloc to the West was punctuated by Ruslana's triumphant, fur-clad "Wild Dances" routine in the Eurovision Song Contest in 2004. That transition was also (and continues to be) hugely complicated by the Chernobyl nuclear reactor disaster of 1986. In its wake, as anthropologist Adriana Petryna argued, the "injured biology" of an entire population became the dominant basis for the "staking [of] claims to citizenship" (Petryna 2002, 258). These claims have been met in a piecemeal fashion by a state preoccupied with the military aggression of its large neighbor, and still dealing with the international shame and recrimination associated with Chernobyl. Basic healthcare for those affected by the disaster continue to be lacking. Ukraine's ruling elites, for their part, have expressed frustration with a culture of dependency and compensation associated with Chernobyl, and the drag this constitutes, in their view, on the transition to a market society.

Citizens, on the other hand, not only yearn for the state, but "demand" it, as Soneveytsky observes, whether as a vehicle of ethnonationalist revival or of civic inclusivity.[38] Song, she points out, is an increasingly vibrant public arena for such demands. In part, this has to do with the presence, and seriousness, of song in Ukrainian public life, in part a legacy of Soviet-era cultural planning, in part a consequence of Ruslana's Eurovision win. Ruslana's voice embodied conceptions of vocal authenticity important in Ukraine, "high in ghostly partials," hovering, as Sonevytsky puts it, on the edge of abandon, of "wildness." A tiny detail, a characteristic yodel, or yell, known as '*huk,*' marking the end of phrases in Ukrainian folk music, is vital—a sure sign of this wildness. Experts in Ukraine say it should sound "like a kettle giving off steam," or "as though you sat on a needle," or "like a goat bleating" (Sonevytsky 2019, 92)—an involuntary sign of physical life, of raw, animal energy, in other words.

A song-competition reality show discussed by Sonevytsky, "Voice of the Nation" (*Holos Kraïny*), involved tense encounters between judges—including Ruslana—and singers. These took place over conflicting claims of *avententika* ("real" folk music), of *fol'klorizm* (Soviet-era manufactured folklore), and of *sharovarschyna* ("ethnic" music blends, currently dominating the market). Having been swayed first by Soviet and then "World Music" ideals, Ukraine's music market now seemed to be swinging in the direction of an authentic "roughness" associated with avententika. Because, Sonevytsky argues, it is here that Ukraine's "acoustic citizenry"—mobilizing at the time of her research around eco-activism and claims for ethnic inclusivity—were increasingly listening for, and hearing, a quality of vocal wildness. Musically speaking, this is a complex projection. Vocalists and musicians had to find legible ways of integrating Hutsul and Tatar sounds with Ukraine's mainstream national folk music traditions. They also had to find ways of giving voice to nonhuman agencies, which, in the broader context of post-Chernobyl restitution, are understood to have rights, too. Folk musicians were thereby able to stage a repudiation of neoliberal, "European" Ukraine's myths of "transition," and the damaged and damaging relationships it has involved with regard to both human and natural environments.

Though they significantly represent places and times and are approached by these authors in rather different ways, let us quickly consider some of the things Cheikha Remitti, Roma Irama, and Ruslana have in common—not forgetting Zeki Müren in the background.[39] Firstly, they all had or have prominent, powerful, and popular voices, voices that dominated emergent media systems and performance spaces in their respective nation-states, and beyond. They sidestepped official media and exploited ambiguities in its cultural programming. Their voices became signs of a nation imagined in expanded terms, conspicuously embracing excluded elements—women (Cheikha Rimitti), the poor (Rhoma Irama), the nonhuman environment (Ruslana). Official recognition in their home countries has consequently been belated and ambiguous.

Secondly, these voices all crossed conventional gendered boundaries—Cheikha Rimitti's acerbic machismo, Roma Irama's weepiness, Ruslana's "wild" sexuality. These transgressions are underlined by the association of their singing with words pointing to complex emotional states such as mihna, cengceng, and huk. Like "*saudade*," or "*duende*" in Portugal and Spain, or "*hüzün*" in Turkey, they belonging to that category of "untranslatable" terms for national states of melancholy, often celebrated by the intelligentsia and literati, but, at best, ambivalently recognized by the state.[40] They involve, after all, an unmistakable gesture of affective defiance, a rejection of the idea that national citizenship, especially when projected to the outside world, is to be worn with a forced smile.[41] Thirdly, in all three cases, the voices of these singers might be taken as signs of life.[42] But they are hardly signs of vigor. Indeed, in two of these cases, and others that one might mention in this context, such as Zeki Müren, it is their qualities of age, tiredness, and illness that have seemed particularly significant.

Of the three authors, it is only Sonevytsky who is explicitly concerned with the question of intimate citizenship. All three studies share some common concerns, however, which are worth noting at this juncture. All are interested in the political resonance of popular cultural voices in postcolonial states, in highly pressured moments of transition toward global markets (Algeria in the 1980s, Indonesia in the 1970s, Ukraine in the early 2000s). All are interested in the ways in which questions about democracy are projected onto these voices by a variety of actors—questions about inclusion and participation; about neighbors, migrants, and minorities; about relations with the former colonial or colonizing powers. All are interested in the effort to claim these voices as politically "representative." All seem to recognize the opportunism of these claims, the difficulty in making them stick, the space they always seem to allow for rivals. All note, in their different ways, that the state's investments in them are belated and ambiguous. Indeed, often they appear cynical, and provoke a reaction.[43]

Recall Plummer's characterization of intimate politics in terms of, to paraphrase, control (or not) over one's body, access (or not) to representations, choices (or not) about identities. This neatly captures the ambiguity and ambivalence at the heart of the questions about "control," "access," and "identity" confronting the citizen today. Neither state nor individual is sovereign in regard to any of these things. The signs of "intimate politics" both reflect and accommodate this ambiguity. The discussion of intimate *voices* both deepens and complicates the picture. It draws implicitly, as I noted in the previous chapter, on key psychoanalytic insights into voice, though insisting on the plural, and situated nature of voi*ces*, in particular moments and in particular places. Indeed, the studies mentioned above have stressed how such voices take shape in performance, in songs, over the course of careers, and in relation to particular processes of mediation. The mobile, shapeshifting qualities of these voices, and indeed of these vocalists, seems to be important in the way they come to stand, following Avelar and Dunn, as "image and agent" of and for certain kinds of citizenship. We have also seen in this section how this mobility extends from voices to entire genre fields—rai, dangdut, Ukrainian ethnopop—across which the tensions and ambivalences of intimate citizenship play out on a broader canvas.

My headings—identity, technocracy, and intimacy—might not always have been helpful, as mentioned before. But they have, however, suggested thematic connections, even when the authors in question do not cite, or indeed appear to be entirely unaware of one another's work. This helps me discern a structure to the field—however roughly and provisionally. And this, in turn, allows me to attempt an appraisal.

2.4 Conclusion

It will be a brief one, however. The chapter has been long, and time is (always) short. The first thing to underline is the lack of a common field of citation in these texts. There is not, as yet, an "ethnomusicology of citizenship," with its own study groups, specialized journals, or designated prizes from scholarly societies. Most of the authors here write about citizenship from the point of view of their own reading about citizenship and their own fieldwork. The citations are typically drawn from a relatively recent literature—Aihwa Ong, Renato Rosaldo, Lauren Berlant—and not from an older philosophical or political science tradition, or from social, cultural, or political history. Sometimes, as previously mentioned, the word citizenship is quite far from the surface of the text, located in footnotes, subheadings, and so forth. This is all understandable. But it means there is little or no sense in the ethnomusicological literature of an accumulating research agenda, little or no comparative frame, little or no sense of the historical depth of questions about citizenship.

Without this sense of an accumulating research agenda, ethnomusicologists will lack a sense of how their own theory develops—how, in other words, key terms, buzz words, jargon (for some)—take shape, when and why and for whom these terms might matter, and on what terms they might be contested. Ethnomusicologists will also lack a framework with which to engage their colleagues in "historical musicology," in anthropology, and in other contiguous disciplinary fields.[44] Without a comparative framework, ethnomusicologists will not be able to explore the perennially interesting question of the relationship between region and theory—what it might be that pushes, for instance, Latin American discussions of music and citizenship one way, and those in Europe (or its fringes) another, or know what is meaningfully comparable and what is not. Without a common sense of the historical depth of intellectual inquiry into citizenship, ethnomusicologists cannot be sure they are not laboriously reframing questions and problems that might have been formulated elegantly and incisively decades, and perhaps even centuries earlier (by Rousseau, for instance). They might miss instructive points of connection—about the acoustics and sonic architectures of citizenship, for instance—that crop up repeatedly in social and cultural histories of the West. They may consequently contort themselves in connecting music and citizenship when the connections—as observed in Chapter 1—are historically and philosophically organic.

Such observations may, to an extent, be justified with regard to the texts discussed here. They may also add fuel to the ongoing bonfire of anxiety about ethnomusicology's inability to "generate its own theory." Timothy Rice's concerns about the failure of ethnomusicology to develop a unified field of theory around "identity" springs to mind (Rice 2017). But where some would observe a failure to interact, I would underline the potential of parallel play. To a greater or lesser extent, the books and articles discussed in this chapter all—in their different ways—perform the necessary and immensely tough labor of pushing back at thinking about citizenship that has relentlessly been imagined as White, Western, and enshrined in texts that somehow float above and beyond history. All explore citizenship with reference to the experience of people excluded, marginalized, or located ambiguously within citizenship discourse. All focus on the *performativity* of citizenship, attentive to its embodiments, its emotional textures, its sensory dimensions; attentive, too, to the struggles that take place within such spaces, the competing desires and interests that will push or pull these performances in one direction or another. None of these authors romanticize activism, but none, too, see themselves as merely observers. They witness the struggles of their interlocutors, participate in them, share their knowledge and expertise when given the chance. It seems likely to me that they, too, are developing their own citizenly competencies in the process, and have an instinctive feel for the positive circularity here. Certainly, all understand that the crafting of citizenship competencies in music both concentrates and releases special social energies, and special ways of talking about them. They all show in their various ways how these flow in and out of other fields of citizenship discourse and imagery. An ethnomusicology *of* citizenship is, it would seem, always already ethnomusicology *as* citizenship.

This is a significant achievement. Far from being limited by a reluctance to designate citizenship an object of unified ethnomusicological theoretical inquiry, our field, I would argue, has benefited from it. We have needed this independent digging into case studies, this patient sifting of material, this finding a way forward to the topic through empirical material. We have not needed—at this stage, at least—a checklist of approved questions and pre-constructed comparative frameworks. The issue now is where these parallel, but gathering, energies might lead. What they suggest to me—if they were to be engaged more fully with the different traditions of thinking discussed in Chapter 1—is the possibility of a systematic and wide-ranging theorization of citizenship as *resonance*. Such an account of citizenship, to deserve the title "systematic," would need to be global in scope. It would therefore, equally necessarily, need to be fully engaged with postcolonial and decolonizing agendas. Ethnomusicologists may (still) need to take a strong lead in such a venture, since it seems unlikely at the time of writing to come from anywhere else. In the next chapter I will push three extended case studies of my own in that direction.

Notes

1. Stoever-Ackerman and O'Toole's important work is acknowledged in Vincent Andrisani's reflection on the term in a special issue of the journal *Sounding Out!* on sonic citizenship. He does so in the light of histories of sound walking, the work of Saskia Sassen and others on global cities, as well as the kind of anthropology and ethnomusicology represented by Stoever-Ackerman and O'Toole. O'Toole's work in Berlin focuses on migrants and the use of music to establish presence, recognition, and the grounds for sharing urban space (see also O'Toole 2022). Andrisani's short article is significant because I believe it provides the only theoretical reflection on the term 'citizenship' to connect the work of two or more ethnomusicologists also using the term. It also describes his sonic ethnography of Havana ice-cream vendors (Andrisani 2015).
2. The expression, belonging to Ana Hofman, came up in conversation with me about this book at a very early stage.
3. An important confrontation was staged by Bohlman and Radano's co-edited *Music and the Racial Imagination* volume (see Bohlman and Radano 2000); this line of critique can be traced to the work of Warren Dwight Allen many decades earlier (Allen 1939). It will be in play, and remain utterly salient, for as long as something called musicology continues to exist. See also Ewell 2021.
4. James Sykes's *The Musical Gift* (Sykes 2018) is perhaps the most forceful critique of "identity" studies in recent ethnomusicology, focused as it is on a zone of shared or overlapping musical practice in a country torn by a civil war fueled by the manipulation of signs of national, ethnic, and religious identity. Anna Stirr's important study of *dohori* in Nepal is less polemically driven, exploring citizenship in Nepal as a matter of "singing across divides" (Stirr 2017), but treads a similar line.
5. On the critique of multiculturalism, and the complicating role of music in it, see Kosnick 2007. Wilford 2017, looking at identity and citizenship among Algerian migrants in London, strikes a similar tone. Cultural "citizenship" for Wilford is a way of talking about struggles for visibility and audibility within this community, acknowledging both the diversity and complexity of these struggles, and the limits of identitarian discourse.

6. See in particular Kirsten Klenke's study of popular music institutions in Uzbekistan, to be discussed at more length later in this chapter (Klenke 2019).
7. The BDS ("Boycott, Divestment, and Sanctions") movement is intended to draw attention to Israel's settlements on the West Bank, in defiance of international law, and its military and economic stranglehold of Gaza. It has had a significant effect on government-sponsored Israeli musicians' ability to tour and to collaborate in international projects.
8. For an extensive review of this literature, see Stokes 2020a; see also Stokes 2021b, concerned more explicitly with migrant aesthetics, its curatorial culture, and associated framings of migrant civility.
9. Significant points of reference over the last two decades include projects such as those of Frances Aparicio and Candida Jacquez (2003), John Baily and Michael Collyer (2006), Tina Ramnarine (2007), Jason Toynbee and Byron Dueck (2011), Simone Krüger and Ruxandra Trandafoui (2014), Maria de São José Corte-Real (2010), Eric Levi and Florian Scheding (2010), and Florian Scheding (2018). Sociologists and anthropologists contributed significantly (see in particular Kasinitz and Martiniello 2019 and Aterianus-Owanga and Guedj 2014). Many of these authors have been concerned with specific facets of the study of migrant and refugee music: Ramnarine with performance, Krüger and Trandafoui with the relationship between migration and tourism, Corte-Real with migrant cultural policy and NGOs, and Martiniello and Kasinitz with music in second- and third-generation immigrant politics. Many of these have a regional emphasis: Corte-Real on the Lusophone world, Aparicio and Jacquez on Latin America, Scheding on contemporary Britain, and Aterianus-Owanga and Guedj on the Black Atlantic.
10. On the media construction of the migrant crisis, see Trilling 2019. On ethnomusicology's migrant crisis see in particular the recent *Society for Ethnomusicology* Presidential Round Table on the subject (Rasmussen, Impey, Beckles Willson, Aksoy, Gill, and Frishkopf 2019), conveying, among thoughtful critiques, a strong sense of the need for a new activism.
11. See, importantly, Joshua Pilzer's research on music in the lives of the Korean women who were subjected to sexual slavery in Japanese military camps during the Second World War in just such terms. Many of those still alive are living out their old age in a government-run community in Korea called the *House of Sharing* (Pilzer 2012, 2015). Those present at the time of Pilzer's research had been forced to travel around the outer peripheries of Japan's wartime empire under the most brutal imaginable of circumstances. The question of how to remember this period is still bitterly

disputed in Korea, Japan, and elsewhere. But the women, as Pilzer shows, clearly had their own agenda. This was to use art and music to remember, and heal, on their own—often idiosyncratic and quite complex—terms. The students and activists at the House of Sharing were both witnesses and chorus, amplifying the message the women's performances contained both within and beyond Korea. To talk, as Pilzer does, about survivors and survival in such a context is to treat these women as agents rather than as victims, as active citizens rather than mute pawns in the ongoing struggles between Japan and Korea over the legacy of the war.

12. See in this regard Pistrick's study of German refugee camps, observing the cherry-picking of refugee musicians by prominent international ensembles (Pistrick 2020); see also Western 2020; Alkabaani, Habbal, and Western 2020. On the curational culture of migratory aesthetics, see Stokes 2021b.
13. *"Bir ulusun yeni değişikliğine ölçü, musikide değişikliği alabilmesi, kavrayabilmesidir."* The quotation is ubiquitous in cultural officialdom in Turkey. This and Atatürk's other pronouncements on music are gathered in Oransay 1985.
14. Citizenship is, indeed, routinely measured according to multiple criteria, extending far beyond formal measures of political activity. Such measurements may, of course, like "quality of life" or "happiness" indices, do little more than confirm already existing pictures of the world, or pictures that support the outlook of powerful meaning-generators such as multinational corporations.
15. Not all ethnomusicologists were (or are) "liberals," looking at state socialism or communism as politically "other." Crucial ethnomusicological work on, for example, Albania was done by citizens of other Soviet bloc states nonetheless closely connected to Western academia, such as Erich and Doris Stockmann (from the former German Democratic Republic). Being a member of the British Communist Party gave folklorists and folk music scholars in the United Kingdom, like Albert Lloyd, privileged access to folk music scenes behind the Iron Curtain during the Cold War.
16. The term 'postcolonial' is admittedly a problematic one here, because it must, at least on the edges, include the Soviet Union, which extended the Russian imperial project; Turkey (successor state to the Ottoman Empire); and Egypt (formerly an ancient empire). Imperial mindsets persist in each of these countries. Still, it might serve to identify twentieth-century modernization projects split between validating a local authenticity and looking to "the West" with greater or lesser degrees of respect for cultural models.

17. "They" in this context refers to a multigenerational group of ethnomusicologists and other scholars reflecting on the making of citizens in (or in reaction to) state cultural institutions in a context defined by the Cold War, the collapsing Soviet system, and the dawning "transitions." El-Shawan Costelo-Branco 1980 was an early and field-defining study of the workings of a modern music institution. Rice 1994 was the first book-length study about how people worked with (and beyond) a major folk music cultural institution in Bulgaria. A slightly later—and, as can be seen from mutual citations, quite closely interacting—group comprising Buchanan working on Bulgaria, Jerka Vidic Rasmussen on Yugoslavia, Margaret Beissenger on Romania, Vesa Kurkela on Bulgaria, Kevin Dawe on Greece, Jane Sugarman on Albania, myself on Turkey, Carol Silverman on Roma, Svanibor Pettan and Mirjana Lausevic on Bosnia, Ted Levin and Margaret Mazo on the Soviet Union, Michael Beckerman on Czechoslovakia, Judith Frigyesi and Barbara Lange on Hungary, Catherine Wanner on Ukraine, Ana Czekanowska on Poland, and Steluta Popa on Romania can be identified through two major essay collections assembled during and reflecting on the period(s) of transition (see Buchanan 2007 and Slobin 1996). Somewhat later, when transition was being looked back on in the past tense, and the researchers were working more independently of one another, the work of Jeffers Englehardt on Estonia (Englehardt 2015), Nick Tochka on Albania (Tochka 2016), Kerstin Klenke on Uzbekistan (Klenke 2019), Andrea Bohlman on Poland (Andrea Bohlman 2020), and Maria Sonevytsky on Ukraine (Sonevytsky 2019) has been significant. On folk dance, which is often neglected by ethnomusicologists working on these regions, see Shay 2002. Kelly Askew's study of the state music traditions and institutions in Tanzania and Thomas Turino's in Zimbabwe established significant points of comparison in African music studies (see Askew 2002; Turino 2000).
18. The extent to which Uzbekistan has thrown the weight of officialdom behind a "popular" music—as opposed to a "traditional" or "art" music—is striking, even allowing for the difficulty in translating such terms. 'Tradition' in this context means folk music and *shashmaqom*, both of which have ethnic associations that the Uzbek state feels a need to manage carefully. These lie more fully within the administrative purview of outside organizations, like the Aga Khan Foundation.
19. On the (often neglected) pleasures of citizenship, see Van Zoonen 2005, whose opening question is "can citizenship be pleasurable?" (Van Zoonen 2005, 1). The question of the pleasure involved in participation in state

rituals is central to Dave's discussion of Guinea, discussed later in this chapter.
20. See political theorist Jeremy Gilbert's introduction to an entire issue of *New Formations* devoted to the proliferating bureaucracies of neoliberalism (Gilbert 2020).
21. The post-Soviet world, as anthropologist Alexi Yurchak has observed elsewhere, is often best understood in "both/and," rather than "either/or" terms, in this regard. He argues for "the dialectics of attachment and alienation" as an alternative lens on late Soviet citizenry, an alternative to seeing only spaces of "officialdom" and countervailing spaces of "resistance" (Yurchak 2005). This, as Dave notes, is a useful corrective to a romance with resistance in World Music circles regarding African music.
22. The calculations at play in these auditions are, unsurprisingly, more exacting for female musicians than for their male counterparts, as Klenke repeatedly notes.
23. For Senghor, "negritude" was internationalist in outlook, attuned to Black experience in the French Antilles, as well as to the Harlem Renaissance and French existentialism. He and its other architects (principally Aimé Césaire and Léon Damas) imagined mutually nourishing interactions between postcolonial Africa and the African diaspora in the New World. Touré's vision, by contrast, was one of development and progress within the nation-state. See Neveu Kringelbach 2013 for a discussion of Senghor's thinking and policies as they related to Senegalese dance in (and beyond) Senegal.
24. On the latter issue see Camal 2019, for a convincing argument with reference to Guadeloupean *gwoka*.
25. See Howard 2012, which gathers the critical thinking in ethnomusicology on ICH as it specifically relates to East Asia. Howard underlines how ethnomusicologists' professional investment in heritage administration both complicates and enriches their critical position. The point is reiterated in various guises in the Norton and Matsumoto collection, which takes a slightly broader ethnomusicological perspective (Norton and Matsumoto 2018). Norton's contribution (Norton 2018), focusing on ethnographic film in heritage work, for instance, enjoins ethnomusicologists to consider the myths about ethnographic representation that they sometimes draw on and perpetuate in their critiques of such projects. The line separating participation and observation can be hard to observe, as is often necessarily the case in most ethnographic work, but that task becomes an important one in such contexts.

26. The matter of external funding and NGO support is complicated in nation-states that are not signatories to various international treaties concerning human rights, environmental issues, migration, and refugee rights. Anthropologist Zerrin Özlem Biner discusses this in her study of architectural heritage issues in eastern Turkish cities (Biner 2020).
27. The emotions Baker's book generated speaks volumes. See particularly Nicholas Kenyon's riposte (Kenyon 2015).
28. Rachel Beckles Willson puts the parlous state of cultural citizenship in Palestine in sharp historical perspective in a book connecting today's international institutional philanthropy with the previous century's religious mission and colonialism in Palestine (Beckles Willson 2013).
29. The authors list the Swedish International Development and Cooperation Agency, the A.M. Qattan Foundation, the Ford Foundation, UNESCO, the Dutch Prince Claus Fund, the German Regional Social and Cultural Fund for Palestinian Refugees and the People of Gaza, the Qatar Foundation, the Khalil Sakakini Cultural Center, and the German Aventis Foundation, which funds the well-known West-East Divan Orchestra, conducted by Daniel Barenboim, bringing together young Israeli and Palestinian musicians.
30. These professionals have mainly been Roma. For the deepest and most systematic analysis of these region-wide projections and their cultural significance both within and beyond the region, see Silverman 2012.
31. Sertap Erener's Turkish Eurovision-winning song of 2003 "Every Way That I Can" felt like a slogan in this regard. See Solomon 2013.
32. The literature is an extensive one. My own points of reference, relevant to this particular discussion have been Greek *rebetika* (Holst-Warhaft 1983; Tragaki 2007), Indonesian *kroncong* (Kornhauser 1978), Turkish arabesk (Stokes 2021), Spanish flamenco (Washabaugh 1996), Argentinian tango (Savigliano 1995; Collier 1986), Algerian rai (Virolle 2000; Schade-Poulsen 1999), Dominican merengue (Austerlitz 1997), Mexican *banda* (Simonett 2001), Japanese enka (Yano 2003), Cuban *timba* (Perna 2005), Brazilian country music (Dent 2009, Reily 1994, Silver 2019), Indonesian dangdut (Weintraub 2010), Peruvian *huayno* (Tucker 2013), Portuguese fado (Gray 2013), and Hindi film song (Morcom 2013). Their emphases differ, of course, but all share an interest in the connections between musical style, popular voice, and political participation at complex moments of transformation into or out of authoritarianism.
33. Space, and the organizational demands of this chapter, have prohibited as full an engagement with Byron Dueck's discussion of intimacy in indigenous music-making in Canada as I would have liked. Intimacy assumes,

as he stresses, particular significance in indigenous communities in North America. His concern with (and distinction between) musical publics and counterpublics is of relevance to this discussion. See Dueck 2013.
34. I was very happy to have the opportunity to discuss cultural intimacy with Dafni Tragaki, some years after *The Republic of Love* (Stokes 2010b), and to do so in more general theoretical terms (see Tragaki 2019).
35. Marc Schade-Poulsen's study of rai and masculinity picks up the story where Virolle leaves off (Schade-Poulsen 1999). He is interested in the ways in which migration intervenes in the story of rai, inflecting its gendered and sexual meanings in significant ways.
36. This turned Hasni Chakroun ("Cheb Hasni"), famous for his *"raï romantique,"* into something of a martyr for the state when he was murdered by the Group Islamique Armé in 1994. See Schade-Poulsen 1999.
37. Of Said Effendi it was said that "those feeling sad will perhaps feel even sadder, whereas those in love will feel even more deeply in love. When the song is over, listeners will either take a deep breath, breathe a sigh of relief or feel unsatisfied" (Weintraub 2010, 51, quoting Indonesian critic Amir).
38. The question of both yearning and demanding is well represented in Anna Stirr's study of dohori in Nepal, a genre that "sings across divides" in a post-civil war context that continues to pose dramatic challenges to the very idea of a Nepalese state (Stirr 2017).
39. Japanese enka's Misora Hibari (Yano 2003), Peruvian huayno's Dina Paucar (Butterworth 2014), and Turkish pop's Sezen Aksu (Stokes 2010b) seem plausible additions to the list of "intimate citizens" in more recent times; Zeki Müren in Turkey (Stokes 2010b), Abd al-Halim Hafiz in Egypt (Stokes 2009), Amalia Rodriguez in Portugal (Gray 2013), and Carlos Gardel in Argentina (Collier 1986) add to the list in the somewhat earlier film and sound-recording era.
40. Cassin, Apter, Lezra, and Wood's *Dictionary of Untranslatables* is a celebration of them, a project based on the ironic proposition that they all are, in fact, eminently translatable, though they do their cultural work on the self-congratulatory assumption that they are not (Cassin, Apter, Lezra, and Wood 2014). Regarding terms like mihna, cengceng, hüzün, *furasato,* and saudade in music, historian William Reddy's concept of "emotives" seems a useful framework: words that capture ambiguous emotional states and provide them with some (verbal) philosophical and psychological definition, cuing action. For further discussion of Reddy's concept as it might concern music, see Stokes 2017.
41. Rachel Harris's discussion of the forced smiles in Chinese folkloric performances is an extreme and interesting case, particularly because they

describe such painful and violent episodes on the margins of Chinese history (Harris 2017).
42. Life, indeed, that goes beyond the grave. Cheikha Remitti's dialogues with Robert Fripp's guitar of 1995 and Zeki Müren's duet with Muazzez Abacı in 2000 postdate their deaths and constitute classic cases of what Stanyek and Piekut describe as "intermundane" communication—the voice as uncanny life. Ellen Gray's discussion of Amalia Rodrigues's drag contests overlaps, cosplay sharing something with these posthumous cohabitations of voice (Gray 2013). On intermundane duetting and "deadness," see Stanyek and Piekut 2010.
43. The Turkish state's efforts to intervene in the emotional politics of arabesk, by promoting, via an aging star, Hakkı Bulut, a version shorn of its "*acı*" ("pain") was something of a failure. It rested on an assumption that arabesk consisted of nothing but acı, from an emotional point of view. Orhan Gencebay was one of many to complain that arabesk was not a single emotional state but, in fact, an entire emotional universe. The subsequent rise of Müslüm Gürses, a singer who seemed to specialize in acı to the exclusion of all else, seems to be connected to these rather fraught interventions. See Stokes 2010b.
44. On environment and climate crisis see the work of James Sykes (2020); on health and disability, see the work of Jessica Holmes (Holmes 2020); and on social movements, see the work of Noriko Manabe (Manabe 2015–2016). These seem obviously points of reference as spaces in which a discussion of citizenship could and should move and make connections across sub-disciplinary space, within music studies alone. Multiple doors are open, in other words.

3
Citizenship Resounding

In a world that seems to be run by criminals, figures of everyday decency, persevering against the odds, become our citizenly heroes. But we pause here, too, because we have learned to question the need for *any* kind of hero—and especially the singular, White, and male versions of them that history conventionally provides. Democracy, we tell ourselves, should not need such figures.[1] The quest for them continues, nonetheless. But it does so now on more complicated terrain—in mass media, in crowds, and in social movements. It occupies more complex emotional territory, too. This is no longer a matter of marble-pillared, major-key triumphalism. It is marked, rather, by the signs of loss, damage, and suffering.[2] It is not always easy to locate such figures, even though some might have a significant history. The iconographic fields in which they take shape have been shifting and opaque.

I suggest in this chapter that music may provide a key to them, though. Music leads our eyes and ears toward things we might miss if our gaze is restricted to writing or the visual alone. It also raises some distinct challenges. Musicology has been making efforts for decades to think beyond the sovereign subject of liberalism, beyond Whiteness, and beyond able-bodiedness (including sound hearing).[3] But the complex of thinking around heroism, "greatness," and Whiteness in music has proved notoriously hard to unravel beyond the professional academic core. The soundworlds of collectivity—of crowds and social movements—continue to be hard to describe, at least, with reference to our habitual ways of describing and analyzing music.

The chapter explores three scenes of democratic iconography—an Egyptian musical revolutionary in his wheelchair, a "sentimental crowd" and its song in England, and a failed social movement and its soundscape in Turkey. Music is both in the iconography and of the iconography: these are all highly reflexive scenes of music-making. But as I will also show, music complicates it. The term 'iconography' is understood performatively here, a constant braiding and unbraiding of discrepant narrative elements as various actors attempt to seize control of them (Ghosh 2011). Engagement with its musical elements might help us see that performativity and that struggle a bit more clearly, in the spaces that often elude narrative capture. The icon's work is never done.

The first section looks at the figure of Egyptian vocalist Abd al-Halim Hafiz, a journey, as portrayed here, from bicycle to wheelchair, from revolutionary icon to a quietly enduring sign of citizenship on the fringes of Tahrir Square. The story—a postcolonial nocturne—takes place in the shadows. A chase scene, in darkness, lies at the heart of it. Love, wit, and agility win the day—with the aid of a bicycle. But I will show that the accoutrements and extensions of the postcolonial subject, at first so life-giving, become a weight, and then prompt a question. When our revolution has pushed us first this way, and then that, exhausted and demoralized us all, and left us with practically no hope—what if the model citizen looks like *this*?[4]

3.1 The citizen on his bike

Abd al-Halim Hafiz rose to fame in the early years of the Nasserite revolution as a star in the movie musical system Joel Gordon aptly dubs "revolutionary melodrama."[5] His training in Western music, his gentle but soulful voice, and his boyish charm positioned him perfectly to represent the "modern" alternative to the dominant voices of Egyptian classical music—Umm Kulthum and Mohammed Abd al-Wahhab—but also as their natural heir. He may not have had their commanding voices, their training in Qur'an, and their apprenticeship with the early-recording era '*mashaiykh*,' and a question mark may have hovered, consequently, over his ability to engage live audiences with the traditional art of '*tarab*' ("enchantment").[6] But he could allude to it and claim to take it to another—modern and revolutionary—level. He would be the character, in his very first film, *Lahn al-Wafa* (1955), to find the lost orchestral masterpiece of his missing adopted father, assemble the score and the symphony orchestra, and put on a triumphant performance, duetting with his female counterpart, Shadia.

The imaginary "lost masterpiece" is a bewildering fusion of tradition and modernity, soulfulness and bombast, lyricism and contrapuntal stridency. "Revolutionary" Beethoven, as imagined by its resourceful composer Riyad al-Sunbati, hovers all too obviously over the scene.[7]

Abd al-Halim's political fortunes grew, if anything, after Egypt's defeat at the hands of Israel in 1967, as the Egyptian state clung to the symbols of its revolution to shore up its legitimacy. This was to continue after Nasser's death, and the dramatic reversals of Sadat's presidency. If Abd al-Halim continued to stand for a revolution, it was a revolution that had, by then, hit the rocks. By the time of Sadat's successor, Hosni Mubarak, and now long dead, he had become a somewhat officialized figure. The lively songs composed for him in the 1960s and 1970s by a stable of composers with cosmopolitan outlooks and a grasp of the Arab world's popular musical imagination—Baligh Hamdi, Kamal al-Tawil, Mohammed al-Mougi—had been reworked for classical Arab orchestras and choruses and become the plodding and predominantly monophonic recitations one could hear at state jamborees in the Cairo Opera. The biopic of 2005, in which Abd al-Halim was uncannily mimicked by the chameleon-like Ahmad Zaki shortly before his death, contributed to the political whitewash.[8]

Abd al-Halim was therefore an ambiguous presence in Cairo's Tahrir Square in 2011, during the revolutionary protests that resulted in the unseating of Egyptian President Hosni Mubarak. Abd al-Halim's association with the previous regime meant that he was not going to be afforded a prominent position in Tahrir's soundscape. But it did not, interestingly, eliminate him entirely (Sanders and Visonà 2012).[9] Collective memories of Abd al-Halim run more deeply, and strangely. Nostalgia for such figures is colored by quietly sophisticated understandings of Egyptian history—quiet because Nasser's legacy is still a divisive matter. There is always more to the iconography of Abd al-Halim Hafiz than immediately meets the eye, or ear. And it is not difficult, as I have had many opportunities to discover, to stir these collective memories. The songs are still well known, the movies well remembered, their original context well understood by the majority.

That he continues to have *any* saliency in the ongoing construction of the *muwatin*, the citizen, in Egypt, says something (Sanders and Visonà 2012). What that salience is, though, is harder to say. One image, an amusing cliché to those who know Egyptian cinema, might offer a key: the figure of Abd al-Halim singing on his bicycle. The amusement lies, in part, in its implausibility these days. In the years I spent visiting Cairo for research purposes (2000–2005) I never once saw anybody cycling in the downtown area. They would quickly have been flattened by the traffic. The few cyclists one saw around were workers delivering bread in the older parts of the city, balancing large wooden frames on their heads—a remarkable enough performance, but one that involved pedestrians, carts, and gridlocked tuk-tuks, not speeding cars. So, on a more recent visit (2017) I was pleasantly surprised to see (female, and clearly local) cyclists on a quiet downtown back street, seemingly on their way back from a shopping expedition. I must have stared—rudely—for quite a while. Averting my eyes, I noticed the road markings indicating an official cycle route. Subsequent inquiries revealed attempts by the municipality to introduce cycling lanes across the city, new cycling racks around metro stations, and the lively efforts of an NGO ("Tebdil"), which liaises with consultancies such as the Dutch Cycling Embassy and Copenhagenize to lobby more effectively for cycling across Egypt.[10]

It is hard to be particularly optimistic about Cairo's "Copenhagenization." The latter's "human centred perspective ... using design, anthropology, sociology and common sense" as their points of departure has, as yet, failed to make to make any discernible impact on Cairo's streets. Official planning has, by all accounts, been inept (including pointless cycle lanes in desert highways far outside the city), and potential cyclists' fears about safety are going to be hard to overcome. The rhetoric of this planning—sustainable transport, health and clean air, democratic mingling on the streets—also seems calculated to appeal primarily to gated-community developers. Cycling imagery in their advertising is a little hard to read, as planner and architect Ahmed Tarik al-Ahwal notes.[11] Most of these gated communities are, after all, far out in the desert, meaning cycling is at best a hobby, an adjunct to a fundamentally car-based existence.

The Cairo that Abd al-Halim encounters on his bicycle in his films is, then, one that is hard to recognize today. The routes he takes, as one so often notices in films of places one knows, are entirely implausible. The lack of traffic seems somehow imaginable, but not the newness and the cleanness of the buildings and the streets. Indeed, when he takes a detour through the "traditional quarters," these acquire a positively hallucinogenic glow. The actors sing their songs and gaze into one another's eyes, oblivious to oncoming traffic or the need to steer or occasionally apply brakes. No matter—we are in a scene of playful make-believe, and this is of course where the enduring charm of these scenes resides. But the persistence of the image of Abd al-Halim on his bicycle, and its ambiguous half-life in Tahrir Square, should give us pause for thought. Might Abd al-Halim's bicycle tell us something about the fate of the revolutionary subject, the postcolonial citizen in Egypt? And beyond?

The postcolonial bicycle does not, at a general level, seem to have received much academic attention.[12] One essay stands out as an exception, though. This is Anthony Appiah's essay on the Yoruba sculpture, *Man with a Bicycle*, on display at the Center for African Art in New York in 1987 (Appiah 1991). It was primarily a critique of then-emerging African art canons in Western art markets, canons in which, Appiah felt, academic poststructuralism and postcolonialism had played a problematic role. His concerns may now feel a bit dated. But a passing comment, drawing on James Baldwin's commentary on the sculpture in a volume devoted to the exhibition, touches on something at issue here. Baldwin's contribution to this volume seemed relatively uninterested in questions about tradition, and departures from it. Instead, he was interested in the cyclist, who he might be, and where he might be going. "He's apparently a very proud and silent man. He's dressed sort of polyglot. Nothing looks like it fits him too well," Baldwin wrote. For all of his "jauntiness" and "authority," there was, for Baldwin, something daunting about his errand. "He is challenging something—or something has challenged him," he observed. But the bicycle "grounds him in immediate reality."

Baldwin alone in this volume interpreted the cyclist in political terms, as a man embarked on a serious mission, determinedly forging his own future. Baldwin's characterization of the sculpture immediately puts Appiah in mind of Yambo Ouloguem's novel, *Le devoir de violence*, and its hero, Raymond-Spartacus Kassoumi. Ouloguem's novel is intended, Appiah argues, as a repudiation of primitivism, anthropology, the Western art market, and the canon of postcolonial African novels—that last ensuring a furious critical response to the novel in Africa in its time. The Yoruba bicycle, as read by Appiah, via James Baldwin, is then primarily a vehicle for a critique of postmodernism and postcolonialism. But if we are to focus, like Baldwin rather than Appiah, not on the bicycle but on the cyclist, and what he might be doing and where he might be going, a rather different line of inquiry might take shape. And it is one that might suggest an interpretation of these Egyptian movie-musical cycling scenes. To follow it further, let me consider a particularly iconic moment: Abd al-Halim's duet with Shadia in the song "Haga Ghariba" ("A Strange Matter") in the 1967 film *Ma'abudet al-Gamahir* ("The Diva of the Public").[13]

It is an immensely well-known scene, the first that devotees of these old films mention when I ask about bicycling scenes, and the first to come up in a web search if you enter the words 'Abd al-Halim' and 'bicycle' in Arabic. It will need a brief description for readers unfamiliar with it, though. It depicts Abd al-Halim and Shadia cycling to a park (probably the Alhambra Gardens in Cairo), wandering among the flowers, sitting by the Nile, looking at the stars, and musing on how love has made the world delightful and strange. The memorability of the song, a rambling eight-minute foxtrot, owes much to composer Kemal al-Tawil's artful duet writing, with its playful switching of *maqam*-s (modes) and *iqa*-s (meters) matching the switching camera angles and the play of perspectives in the lyrics.[14] It is typical of the genre, and the Latin, jazzy cultural moment. A few years later in Abd al-Halim's oeuvre these long songs would take on a more Middle Eastern tone, more wedded to a single maqam tonality, less reliant on the Western orchestra for color and dynamism. The foxtrots, cha-chachas, rumbas, and tangos would soon become period pieces.

A darkness hovers over the scene, however. Firstly, a literal darkness: it is night. For reasons I will come back to, this in itself does not necessarily confer menace or threat. But it makes for a pointed contrast with the film's first "bicycle song," "Ahibbik" ("I love you"). Abd al-Halim's route in this particular song is weirdly implausible, but momentarily worth an attempt to reconstruct, since it amplifies the meaning of the second. At the beginning of it, we are zigzagging around central downtown, momentarily passing Ataba square. Then, abruptly, we are in a tree-lined boulevard, possibly in Zamalek a couple of kilometers away in the opposite direction, or perhaps in Heliopolis—a leap of a similar magnitude in another direction entirely. Then, equally abruptly, we are in a "traditional" neighborhood, possibly Bulaq, even though that would have necessitated a tricky journey back across the river if we had been in Zamalek earlier. Nevertheless, here Abd al-Halim dismounts and greets local folk in the cafe who are playing backgammon, working in their shops, and playing football on the street. He enters his house, greeting womenfolk and his cat, and busies himself with household chores, continuing to announce to all and sundry his hopes and anxieties concerning love. The lyrics offer gently shifting angles on his predicament. The long, meandering, multi-sectional structure of the song, with its sudden shifts of mood, tempo, and tonality, is where the real interest lies, providing an interesting musical analog to the shifting, zigzagging urban perspectives of this implausible bike ride. On this first bike ride, all is sunlight. "Haga Ghariba," in stark contrast, takes place at night.

Secondly, the lovers are not alone. In the film narrative, Abd al-Halim's career as a singer is just taking off. Shadia is a singer, too, but, in the film, her career is just then on the point of decline. But at this moment, both are famous, and the paparazzi are hot on the trail. Their bumbling efforts to get a picture of the lovers add to the comedy of this scene. But afficionados of these films already know that things rarely go well between Abd al-Halim and Shadia. *Ma'abudet al-Gamahir* reprises not only *Mu'id Gharam* but also *Dalila*, both from an earlier period.[15] All of these films also involved Shadia as Abd al-Halim's beloved, and storylines about fame that run on parallel, indeed, almost identical tracks. But where *Mu'id Gharam*, for instance, shows an abandoned Shadia sobbing on her own as she listens to the newly famous Abd al-Halim singing on the radio, *Ma'abudet al-Gamahir* makes a more lurid—indeed, a technicolor—spectacle of Shadia's decline and abjection. Abd al-Halim's agonized realization that he has stolen his lover's fame, and condemned her to artistic irrelevance, seems to be the fundamentally important issue in *Ma'abudet al-Gamahir*. Fame, we learn here, is a zero-sum game. One person's gain is another's loss. It is no friend of romantic love, either. Women will inevitably suffer, on both counts. The paparazzi in the film, in other words, signify the pain to come.

Thirdly, Abd al-Halim Hafiz and Shadia are being pursued, at the outset of this scene, by a car. It takes the viewer a while to grasp exactly what is going on in the strange nocturne with which the scene opens. First, we see streetlights wheeling in a night sky; eventually it becomes clear that this is a view from a speeding car. The car does not confer much of an advantage on the pursuers, however. Abd al-Halim and Shadia swerve off into the park, and the paparazzi (we assume) must park their vehicle before following them on foot, at which point they struggle to catch up. As far as the film is concerned, the lovers may have won this battle, but not the war. The paparazzi destroy them in the end. In "real life," meanwhile, Abd al-Halim's illness and physical decline were about to begin, in a merciless glare of publicity. His "real life" lovers would be hounded by the press, too, in Suad Hosni's case (it seems) taking their own lives. And the bicycle would disappear from Cairo's streets. At precisely the moment the Egyptian state had started to manufacture its own bicycles, then, *Ma'abudet al-Gamahir* makes the bicycle—and these iconic cyclists—a sign of vulnerability and nostalgia.

Earlier representations of the bicycle in Egyptian musical film—an intensely self-referential artistic practice, as many have noted—bear this interpretation out.[16] In a memorable scene in the 1937 film *Salama Fi Khair*, for instance, Neguib al-Rihani is entrusted with a suitcase full of cash, and immediately starts to notice bicycle thieves snatching handbags and purses. His alarm grows. Suddenly, following a series of visual puns reminiscent of a Jacques Tati film, he is surrounded by a peleton of sports cyclists. He panics and tries—absurdly—to outrun them. In this film, the bicycle is something of a threat, associated here with opposite ends of the urban social scale—Neguib al-Rihani's pedestrian citizen is caught in the middle. The bicycle may have been ubiquitous by then, according to Ahmed Tarek al-Ahwal, but—to judge by the photographic evidence—it was primarily a work vehicle for the urban poor and fez-wearing office workers, or a sporting accessory for groups of young men.[17] By the end of the 1960s, however, cycling seems to have conquered the middle ground and crossed the gender divide. It was now associated with smart, upwardly mobile, modern women. It could thereby be associated, in song, with romantic love.[18]

The basic premise of the "revolutionary melodrama" of the 1950s and 1960s was to co-opt sentimental plots, artful cinematography, and great songs into the fashioning of the Nasserite citizen (Gordon 2002). Romantic love in these films, and music, too, was shown improving the lives of those it touched. These revolutionary films depicted men learning, through love and music, to serve others and participate in society, to understand the relationship between tradition and progress, to live sensitively but happily, even exuberantly. These films also recognized—very frankly—the unequal demands they placed on men and women. This acknowledgment did not diminish their revolutionary claims. In its gendered and sexual arrangements, the world they had inherited was a harsh and a broken one, after all. Women were to be under no illusions about the challenges of modern, revolutionary citizenship in a country like Egypt. But the lessons men and women were expected to learn, as couples, were fundamentally the same. The exercise of democracy in revolutionary Egypt, as elsewhere in the 1960s, was to "begin with two" (Irigaray 2001).

The bicycle, I would suggest in the light of *Ma'abudet al-Gamahir*, both underlined and extended these lessons. Firstly, it clarified what we might call, following Iris Marion Young, the *necessity* of the city (Young 1986). Without, as she put it in a well-known essay, the "physical historicity" of the city—the architectural sedimentation of different histories rather than the imposition of a single vision; without "the experience of aesthetic inexhaustibility . . . the pleasure in detail and surprise" such a city provides; and without the active constitution of public spaces—"streets, restaurants, concert halls, parks" and the possibilities these afford for intimate interactions with strangers—democratic citizenship cannot survive (Young 1986, 20–21).[19] The bicycle is portrayed in *Ma'abudet al-Gamahir* not just as a kind of urban connecting device, but as an urban *agency* as well. By allowing an individual, on a whim, to traverse the city, from old to new, from its elites to its poor, in minutes, it fashions an awareness of the city's sedimented history, its capacious but sensitive sociability, its constantly changing landscape of "detail and surprise." Remember that it is (revolutionary, democratic, and romantic) love that makes these journeys necessary in the first place.

The bicycle is also portrayed in *Ma'abudet al-Gamahir* as a key to the night. The Nasserite state invested heavily in nocturnal festivity. Umm Kulthum's concerts, which would start late anyway, could last six hours. As ethnomusicologist Virginia Danielson observes in her study of Umm Kulthum, these were displays of stamina, not without revolutionary significance (Danielson 1997). But the "conquest of the night" has a longer history in Ottoman cities (among which Cairo must still, historically, be counted). Ottoman historian Cem Kafadar connects this to the growing coffee trade and the manufacture of lighting materials (oil and glass) accompanying Istanbul's transformation into an imperial metropolis in the mid-seventeenth century (Kafadar 2014). Coffee was, in its time, bitterly resisted—a position amusingly satirized, with an eye on today's religious opponents of urban nightlife, by novelist Orhan Pamuk in *My Name Is Red* (Pamuk 2001). Night was a scene of contest and anxiety in the early modern Ottoman city, too, as Kafadar shows. It was the domain of ancient drinking cultures maintained by the Greeks, Jews, and Armenians; of rowdy gangs of young men from the Anatolian countryside who were looking for fun; of millennial mystics chanting and spinning the night away. No wonder the Ottoman state saw the night as a challenge. It became a space on which it would impose an alternative vision of society, build an industry upon it, and present it to their subjects as a sign of civility.

Consumerism and rural-urban migration in the 1950s boosted nightlife in cities like Istanbul and Cairo, as it did across the developing world. But so, too, did revolution. As in Shanghai, as in Havana, as in Kinsasha, nightlife was a postcolonial proposition, vital to the symbolic and emotional recruitment of the new state's citizens.[20] Farrar and Field note of nightlife in Shanghai in the 1950s that it involved a symbolic rejection both of Chinese courtesan culture (with its decadent connotations) and of Japanese colonialism, for example. Building on what remained of the nightlife infrastructure of the 1920s, a socialist ballroom dancing culture (known as '*jiaowjiyu*') thrived briefly in the 1950s, before couple dancing was eventually banned in the Cultural Revolution. As Farrar and Field note, "a kind of socialist class habitus" took shape here, involving ideas about 'character' (*renpin*), 'personal quality' (*sushi*), and 'civility' (*wenming*), and an appreciation of the "grace" and elegance of dancers (Farrar and Field 2015, 59). This may, in reality, have served only the upward mobility of party elites, as Farrar and Field observe. Deng Xiaoping's efforts to revive it and extend it into working-class areas of the city and the countryside in the 1980s came to nothing, perhaps for this reason. In the 1990s, the new market economy and the importation of Taiwanese and Hong Kongese club culture were to transform Shanghai's nightlife in its entirety. But they show that nightlife in China in the 1950s had clearly been understood—by both state and citizen—as an ancillary to revolution, and a site of postcolonial self-fashioning.

The night is not just daytime extended by artificial lighting and stimulants. It is quite its own project, as cultural theorist Will Straw has observed. Gas and electricity produced not just light, he reminds us, but flickering shadows as well. The night's ambiguous meanings have always drawn on this unstable dialectic. So, too, have they drawn on social anxieties about the shifting composition of the nighttime crowd, as urban work patterns, transport systems, and media systems change (Straw 2014, 2015). More recently, the neoliberal management of the night as "an economy," a means of attracting tourists, developing the field of heritage, and boosting the gentrification of downtown real estate, strikes dispiriting notes today (Cohen 2007). But in the 1960s, nightlife was understood in many parts of the world as inherently progressive, as a legitimate interest of the state, and as a space of citizenly self-fashioning. The song "Haga Ghariba" is to be read, I would suggest, as a kind of postcolonial nocturne. The bicycle in it underlines the opportunities the night affords a young couple not simply for escape, but for a particular kind of *access to* urban public space, for a particular modality of urban *participation*.

If Abd al-Halim's bicycle invites us to think about access to and mobility within urban space as a facet of citizenship, it also invites us to think about the temporality—and speed—of that mobility and access. The city in these films is always encountered at speed. Technicolor, an important industry innovation in these years, with its wide screen ratios and more sophisticated sound, encouraged long tracking shots supplementing the "shot-reverse shot" of classic black and white cinematography.[21] Egyptian filmmakers and their audiences quickly developed a taste for city scenes observed as though from, or taking place within, a speeding vehicle. The camera often swoops and swerves through the city at speed in Abd al-Halim films, evoking the excitement and bewilderment of a world not simply changing, but changing for the better. The pursuit of bicycle by car in *Ma'abudet al-Gamahir* suggests these films drew on the distinctions their viewers might make between *kinds* of speed, though. Or, more accurately, the question they might ask about the payoff between speed and agility. The lovers outwit the paparazzi in the first round of this contest, as we know. This is not a race, after all, but a battle of wits. A "slower" vehicle might get you to where you (and your lover) need to be more quickly—a place of privacy away from home. It might allow for a more agile traverse of the urban social landscape. It might simply be more fun, keeping your spirits high, your joie de vivre bubbling.[22] In Abd al-Halim's films, these are presented as the cardinal social—and citizenly—virtues. They are made possible, I would underline once again, by the bicycle.

In 1973, not long after *Ma'abudet al-Gamahir* was made, French social theorist Andre Gorz wrote a jeremiad entitled "The Social Ideology of the Motor Car" (Gorz 1980, 69–77). His central argument seems unassailable these days: the "freedom" promised by motor transport had already been undermined by its compulsory nature; the social distinction it promised ("get there more quickly!") has been undermined by the uniformly slow speed of traffic; the distance it "made" (by extending spatial relations) is greater than the distance it overcomes; the time spent in driving and earning the money to keep cars on the road meant that the average person—when the sum total of their movements were averaged out over a lifetime—was now moving around the city at less than walking pace. What is the answer to this absurdity, he asks? If cars are to be compulsory, the solution is simple, he says, and with biting irony: abolish the city. He felt North American suburbanization had in fact already done so.

Reflecting on these years in his recent semiautobiographical study of "Motor City," Detroit, Mark Slobin puts the opposing North American case with panache (Slobin 2020). Detroit was, obviously enough, a city made by cars and for cars. And, as the world knows, Detroit's cars lay symbolically and experientially at the heart of North American popular culture and music. In a book filled with driving and road-planning metaphors, Slobin shows how the car, and the city built around it, anchored a fragile civility, bringing Black and immigrant music-making together, and unleashing a powerful creativity.[23] Indeed, Detroit's musical achievements rested on it.[24]

The views from Paris and Detroit about the car's relation to the city, civility, and citizenship would seem to be irreconcilable, at least, as expressed by Gorz on the one hand, and Slobin on the other. Abd al-Halim's bicycle offers an alternative, though, and one that is not entirely incompatible with either.[25] It acknowledges that the citizen "needs" the city, in the senses proposed by Iris Young—the experience of diversity; of layered, built, sedimented history; of "detail and surprise." It shows how this experience might be pleasurable, exuberant, progressive, and above all gregarious. Indeed, how very gregarious it might be. On his bike rides, he sings to the trees and greenery; he greets workmen and shopkeepers in the street; he kisses his mother; he strokes his cat. From the outset, they are motivated by love.[26] Here is a picture, then, of how the city's "detail and surprise" might be reconciled with the re-enchantment of "territory," in a society in revolutionary motion.

What does *song* have to do with it, though? Why does it matter that he is singing on his bicycle? In part, as we have already seen, these "movie musical" moments are genre driven, satisfying a need for a lively and entertaining way of making an eight-minute song visually vibrant and appealing, and taking full advantage of the opportunities (long tracking shots, camera and subjects in motion) offered by the new CinemaScope format. In part, they are shaped by the politics of the moment, connecting complex, mobile, and energetic songs and singing to the idea of the revolutionary subject—himself, complex, mobile, energetic, and, above all, in love. But singing also casts a shadow on the scene. As we have seen, in the highly reflexive world of the films, it is a route not just to revolutionary citizenship but also to stardom, and stardom—the film is terribly clear on this matter—can be destructive. To be more specific, it destroys love. The more Abd al-Halim sings, after all, the more he separates himself from Shadia. In this context, one established by the films and by knowledge of the star's life, singing is marked by a certain ambivalence.

So, too, is the orchestral sound. As already noted, it is one filled with signs of vivacity and energy, but also of expertise and technique. The composers of these songs—Kamal al-Tawil, Baligh Hamdi, Mohammed al-Mougi, Mohamed Abd al-Wahhab—put together maqam and *iqa* in technically innovative ways. The arrangers—Ali Ismail, Andreas Rider—pulled together the resources of Arabic '*takht*,' jazz big band, Western symphony orchestra. The conductors sat at the apex of this technocratic scene, directing the flows and energies that pass between the various elements of it. The soundscape is an image of technocratic mastery—another zone of what historian Timothy Mitchell has described as the "rule of experts" in Egypt at the time (Mitchell 2002). The bicycle, whose proliferating use in Cairo was a small but transformative triumph of engineering, planning, and social ingenuity, is symbolically connected. However, for people who know the films, the image of Abd al-Halim singing on his bicycle is also, indissolubly, linked to another, more painful image. This is of the ailing, bilharzia-afflicted character of later life, dependent upon wheelchair and microphone to manage rehearsals, and visibly struggling with illness on stage. A famous picture shows Abd al-Halim at rehearsal, flanked by his composer and his ensemble director, in his pajamas, frail but energetic on his wheelchair, speaking, microphone in hand, to a room full of musicians we cannot fully see.

It is not only an image of vulnerability. It is, at least equally, a picture of will, determination, and energy. It is an image, above all, of the forceful management of an intricate musical division of labor. Tarab enchantment, long prized in Arab aesthetics, once described, and attached a value to, the emotional feedback loop between performers and (vocal) listener, co-participants in the music. Here we see it transformed. It is, visibly as well as audibly, a matter of organization, hierarchy, technology, professional expertise. It is a matter of vocal enchantment enhanced by orchestration, harmony, and counterpoint, the rationalization of instruments; the self-conscious blending of East and West. It is a musical order that has extended the emotional range and organizational capacities of the sounding human body—like Abd al-Halim's bicycle, and his wheelchair. Admittedly, tarab is, at this point, significantly in question. Some would describe Abd al-Halim as a moment of transition, in touch with the old ways, but also showing how tarab itself would eventually be supplanted by other, more modern, forms of enchantment. Momentarily, though, the singer on his bicycle figures as an extension of the human into both the urban and sonic dimensions of a revolutionary postcolonial modernity.

Nostalgia for this meaning is inevitably at play today. With the steady disappearance of Cairo's expert bandmasters and arrangers, attrition in music higher education, and the reorientation of the Egyptian recording and film industries at the end of Abd al-Halim's life toward Lebanon and the Gulf, performances of the songs increasingly managed without the intricate counterpoint, jazzy harmony, and sumptuous orchestrations. A maqam-based monophony became the stylistic norm. At the same time, they increased in size for gala performances. In 2015 I decided, with a group of music students at King's College London and friends in the Oxford Maqam ensemble, to re-orchestrate and perform some of the bigger numbers for a public concert in London. Chief among these numbers was the Riyad al-Sunbati "masterpiece" discussed above, from Abd al-Halim's first film, *Lahn al-Wafa* (of 1955). The motivation was curiosity. Might we come to understand something about why these orchestral numbers have been so neglected? "Scores" of the older songs do not exist, so we worked with what we could hear on the soundtrack, and with our imaginations. Rescoring was a labor-intensive task, but only, in the event, the beginning of our problems. The coordination, in rehearsal as well as in performance, of Arab takht, choir, jazz big band, and symphony orchestra—very separate worlds today, though not necessary then—turned out to be an exceedingly complex matter.

Despite the challenges, the concert went off without too many hitches. The warm reception from a large cross section of London's Egyptian community made me stop and think, however. I quickly realized that the exercise had been more than a matter of, as it were, restoring a faded picture.[27] The "fading" in question has, after all, been a deliberate, and official, process of reframing this song repertory politically, not, as it were, a natural or chemical process. The exercise seemed to have appeared to this community as the restoration of a *principle*: that this music, and the tarab enchantment associated with it, might not just accommodate out of necessity, but actively thrive on its complexity, its heterogeneity, its cosmopolitanism. Such elements, as far as the audience was concerned, could be deemed neither disposable nor inauthentic. This was a vision of the future of Egyptian—and by extension Arab—music that had once seemed possible: a vision of music on wheels.

The case of Abd al-Halim Hafiz is nostalgic, but it continues to resonate in the challenging political and cultural contexts that pertain across much of the Global South. Here, the questions will often be thus: if a participatory politics is to be forged in a non-democratic environment, then how? If city life is to be made meaningful, pleasurable, and creative, then how? If an alternative is to be found to the ethnic and exclusionary nationalisms of the day, then how? If love is to be possible, when economic and political conditions pull people apart so relentlessly, then how? These questions continue to connect and cross-fertilize in post-revolutionary Egypt, and elsewhere. Our next case study concerns a sign of more recent times, and the United Kingdom. But it is also one in which ideas about citizenship, mobility, and popular song connect and cross-fertilize. It concerns Captain Sir Thomas Moore, veteran fundraiser, and his rendition of "You'll Never Walk Alone," with entertainer Michael Ball, in April 2020. It concerns, too, the place of the crowd in today's citizenly imaginary.

3.2 The citizen in the crowd

Few people in the United Kingdom during early days of the COVID-19 pandemic will not have known the remarkable story of Captain Sir Thomas Moore. "Captain Tom," as he was popularly known, was a decorated war veteran, who had served in the Royal Armoured Corps in India and Burma. During the pandemic, at the age of ninety-nine, he set out to walk a hundred laps of his garden to raise money for Britain's National Health Service. His intention was to raise £1,000 by the time of his hundredth birthday. Popular singer and entertainer Michael Ball—who will play a more prominent role in this story shortly—featured him on a Sunday morning BBC radio phone-in show. Media attention snowballed. Soon everybody was familiar with the image of this determined man making his way up and down his garden in Bedfordshire with the aid of his walking frame, lap by painstaking lap.[28]

By the time of his hundredth birthday, he had raised nearly 33 million GBP. The final laps were completed in the presence of a guard of honor supplied by the First Battalion of the Yorkshire Regiment, his old unit. He was knighted in the 2020 Special Honours, promoted to honorary Colonel by his old regiment, awarded honorary doctorates by Cranfield and Bradford universities, and described by then Prime Minister Boris Johnson as a "point of light." On his birthday he received a personalized greeting from the Queen, a Spitfire fly-past by the Royal Air Force, and a video call from the Secretary General of the United Nations, António Guterres. Buses and trains were named after him. He died on 2 February 2022 after contracting the virus himself. His death was the first item of news on the BBC that day. Flags flew at half-mast across the country; politicians and royalty declared their respect for his achievements.

Popular song culture—of a distinctly British variety—made Captain Tom a figure of national sentiment. It also made some strange connections. Scottish pantomime star Allan Stewart and director Ryan Dewar released a version of David Bowie's "Space Oddity," with the words changed to address "Captain Tom" rather than Bowie's "Major Tom."[29] Others subsequently jumped in with their own "Space Oddity" tributes and social media parodies. Allan Stewart's version may have been little more than a passing social media event, but it built on a deeply felt relationship in the United Kingdom between technocracy (emblematized by the National Health Service), popular culture, charity, and civic life. At the heart of this relationship are the figures of quietly eccentric men on quirky, willful missions.[30] The parodists themselves identified with it. Allan Stewart observed that his parody had "started out as an exercise to keep my mind active" during the pandemic, but that it had "taken on a life of its own"—with 750,000 downloads, and considerable sums raised on its back for Captain Tom's charity. With Second World War nostalgia on the rise in the United Kingdom, "heroism" is repeatedly described in terms of selflessness and uncomplaining hard work, civic decency in the face of an implacable enemy, and overwhelming odds.

Michael Ball's celebration of Captain Tom's one hundredth birthday with a rendition of "You'll Never Walk Alone" on a BBC breakfast show moved the story into entirely new territory. It was followed by a single, featuring Ball and Moore duetting, and the NHS "Voices of Care" Choir in the background. It is, at the time of writing, easy to find online and worth listening to attentively, with particular attention to the relay of voices.[31] Moore introduces this song in spoken recitation. Ball then takes over, singing. Both sing the chorus. But Moore, whose voice is frail, drops out on the first iteration well before the extended top note (on the first syllable of "never"), a significant choric "event" of the song that will be discussed shortly. He joins in again on the downward slope to the cadence. The second verse pushes things up a semitone. This is a familiar cliché evoking collective singing, but it considerably ups the stakes for Moore, who is already stretched in reaching the high notes. Somehow, and a little unexpectedly, Moore sticks with Ball for the entirety of the chorus, delivering the final lines on his own. On 24 April 2020 the single hit the top of the charts, making Moore the oldest person in the world to have had a number-one single. The singer who was at that moment number two in the charts. The Weeknd (aka Canadian Abel Makkonen Tesfaye), joined in the campaign, urging people to download Michael Ball and Captain Tom's song rather than his own—a gesture that may well have prolonged its chart presence.[32]

"You'll Never Walk Alone" firmly located the figure of this self-effacing but eccentric citizen in well-trodden national narratives. But how did it do this? In the first instance, the song carries meaning associated with its familiar musical contexts. One of these, quite far in the background, is *Carousel*, the 1945 Rogers and Hammerstein stage musical, later a film. The song, here, is a narrative of endurance. Billy Bigelow, a small-time thief, has committed suicide after a botched bank job. (The film version differs from the stage musical, perhaps to make Billy more redeemable: he dies after accidentally falling on his knife.) The musical follows the story of his wife, Julie, and his daughter as they struggle through life without him. Bigelow is granted a day's return to earth as a ghost. He watches his wife and daughter graduate, tearfully joining in the final chorus of this song. It is a song about the struggle with grief and loneliness, obviously enough. It is about the supportive presence of invisible others, then: one is never alone. It was picked up and recorded by various singers over the ensuing decades, including Frank Sinatra and Elvis Presley.

In the United Kingdom, however, the song is associated almost exclusively with Liverpool Football Club. This association dates from the early 1960s, coinciding with the advent of live football on television. Liverpool FC, a northern English team with attitude and a desire to impress the (southern) national media, led the way in musical entertainment on match day. Prematch entertainment from a DJ was already a regular feature of stadium life, with the top ten being played in reverse order as kickoff approached.[33] The songs of the day were taken up by the Liverpool crowd with particular vigor—a phenomenon that made it the subject of a BBC Panorama program in the early 1960s.[34] Gerry and the Pacemaker's 1963 version of "You'll Never Walk Alone" was a number-one hit at the time. It might have slipped into oblivion, like other number one hits from these years. But the Liverpool crowd latched onto it and did not let it go.

Thanks to the Liverpool fan's zesty performances on TV, "You'll Never Walk Alone" spread as a club anthem to other football clubs, not just in the United Kingdom but in Europe as well. But its association with Liverpool deepened, and changed, with the Hillsborough disaster on 15 April 1989. Poor stadium design and police mismanagement of the crowd resulted in the deaths of ninety-six fans. The conservative press covered up the botched handling of the disaster, blaming the fans for the deaths, which they have never forgotten or forgiven. The most recent official inquiry, in 2012, came at least somewhere near to exonerating the victims. "You'll Never Walk Alone" could be described as the soundtrack of the entire process. It featured in the 1989 memorial service at Liverpool Cathedral, when the words were read out by actor Peter Jones, and then sung by the Cathedral Choir. It continues to be the culminating event at official memorials. On the day of the official inquiry in 2012 it echoed down the Strand in Central London, outside the Central Law Courts. I walked past the fans gathered there on my way back from work that day. It was about 7:00 in the evening, and the streets were emptying. But the fans were still going strong, twenty or so standing for many times that number in their own minds, and in those of anybody familiar with the song.

The association with solidarity in mourning was picked up by other clubs. Celtic FC in Glasgow adopted the song in 1966, Glasgow also being bitterly divided between Catholics and Protestants.[35] Gerry Marsden and others recorded a charity version of the song to support the fifty-six victims of the Bradford City stadium fire in 1985. Alina Schmidt sang it with guitar accompaniment at a stadium memorial for Robert Enke, the Hannover goalkeeper who committed suicide after a long struggle with depression on 15 November 2009. It is, in other words, a song that is transferable to other disasters, other scenes of suffering. It has often been sung as a mark of respect for, and solidarity with, the Hillsborough campaign by opposing fans as well. This also makes it an object of desecration and ridicule. Parodies sung by opposing fans or attempts to sing over the Liverpool supporters (e.g., Manchester United fan's notorious "Always the victims, it's never your fault" chant) are the object of spluttering denunciations by visiting managers when it becomes clear they have hit their target and caused offence.[36] Desecration and ridicule only deepen the song's significance and power, of course.

It is a borrowed song, and it lends itself, in turn, to other situations, and more generalized sentiments. But these borrowings, at least in the United Kingdom and the neighboring countries that share its football culture, carry with them, whether implicitly or explicitly, the sound of the Liverpool FC *crowd*. The song, in other words, carries with it an idea of 'crowdness.' With its, by now inextricable, associations with the Hillsborough disaster, this is the crowd understood in a rather particular way—as a scene of affective solidarity, social memory, and political intent. The Liverpool FC crowd could be said, in other words, to have imposed these particular ideas about the crowd, and, indeed, about "crowdness," on the song. It has shaped the meanings of its citations in popular culture—from Pink Floyd's *Meddle* of 1971 to 2020s cult Netflix heist drama *La casa de papel*. It has raised the interesting question of when use of the song is legitimate, and when it is not, and who gets to decide. Tam Yiu Chung cited it in support of the police during a Legislative Council meeting in Hong Kong during the 2014 pro-democracy protests, for instance. Fan associations in Liverpool vehemently objected, recalling the Merseyside Police's behavior during and after the Hillsborough disaster.[37] How has the remarkable political iconicity of this song been forged? Three questions present themselves immediately. One is *what* it is about this song that that has made this possible. A second concerns *how* it is—most often—heard sung, in a crowd. A third concerns what this crowd might itself *mean*, politically speaking. An attempt to answer these questions will eventually lead us back to Captain Tom's rendition of the song and the question of citizenship. But they deserve to be answered in a bit of detail.

With regard to the affordances of the song, we might start by qualifying my earlier statement that the song "lends itself to crowd singing." The chorus certainly does, but the verses arguably do not. When sung by the crowd on its own, without the help of the Kop's sound system, the verse section is indeed often a lackluster mumble. The melodic arc of each phrase is a shallow and somewhat indistinct one. Musicologists might enjoy the contrast between the placid, gently contoured lines and the relatively complex tonal design—spelled out in spiky arpeggios by the keyboards in the Gerry and Pacemakers version. But the crowd has little to get its teeth into here. Things change immediately in the chorus. This rises steadily, but powerfully, to a false summit at the end of line 2 ("Though your dreams be tossed and blown") and then to a true summit, with its conspicuous soaring arc, at the end of line 4 ("You'll never walk alone"). Musicologists might enjoy, and find meaning in, the fact that the top of this arc is approached by a fourth, the largest upward leap in the song, indeed, the only one of this magnitude. Singing in a crowd, it is, of course, anticipated from the outset and focuses, in the event, an extended roar, a vocal gesture of assembled lungs, chests, vocal tracts; raised arms and faces. It is to have a very particular experience of the song's message of challenges faced and overcome, of tears mastered and controlled.

Musicologists, less anxious than they once were about the specter of "regressive listening," will have various ways of understanding how a fragment of melody—here, the ascending fourth—might constitute a crucial element in the hermeneutic framing of a song.[38] The crowd, for its part, has a *collective* experience of the song—indeed, an experience of associating the collectivity with it. In the singing of this arc, the crowd hears its own singing. Its crowdness becomes present to it, in other words. Interestingly, Gerry Marsden clips this arc in his recorded version.[39] The Liverpool FC crowd would seem to have extended it from the very outset.[40] That extended choric arc—fusing physical gesture, vocal sound, and stadium architecture—quickly became iconic not only of Liverpool FC, but also of "crowd" itself, an iconicity Pink Floyd's 1974 citation in *Meddle* relied on. Though unheard, it can be supplied by any listener familiar with British popular culture, to Captain Tom and Michael Ball's singing of the song in 2020. So, in the last chorus, where (you will recall) he *does* join in, Captain Tom's fragile, centenarian voice is born aloft by this invisible and inaudible crowd. One knows from experience, even if it is vicarious experience, how voices at this point audibly lift and sustain one another. If one cannot hold that top note, one can be sure others will, and know that one's own efforts have somehow contributed to theirs. Vocally, it is impossible to be "alone" at this moment, even if one is singing to oneself. Steven Connor, interested in the haunting of voice by the idea of the crowd and what he calls "fantasies of amplification," speaks of voice "that is compounded of, rather than subtracted from (crowd) noise"; this would seem to be a good example (Connor 2016, 6). "The arc," in other words, affords a certain appropriation by the crowd, and recursively imposes a very specific set of meanings on the song to do with collectivity, meanings that are now indissolubly linked with it.[41]

The crowd might recognize its crowdness at that moment, a crowdness that persists in the imagination, in the appropriate cultural contexts, in all subsequent iterations, whether actually sung by a crowd or not. Part of that process of recognition lies, as argued above, in the song's particular affordances for crowd singing. But it also lies in the matter of *how* crowds sing. This is trickier terrain. We know something, these days, about *what* crowds sing, and, to an extent, *why*. The question of *how* poses some intractable questions. Elias Canetti put sound at the heart of his 1960 phenomenology of the crowd, *Crowds and Power* (Canetti 1984). Early in this book he observes that it is the sound of feet—left feet and right feet, in his view, sounding different—that communicates to the crowd knowledge about its size, its motion, its position in urban space (Canetti 1984, 31). In its details, this seems far fetched. But he is correct that crowds want to know their size (and thus their strength), and their direction (and thus their purpose, which may not yet be entirely or uniformly clear). And sound assumes importance when other sensory sources of information are restricted.

Anybody doubting this phenomenon might reflect on something, I expect, many readers will have experienced. A crowd that has gathered in a park to march on a city-center government building will know the growing resonance of footsteps and chanting as it moves from trees, leaves, and grass to narrowing city-center streets. The knowledge that the crowd is approaching its destination is conferred, to a significant degree, by the changing resonance. In part, this is simply knowledge of a location on a map, and speed of progress to its destination. But it is also knowledge of the crowdness of the crowd—its capacity to halt everyday life in a city and stop cars, to bring out the police, to attract a hostile counterdemonstration, to be met by closed doors indicating official silence, to push a political issue to the brink, to make the evening news. This is, as Canetti signaled, the self-constituting knowledge of the crowd as a historical and political event.

If discussions of crowd singing have tended to focus on the playful looping of repurposed popular song fragments, on call-and-response improvisation, and on the exploitation of the acoustic properties of architectural environments,[42] Liverpool FC's crowd's singing of "You'll Never Walk Alone" adds another element worth considering in this context. The effects of all this, too, are concentrated around "the fourth." That is the way the crowd reconfigures the meter of a song. Gerry and the Pacemakers' version is a gentle R&B 12/8 shuffle. The crowd pushes toward a zesty 3/4. The result is often what ethnomusicologist Jean During would label an 'ovoid' rhythm, occupying a metrical space somewhere between, as one can hear clearly on match recordings in the 1980s (During 1997). Later, a new generation of sound installations in football stadia meant, often, competing recorded and crowd versions, where the clash of meters and the slipping out of phase of the crowd version becomes conspicuous—to the ethnomusicologist, at least. But even without this conflict, it is a complex metrical maneuver. The shift can be represented in Western music notation as seen in Figure 3.1. For those who do not read this kind of notation, try counting a slow four to the Gerry and the Pacemakers

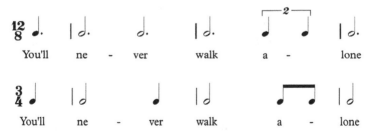

Figure 3.1 Metrical transformations of "You'll Never Walk Alone."

recording. Then listen to a recording of the Liverpool crowd singing, uncomplicated by competing recorded versions played simultaneously on the public address system; count a brisk three or imagine a waltz.[43]

At issue, then, is not a particular kind of meter ("ovoid" or otherwise), but a metrical *process*. Some insight into this can be derived from Bernard Lortat-Jacob's analyses of a similar metrical transformation in the Berber highland-pasture migration festivities known as *ahwash* (Lortat-Jacob 1994). This transformation features a progressive clipping of the central rhythmic cell, over the course of twenty minutes or so of antiphonal singing and dancing. This might be represented as seen in Figure 3.2.[44] In WAM terms, this represents a shift from a triple to a duple meter, phased across a continuum, so not involving the abrupt shifts implied by the technical terminology here. A combination of intensifying excitement, the quickening of breath caused by exertion, and the nudges provided by the more experienced vocalists and dancers is at work to produce that change. It is, in effect, the work of an assembly *on* a musical motif. For Lortat-Jacob, it is a sonic sign of the collective, present to itself in this seasonal festival as at no other time. In "You'll Never Walk Alone," in these crowd-only versions, we can hear a similar push and pull of bodies, the nudging away from the recorded version led by sections of the crowd, and the affirmation of the ♩ at the arc of the melody, at the fourth. Chests are puffed out, heads are lifted, arms are raised, collective energy surges, accelerating the process, which is as much choreographed physical gesture as sound. Masculinity is, obviously, at play.

Secondly, the question of who and what that crowd represents—beyond, as we have seen, crowdness—is not easy to establish. And the link with questions about citizenship seems, at first glance, particularly remote. Liverpool FC has an unfortunate role to play here. A riot involving Liverpool and Juventus fans at the Heysel stadium in Belgium

Figure 3.2 Metrical transformations in the Berber ahwash (from Lortat-Jacob 1994, with reference to During 1997).

in 1985 caused the deaths of twenty-nine and injuries to over six hundred. The blame was firmly laid on Liverpool FC by the UEFA.[45] 26 Liverpool fans were charged with manslaughter, and an indefinite ban on English clubs playing in Europe immediately followed. For at least a decade, the sound of English football club fans in Europe's historic city centers had meant only one thing—a night of running street battles between rival groups of fans and police, and a landscape of wreckage the following morning. Europhile Britons looked on in shame. It is hard, with hindsight, not to see at least some of the lines of Britain's rancorous Brexit debates three decades later being drawn at that moment. Some would continue to see Europe, across the English Channel, as a beacon of culture and civility, and England as a bewildered nation unable, without its Empire, to find a place for itself in a modern world. Others would continue to see Europe as fundamentally authoritarian and bureaucratic, haughtily disrespectful of Britain's identity, history, and political values.

In his celebrated book *Among the Thugs*, American writer Bill Buford devoted an attentive ear to these soundscapes (Buford 1992). In what has become a well-known passage, he accompanies Manchester United's notorious Intercity Jibbers to the European Cup Winners final against Juventus FC in Turin in 1984.[46] Violence starts with the sound of a shattering windshield. "It had been the range of sounds, of things breaking and crashing, coming from somewhere in the darkness, unidentifiable, that was increasing steadily the strength of feeling of everyone around me" (Buford 1992, 90). "Temperature'" rises; there is a "chemical moment" as adrenaline kicks in, a roar, a second crashing sound. "Frenzy" and "weightlessness" take over. It is the first of many sequences in this book that describe the gathering of fans on public transport and at airports; the singing, vandalism, and insulting the local citizenry; the tipping point, a sonic event of one kind or another, as we have just seen; the running battles in darkened streets; the actions, in the heat of the moment, of the various characters Buford has identified, variously, as leaders, foot soldiers, clowns, and mischief-makers; the frequent stops to top up on alcohol; the weary dawn, the match itself, as it always had been, a complete irrelevance; the reassembly of the scattered and exhausted company to catch the plane back; the declaration, somewhere along the way, of "victory."

From today's perspective, two things stand out. One is the attention Buford devotes to singing and, more generally, to sound. Singing provides the cocoon, the solidarity, the feeling of invincibility, the nostalgia for Empire and the Second World War, feeding hostility to everybody the company encounters. It provides a powerful sense of community, but it is also, for Buford, where the violence accumulates. And it is sound, as we have already seen, that creates the "tipping point," pushing events that one could, until that tipping point is reached, describe in sociologically conventional ways (to do with class, age, gender, sexuality), and after it in terms of sociologically ill-defined "crowd behavior." There are elements in these descriptions of what Jonathan Sterne described some time ago as "the litany," a repetitive evocation of the difference between seeing and listening as opposed modes of cognition, the first to do with order and ordering, the second with their negation (Sterne 2003, 15).[47] The relations between the senses are, Sterne insisted, historically constructed, not rooted in the working of the cognitive system. More specifically, sound's "negation" of vision is a product of European romanticism. Vivid and thoughtful though this account of crowd behavior is, it rests on something (sociologically) quite conventional in its focus on tipping points, and the linking of sound with them.

These conventions are, sociologically speaking, Durkheimian. In the famous passages that opens *The Elementary Forms of Religious Life*, Durkheim asks readers to recall the experience of being in a crowd, to make vivid to them how "the social" makes its appearance, brightly lit by that "state of mind" Durkheim labels 'effervescence' (Durkheim 1893/1965, 9). Totems, like all subsequent religious experience, draw on this effervescence, without which our emotional commitments to "the social," more broadly, could not take shape and flourish. Crowd sound is an afterthought in Durkheim's opening scenarios, but it makes a symptomatic appearance in a few key passages. "Cries, veritable howls, and deafening noises of every sort" in the crowd, he says, "aid in intensifying still more the state of mind which they manifest" (Durkheim 1893/1965, 247). This is consonant with an idea of "the social" as a sudden manifestation, a qualitative change of consciousness.

Buford, as mentioned, reads the crowd negatively. The crowd might be social, lit, in Burford's echoings of Durkheim, by a strange effervescence. But for Buford, it is far from civil or citizenly. Indeed, it is quite the antithesis of these things. Recall that the crowd, for both Durkheim and Tarde—in their opposition to Le Bon—was an inherently progressive phenomenon. But Tarde saw the crowd significantly differently from the way Durkheim did. Tarde understood the crowd in terms of "invisible, infinitesimal [and] molecular" processes of gestural imitation, processes that lay at the heart of sociality in general (Brighenti 2010, 300). There was, for Tarde, no qualitative experiential moment separating "the individual" from "the collective," as there was for Durkheim. There was no tipping point in the crowd, only an acceleration of the mimetic process, a process of emergence. The opposition between these two conceptions of the crowd deepened as competing political factions gathered around Tarde and Durkheim at, respectively, the Collège de France and the Sorbonne (Brighenti 2010). But both could be said to have been reacting to Gustave Le Bon's picture of "crowd psychology," characterized by its blind adherence to leaders. Writing in the aftermath of the Franco-Prussian war and the Paris Commune, Le Bon had seen the crowd, quite unambiguously, as a threat to order, and as a matter for criminologists, not sociologists. But the Tardean crowd has fared better than its Durkheimian counterpart in recent decades.[48]

A somewhat neglected social theorist pulls Tarde's intuitions about the crowd's "immanent" and "emergent" qualities explicitly in the direction of citizenship. This is Robert E. Park, an American sociologist who studied with Georg Simmel in Berlin in 1899 before completing a PhD at Heidelberg under Wilhelm Windelband and Alfred Hettner in 1903. His doctoral dissertation was published in German as *Masse und Publikum: Eine methodologische und soziologische Untersuchung*. This work complicated the important distinctions he wanted to make between 'mass' and 'crowd,' German having only one word for both— *Masse*. But the English translation, published when he was teaching sociology at Harvard, allowed him to tease out the distinctions and connections (Park 1972). In both cases Park was interested in the 'volitional attitudes' (*Willenshaltungen*) of individuals interacting in group situations. A fundamental issue for modern political subjectivity is, according to Park, the individual's inherent lack of "self-awareness." "Imitation," within the group, "induces new dispositions" to individuals, a reciprocal and reflexive process for Park as it was for Tarde (Park 1972, 44).

Park was more interested, however, in the political consequences of this mimetic principle, explicitly as it concerned democracy and the citizen. The "susceptibility" and "suggestibility" of the crowd, for Park, were positive qualities. They generated "collective attention," and thus a "general will," and produced "the mutual affecting and reconciling of human drives" (Park 1972, 77). Without such attention and such "mutual affecting," the most important work of the collective, which is "the establishment of facts," cannot be fulfilled. The importance of facts, for Park, was that they demanded collective recognition even as they acknowledged difference of feeling and opinion. Without facts, for Park, there is no public. If Park distinguished crowds by their inability to produce "facts," he also saw crowds and publics as related, as points on a continuum. Historically and politically, each could become the other, under certain circumstances. The crowd is seen by Park, then, not just as formative of modern democratic political subjectivity—of citizenly values and attitudes, in other words—but, like the public itself, as a process of self-reflexive actualization and transformation from within—"forms used to make new groupings" (1972, 79).

Park's nuance is worth remembering, because old, and ultimately perhaps unshakable, sociological anxieties about crowds seem to be returning.[49] Sound has a role to play in this revisionism, as a recent and luminous article on "chorality" by Steven Connor suggests. Connor is interested in the crowd as a "reservoir of unbounded noise," and in the way sound, rather than depleting, accumulates and redistributes its energy. But he hears the crowd singing to itself only. It is "thymotic" in its quest for recognition, and is correspondingly sealed in, open to no outside influence. Crowd singing, as he understands it, moves between noise (the roar of the crowd) and redundancy (the unisonality of song). When it constructs a dialogue, as in call and response, it is in dialogue only with itself. Connor draws two conclusions from this. Firstly, the singing crowd maintains the "hallucination" of "collective voice," which he considers an impossibility, the mere fantasy of it threatening. A key passage concerning this is worth quoting in full:

> I think there are compelling reasons to doubt the existence of such collective subjects which might be able to feel, deliberate, and communicate on their own account. Despite, or perhaps because of, the fact that the voice is so closely associated with the individual subject, the choral voice is one of the most potent carriers of the fantasy of the collective subject; it is the embodied fantasy of a fantasy of embodiment... Chorality is the means whereby we allow ourselves the collective hallucination of collectivity. We understand much of the pressure and pleasure of the voice in understanding its choral forms; but the point of trying to understand the power we allow ourselves to exercise over ourselves in the fantasies of chorality is also to be able to refuse and as necessary rescind its demands. (Connor 2016, 20).

Secondly, he sees it slowly disappearing from modern life. This is a somewhat hopeful position, given the first. With twentieth-century modernism, as "quoted" in Ligeti, Stockhausen, Adams, and Reich, the crowd becomes a figure of involution and decline. If choral music has become "marginal" in the twentieth century, and choral societies are now bourgeois and graying, it is because the ideas that once associated the chorus with the revolutionary crowd, and with the nineteenth-century march of democracy, have by now become redundant. "The enactment of the idea of the crowd no longer carries the force that it used to," in short (Connor 2016, 21). Chorality disappears in an involuted fashion into experimental literature, the strange reflexivity of flash mobs, the vicious politics of the football crowd, the hollow rhetoric of "crowd sourced" questions at Prime Minister's Question Time, involutions that seem, for Connor, to be retrograde and inherently uncivil.

My own starting point is, with Canetti, more positive. It also to approach the crowd at a rather specific historical moment. The "sentimental crowd," gathered simultaneously to mourn, protest, and reflect, has, I would argue, taken shape at a particular historical and political juncture. Hillsborough marks one conspicuous event within this juncture. One can think of others within the United Kingdom alone. One would be the gatherings in Central London associated with Princess Diana's funeral in 1997. Another would be the million-strong crowd that marched to protest the United Kingdom's involvement in the Iraq

War in 2003. The juncture, in UK terms, can be characterized in terms of a crisis of traditional authority (the police, the royal family), a crisis of public communication (distrust of the press and the BBC, the rise of social media), a crisis of public space (out-of-control real estate markets, intensified surveillance and policing of city centers), and a prevailing set of neoliberal tenets in government that has been happy to see these crises grow. Under these sharp and difficult circumstances, the crowd—the crowd gathered to remember, to protest, to express a mood—has had specific meanings. These, I would argue, are to do with the crowd's collective and performative modeling of its own civility.

"Sentimental citizenship"—citizenship informed by emotional literacy, reflexivity, and the issue-driven quest for social justice (see Marcus 2002)—may not involve only individual rumination and calculation. It may also be crafted collectively. I propose the term more as a historical marker than as one more sociological type. It also helps me understand the place of song in them. But that history is a British, or, at least, a northwest European one. It has its limits, then. It assumes a crisis of liberalism, rather than a crisis of authoritarianism. It will be useful then, in the next section, to consider an example at exactly that limit point. This concerns the Gezi Park protests in Istanbul in 2013.

3.3 The citizen in the square

The crowds that gathered in what were quickly, and collectively, labeled 'The Squares' both reframed and added considerable urgency to the question of citizenship. The "Arab Spring" of 2010, sparked independently in Tunisia, Syria, and then Egypt, caught global attention. City-center occupations elsewhere—in New York, Tel Aviv, Ukraine— seemed to be part of the same story. The protests in Montreuil (Paris), Rinkby (Stockholm), and Tottenham (London) also seemed connected, if more clearly about race. But it was hard to see exactly what, in terms of their stated goals, these connections were.

Seen from a comfortable distance they signified a slumbering citizenry, stirred to revolutionary action by poverty and desperation, and the brazen corruption of their leaders. At "home," the press was, by contrast, quick to label them race riots, violent disturbances of the civic order. Somewhere in between—Istanbul, Tel Aviv, and Kyiv—their meanings were less clear, pulled one way or another, depending on how the West's media chose to understand their leaders, Erdoğan, Netenyahu, and Yanukovych. It was often difficult, from a distance, to decide exactly whose behavior was to be labeled civil and whose not. It was readily apparent, nonetheless, that these movements were heavily invested in the idea of civility and responsible citizenship, and in the questions surrounding rights of access, mobility, and residence within the city. Their exuberant convergence on downtown city squares reinforced this impression. Were we witnessing, in desperate times, the rebirth of the classical agora? Labeling this the age of "The Squares," many commentators clearly hoped so.[50]

A powerful—and long-standing—nostalgia was at play, however. As philosopher Marshall Berman reminded us, political nostalgia for the Athenian agora goes back to the fourth century BC. The "Old Oligarch," a fifth-century BC commentator, was fascinated by the Athenian agora's "sloppiness"—the lack of a visible hierarchy in its dress codes, the informality of its speech, the leveling effects of shopping.[51] The bonds this built, according to the Old Oligarch, meant people were able to learn, and learn peacefully, "how to rule and how to obey." This concept, as Berman shows, became the classical formula for democratic citizenship. But even then, it had its critics, Plato among them. From the outset it was under pressure. By the time Alexander the Great conquered Athens and other Greek cities in the late fourth century BC, Berman reminds us, both the ideal and the practice had disappeared. The agora as crucible of citizenship in antiquity was already a fantasy.

Rousseau's depictions of the assembled mass addressed by the human voice, and the French Revolution's gathering of the people at the Bastille and the Champ des Mars were a—nostalgic—attempt to revive its spirit. What ensued was the Terror, as we know. Public squares in which the masses might be assembled, addressed, and instructed became an adjunct of totalitarianism, in Europe and beyond. They emptied of life, to have a semblance of political energy only in the staid televised rituals of the totalitarian state. The aching emptiness of these squares—Red Square in Moscow, Tiananmen Square in Beijing—spoke eloquently to observers in the West. Recall one of the most iconic political images of the late twentieth century, the lone man defying the tanks in Tiananmen Square. Art historian T.W.J. Mitchell notes of this image that its power lies in the (imagined) emptiness of the square, the terrible solitude and utter vulnerability of the lone protestor. This symbol fed a powerful desire, far in advance of the Arab Spring and the global city centre protests of 2010, to reimagine the square as a sign "of potentiality, possibility and plenitude" (Mitchell 2013, 112).[52]

If nostalgia for the classical agora was at play, so, too, was a reluctance to consider the way colonial histories bore on these locales. Tahrir Square in Cairo is particularly instructive in this regard. Cotton, and in its wake British commercial and military interests, dominated the city in the late nineteenth century. In the colonizing of Egypt, as historian Timothy Mitchell argued a while ago, power was to take shape in the act of seeing and being seen (Mitchell 1991). Significant parts of the city were rebuilt to facilitate the process. If the downtown area, with its Hausmannesque étoiles and boulevards, "performed" a colonial modernity in this fashion, they did so in relationship to a no-less curated vision of "traditional" Islamic Egypt—the jumble of streets and alleys around the old city core. Colonial "metaphysics," Mitchell argues, took shape around this juxtaposition, those with the ability to plan (and impose plans) decisively separated from those lacking such an ability.[53] If "the squares" of the Middle East and North Africa were to be imagined by the West as a resurgent agora, we must remind ourselves that the colonial powers redesigned these cities, working squares, étoiles, and Hausmannesque boulevards into their design, not with the intention of nourishing democracy but of subjugating a local population.

The question of the agora takes shape differently when we put the question of sound center stage. To an extent, the matter has been anticipated, as we have already seen, by Rousseau. We do not need to subscribe to his incipiently authoritarian fantasies of the audible single voice, though. In 2010, the squares presented themselves to the world as an image of sonic creativity and multiplicity. To return, briefly, to Tahrir Square, the shifting circles gathering around chant leaders in the square, the impromptu concerts momentarily focusing the entire crowd, and the more fragmented performances scenes within the crowd are vividly remembered and well documented by historians and ethnographers.[54] Tahrir Square made international stars of some of the activists, notably Ramy Issam (Levine 2014). It also, as mentioned earlier in this chapter, underlined the names of historical singers and musicians associated over time with Egypt's revolutionary struggle—Sayyed Darwish, Sheikh Imam, Abd al-Halim Hafiz, and others. We have an impression of *what* was sung, thanks to a (heavily mediated, heavily curated) process of memorialization and documentation. But we have—largely because of that mediation and curation—much less of a sense of *how* it was sung. As the previous section of this chapter has already indicated, this might be where some important questions lie.

The Gezi Park protests in Istanbul of 2013 allow me to develop them a bit. Collective memory of these, in and beyond Turkey, is now somewhat blurred. Neither government nor protestors can confidently claim success. Prosecutions against activists continue. Shops in the vicinity that supported, or denied access to, protestors are still remembered for the purposes of boycott or patronage. At the time of writing, the park continues to feel like a building site.[55] If memory of this event is blurred and fragmented, this is probably a consequence of an even more momentous event that took place three years later—the botched coup of 15 July 2016. President Erdoğan survived it and seized the moment to identify Fethullah Gülen, who appeared to have orchestrated it, as a public enemy. The relentless struggle against the Gülen movement continues to this day. It continues to be a bewildering and exhausting process for most of the population, and it has hugely complicated efforts to organize antigovernment protest. Unlike the Tahrir protests, then, those in Gezi have not, quite, been monumentalized (and thereby silenced) in collective memory. I turn to them, in part, for that reason.

Gezi Park sits on the edge of Taksim Square in Istanbul. Like Tahrir Square, it became a home to protests almost accidentally. As the name (meaning 'division') indicates, Taksim was where water brought in by aqueducts from the Belgrade Forest was divided among the surrounding neighborhoods. The Ottoman sultans concentrated their westernizing city planning fantasies in the Muslim, not the Christian, part of the city, far away on the other side of the Golden Horn. Like Tahrir, Taksim was dominated by military barracks for much of the nineteenth century. The barracks were largely destroyed during the 1909 constitutional crisis, briefly becoming a stadium. It was only in the modern republic, in the 1930s, and as part of Henri Prost's reconstruction plan, that Taksim was bought into a city-wide (though never completed) project to ring the entire city with parks and public amenities (Çelik 1992). Gezi Park dates from this period. It does not, then, have a significant claim to antiquity, prestige, or even, really, centrality.[56]

The revelation of plans early in 2013 to build a neo-Ottoman shopping center, closely modeled on the old barracks, and containing a mosque, caused outrage. The plan was provocative at a multitude of different levels. Gezi Park is a small sea of green in a heavily built-up area in the heart of Istanbul's formerly "European" commercial district. It is felt by many to be a secular space, as distant from mosques and minarets as you can be in this city. It is close to one of the Muslim world's first ever pieces of public statuary, close to the Atatürk Cultural Centre (AKM), close to the Greek Orthodox cathedral, and close to Turkey's first ever McDonalds. It has long been the place where protestors have assembled and sought refuge during demonstrations and protests in this part of the city. But it is also a place to catch your breath, meet friends, have picnics, have a glass of tea, catch up on your phone messages, and so forth. A space of intimacy, in other words.

In the context of Turkey's culture wars, which pitted an increasingly authoritarian and religiously conservative Recep Tayyip Erdoğan and his AKP against secularist, liberal, and leftist critics countrywide, it was a provocative declaration. It happened to coincide with debates about the AKP administration's efforts to curb alcohol consumption and public kissing. His critics were beginning to feel the effects of a concerted attack on their (secular) way of living in and moving around the city. A sit-in, sparked by early efforts to uproot trees, began late in May. It was violently dispersed by the riot police on 15 June, the manner of the dispersal generating further outrage. It sparked mirror protests across the country and the Turkish and Kurdish diaspora in Europe, and weeks of street fighting in and around the Taksim area.

I had, coincidentally, arrived in Istanbul on the morning of 15 June to attend a conference. I had been following the protests online. The atmosphere, until that point, had been festive, and I was looking forward to wandering over when I found a moment. That evening, I had an extended drink in Sultanahmet with a visiting English colleague whom I had not seen for a long time. I was vaguely aware of my phone buzzing frantically in my pocket as we ordered our second round of drinks. By the time I had found out what was going on, the Taksim area had been sealed off by riot police.

When a route there finally proved possible several days later, I attended a silent vigil in the Square. I recall police, journalists, and a hundred or so silent protestors, amid signs of the previous evening's clashes. A pattern had momentarily established itself: quiet protests in the Square during the day, running battles between protestors and police during the night. This vigil I attended quickly extended itself across the city, with isolated protestors standing silent and still in streets, at bus stops, in parks, and reading books. My first engagement with the soundscape of the protests was, then, one marked by silence. Its message could not have been clearer: reading (and an education, and "culture") may be a necessary condition of citizenship, but it was no longer a sufficient one.

To turn to the "sounded" soundscape, three independent elements could be distinguished.[57] The first involved the fashioning of chants, slogans, and songs in ways that involved wit, arcane intertextuality, and dense subcultural reference, looping between park and social media. Perhaps the most celebrated was provoked by Erdoğan's early reference to the protestors as 'looters,' or *çapulcu*. Overnight, those in sympathy with the protest added çapulcu to their social media names or used it as a term of address. The words "Every day I'm chapulling" (in English) were to be seen scrawled over walls around the Taksim area. A YouTube video grafting images of the protest onto the music of LMFAO's 2011 hit "Party Rock Anthem (Everyday I'm Shuffling)" went viral. LMFAO's hit alluded to and incorporated some of the lyrics of rapper Rick Ross's song, "Everyday I'm Hustling," but turning its grim tone of ghetto defiance into a joyous celebration of street dancing. The slogan "everyday I'm chapulling" underlined, therefore, not only the secular subcultural cosmopolitanism of the moment, but the spirit of play—play with language, play with sound, play with popular cultural knowledge—at the heart of the protest.

A second was the beating of pots and pans on apartment balconies across the city. Some argued that this was a "traditional" protest technique in Turkey, dating back to Ottoman times. It clearly has some relationship with European practices of *charivari* or "rough musicking," widespread, still, in southern Europe.[58] It seems probable that it was picked up in Turkey from news coverage of the anti-austerity protests in Argentina early in the 2000s. Here, though, it was more directly a response to Erdoğan's dismissive comment to a journalist concerning the protests, "*tencere tava, hep ayni hava,*" "the same old story, pots and pans": i.e., "here we go, the usual rubbish." It was an unfortunate choice of words, once again putting a powerful weapon directly into the hands of his opponents. Women in working-class neighborhoods who might not have been able to travel downtown to join in were now able to make their views known publicly without stirring from their own homes. A prominent protest group, Kardeş Türküler, associated themselves with the protests by singing a newly composed protest song in the neighborhood streets, self-accompanying with an intricate array of pots, pans, tea glasses, plates, spoons, forks, ashtrays, graters, and so forth. The video quickly went viral.[59]

Thirdly, the pre–June 15 protests involved free concerts in the park. The protestors had organized a playfully miniaturized state, with its own medical facilities, schools, advice bureaus, a library, and, naturally, a symphony orchestra, the so-called Gezi Philharmonic. Students from a big music conservatory nearby had a role to play in supplying the talent and organizational skills. The performances, to judge by social media clips, had a rough and ready edge to them, but they were performances, and they involved some elaborate street productions, for example, of *Les Misérables*. Musical performances contributed to the ironic, playful, and reflexive spirit of the protests. But they were to be transformed on 12 June by the unexpected arrival of German musician Davide Martello. He performed throughout the day, playing, in the evening portion of this long and often improvised recital, some Beatles songs, some Bach, and some of his own compositions. After days of fighting between police and protestors, both sides, by all accounts, sat down peacefully to listen. And while this moment of peace was not to last, an enduring piece of Istanbul folklore had been forged—a protest movement capable of organizing a piano recital by an international artist, including the delivery of a grand piano. This was an extremely powerful image for the protestors. If the state would no longer fund progressive and Western music—the dilapidated state of the Atatürk Cultural Centre at the edge of Taksim Square a silent but eloquent symbol of official disdain and neglect for the ("Western") arts—the protestors could make it happen.

Davide Martello's story is a remarkable one, and worth a brief digression.[60] He is a German pianist, with an Italian background. He carries his grand piano around Europe, playing pop-up concerts at sites of memorial and mourning wherever he goes. The piano has been modified to allow for amplification and transportability, but it remains a distinctly grand piano. He has also modified it to attach to a bicycle. He has a small team to help him get around and retrieve him from scrapes. A recent event in California resulted in the entire apparatus crashing after it had run out of control on San Francisco's steep streets. He tends to work on the basis of spur-of-the-moment decisions and invitations. His concerts usually include some classics intended to be listened to quietly, as well as some of his own compositions, and songs to sing along to. The Gezi concert was, in other words, a routine one for him. He had been in Sofia for a concert, heard of the protests, and decided he would make an appearance. But he was to become, in the opinion of a great many, *the* enduring icon of the entire movement.

It is worth asking why, because there were others. His considerable charisma, charm, and eccentricity played a role, of course. So, too, did his status as an outsider, simultaneously witness and supplier of an international dimension to the protest. And so, too, did the timing, an extended moment that defused mounting tensions and seems to have been enjoyed as much by the police as by the protestors. I would add another element to the picture, which is the metaperformative level on which Martello worked. It was not just a performance, in the eyes of protestors and commentators, but a performance of a performance, a claim on performativity itself. If the state wanted to see citizens parking their cars and shopping like zombies, very well: here were people coming together for free, quality art. If the state preferred to mothball the Atatürk Cultural Centre and with it the legacy of secularist cultural westernization, very well: a German maestro would give a free concert out on the street, right in front of it. If the state preferred to build mosque after mosque and fill the city with the sound of the call to prayer, very well: here would be a grand piano and a Beatles classic, "Hey Jude."

The performativities at play were small scale in the sense that the state's westernization policies once used to envelope and enfold the citizen-subject, like the gigantic statues, flags, and posters representing Atatürk of earlier years. In the Gezi protests, these policies—the secular, Western nation-building process itself—was symbolically presented as small and fragile objects, almost engulfed by the larger-scale—indeed, "global"—processes at play in downtown Istanbul—commerce, Islam, neoliberalism, populist authoritarianism. They were, in a quite direct sense, performativities of citizenship. They were designed to shame the state into a sense of responsibility—responsibility for education, culture, social justice, diversity; for a vision of the city that extended beyond praying and shopping.

The centrality of music both as image and practice of the protest was striking throughout. Three recent ideas about music in protest movements are worth reflecting on here. Firstly, as anybody who has attended a street protest recently knows, simple crowd improvisational practices are, with experienced hands at the helm, capable of fashioning a lively and sustained sonic *presence*, occupying not just space but time. Call-and-response chanting provides an example, as do strophic forms allowing new verses to be improvised by simple word-substitution processes, like verses of "We Shall Overcome" that can be made up on the spot.[61] Keeping sound going creatively and inventively is a core crowd skill, relying on small groups of people ready and willing to assume sonic leadership, and others to follow. But these vocalizing techniques are not just about occupancy. They are about establishing temporalities and historical presence, as Eyerman and Jamison emphasized a while ago (Eyerman and Jamison 1997). Singing is crucial, they point, out, not just to the activation of protest, but to the cognitive process of remembrance. It builds in historicity—a sense of where the event comes from, what its core historical meanings and sensibilities are—from the outset. Participants thereby become conscious of its nature as "event" with roots in the past, conscious of a future in which the meaning of the event might be disputed. Martello's extended "Hey Jude" showed the protestors to be capable not just of occupying the park, but also of prolonging that occupancy, of imposing their own tempo upon it, of ensuring, thereby, lasting collective memory.

Secondly, as Noriko Manabe has shown, protest soundscapes today exist in a state of constant relay with social media (Manabe 2015-2016). Protest signs thereby accumulate additional meanings and points of reference with lightning speed, pulling their original meanings in unexpected directions. Indeed, often they seem to come out of nowhere. Much has been made of the role of social media in the social movements of the early 2010s, and particularly in Tahrir Square. They were the source of news outside heavily controlled state media, ensuring that anger with the Mubarak regime could build and develop a coherent focus. They enabled demonstrators to plan, and to speak to a broader public. Regimes and their security forces—then— were slow to understand the threat, or what might be done in response. Manabe's questions underline the *cultural* dynamics of social media in such situations, and thus its capacity, in real time, to generate signs, understandings, moods. The Gezi protests exemplify her point well. Breaking news coverage of the Gezi protests by Turkish news channels was replaced, with comic abruptness, by a nature documentary about the Antarctic. Penguins became, within minutes, the emblem of the Gezi protests—a cute image of the protestors themselves, as well as a reminder of the lengths to which the government would go to cover the protests up. At every step, the protestors were able to make the government and the police look dull witted and heavy handed, to show that the protestors had control of the signs and symbols *that would be remembered*.[62] Music—in hastily constructed, improvised performances in the park and click-friendly social media sharing— both absorbed and projected these values speedily and effectively.

Thirdly, protest movements in the early 2010s shared a common problem. They may have had a shared focus, as at Gezi—in this case, preventing the destruction of a park. But they did not share a unified politics. A multitude of groups had a stake in the matter—leftist, religious, LGBT+, feminist, secularist, environmentalist groups, football fanbases, and more. The shortcomings of single-issue politics have long been noted by political scientists; social movements themselves have long known how to contain them and turn them to advantage. Looking at the protests taking place at the time in Japan following the meltdown of a nuclear reactor in Fukushima in 2011, for instance, David Novak describes how quickly the protest movement became a kind of street festival. At first sight, this does not look promising. Indeed, it looks very much like a heavy-handed bureaucratic effort to control dissent and contain the noise. But as Novak shows, the festival was informed, from the very outset, by a sophisticated understanding of the problem of multiple interests. The movement could not speak with one voice. But in actively refusing to do so, it could, as Novak argues, perform its own diversity, and thereby make the more telling point to the government: that the protest was not going away.

For Eyerman and Jamison, reflecting on the protest movements of an earlier generation, music was a way of forging ideological and affective unity out of a multitude of positions and interests.[63] Novak suggests the opposite. The unlikely "festivalization" of the Fukushima disaster performs the *sharing* of space, ideas, and symbols. The "noise" of the festival was a matter, he shows, of making audible "the diverse political assemblies, who respond with ambivalence to demands to speak with one voice" (Novak 2017). The Gezi protests suggest an extension of Novak's insight. Music here highlighted the diversity of these assemblies, but also the strategic and creative ways common symbols could be forged. The movement was to perform, in other words, not just multiplicity, but creativity as well. It had no overarching function. The Davide Martello "concert"—which, you will recall, momentarily unified not just protestors but also police—did so as a random event, able to unify to the extent that it appeared from outside the frame of Turkish politics.

The momentary and strategic forging of shared symbols can be illustrated by another icon of the movement, the strange image of a black-satin-clad Mevlevi dervish, wearing a white gas mask, whirling to unheard music. The satin evoked subcultural fashion, with a hint of camp. The "whirling" evoked the most vital, and the most internationally recognizable, image of traditional Turkish Sufism. Musicians associated with Mevlevi culture, such as Sufi electronica artist Mercan Dede, had conspicuously supported the protests. The range of musical expression at the protest, the "concerts," the flash mobs, the chanting, the playlists, the "impossible-to-categorize manifestations of instantaneous creativity on the streets" served to underline, without any form of overarching aesthetic control or artistic manifesto, that this was, as critic Mutlu Yetkin puts it, "an alliance of the unhappy cemented by feelings of mutual respect and solidarity" (Yetkin 2014).

When we reflect on "the squares" from the distance of a decade or more, the story is clearly an ambiguous one. On the one hand, they spoke of a yearning for a more satisfying, a more compelling public narrative of citizenship and democratic participation. Beyond the possession of an identity card, "citizenship" in Turkey had started to appear, as elsewhere, primarily to be a matter of shopping, praying, and car ownership. The reshaping of downtown areas in cities across the world at that time underlined the message. With its "sloppiness" and informality, with the intimate and cumulative lessons it supplied in learning "how to rule and how to obey" (Berman 2012, 200), the agora was more than nostalgia in 2010. It was a desperate experiential, emotional, and symbolic need. If these public spaces were now building sites, imposing the state's new priorities on its citizens with little or nothing in the way of public consultation or debate, they could at least be animated sonically. Memories of these events will not fade quickly.

On the other hand, these events supplied these cities' rulers with all of the information they needed to ensure that the events would never happen again. Access and circulation in downtown areas would now be carefully supervised. The Taksim project was, momentarily perhaps, derailed. The shopping center has not been built. Gezi Park itself remains intact. But traffic and Metro now whizz by underneath. The newly cleared area to the west of the park is dominated by a large mosque. A fleet of armored cars are permanently stationed outside the police station. Atatürk's statue—a monument to the secular nation-building project—is now marginal, rather than central. Meanwhile, crowds are bused to sports arenas and other purpose-designed spaces for choreographed rallies, to provide the government with friendly "crowd scenes" for public consumption. Social media is firmly under government supervision and print media all but extinct. A similar story could be told of Tahrir. Even in its negation, however, the centrality of the agora in the imagination of citizenship could be said to have deepened, and perhaps, even, be deepening. Cities may have irrevocably changed, but the agora's musicking and sonicizing seem capable of keeping the idea of it alive.

3.4 Conclusion

This chapter has engaged with a counterintuitive, perhaps even impossible, set of subjects. The human frame—in its heroic and almost invariably male guise—has dominated the conventional citizenship narrative. My first case study, concerning Abd al-Halim Hafiz, showed the pressure on this figure, and the complex iconographic properties—under strained postcolonial and revolutionary circumstances in Egypt—it now possesses. The second inverted this citizenly iconography by looking at a "figure" that conventionally plays either a background or an actively oppositional role in it, that of the crowd. As we have seen, recent circumstances in the United Kingdom have pulled the crowd back into the symbolic imaginary of democratic participation, not as revolutionary mob, but as affective multitude—what I have labeled here the sentimental crowd. The third explored the conflicted landscape of social movements today, and citizenship imagined, through the figure of Davide Martello at the Gezi Park protests in Turkey, as a crafting of intersectional solidarities around shared symbols and other affective foci. The key to these extremely complex scenes, I have suggested, lies in the music, which helps us understand something important about the mobilization of citizenly iconography, its transmission, its mediation, its affective and temporal dynamics.[64]

The previous chapter showed how ethnomusicology has absorbed the term citizenship since 2011, and in doing so, taken it in different directions. I contended that this absorption spoke to an underlying concern with ongoing, and perhaps deepening, problems of writing about music and politics. These problems include dealing with assumptions in the world at large that these two terms simply do not belong together; with the fact that the Global North views the music and politics of the Global South, still, in ways that suit its own agendas; with the demands of activism, engagement, and a "task-oriented" ethnomusicology, as opposed to furnishing the center with reports from distant lands. For all their differences of direction and intent, the case studies discussed in Chapter 2 suggest that, at the very least, the term citizenship seems to be injecting these questions with life.

The risk, though, has been one of losing touch with contiguous discussions in other fields of music study, wherein the term citizenship has, with a few exceptions, been conspicuously absent. That does not of course imply withdrawal from broader questions about politics, which are clearly not just a common but an intensifying concern. The case studies in this chapter have pulled me toward the language currently being used in other fields of music study, engaging with questions of disability, voice, crowds, the "posthuman," with distributed forms of agency and social practice. This vocabulary helps in two ways, I believe. One is to suggest a few routes forward in ethnomusicology's current "citizenly turn." Another is to see whether this practice might yet forge connections across the broader field of music study, rather than cut ethnomusicologists off from it.

This raises the question of what ethnomusicologists might—still—be claiming to do differently, and why. The answer implicit in this volume, from the outset, has been "globally, and from below"—a postcolonial claim. It will be worth reflecting on this one last time as I draw toward a conclusion.

Notes

1. Democratic heroes, Adlington and Buch observe, are a contradiction in terms. "Democracy is the only political practice that admits, indeed, encourages, its own critique. One of its consequences is to undermine exalted, epic versions of itself. The democratic subject is no hero and is not supposed to be one" (Adlington and Buch 2020, 8).
2. Vital texts on political belonging, affect, loss, and trauma include Ahmed 2004, Berlant 1997, and Mookherjee 2005.
3. There is a huge literature on these topics. On music's sovereign subjects and their vicissitudes, see Head 2013. On race and the problems of musicology's Whiteness, see Bohlman and Radano 2000. On disability, with attention to deafness among other things, see Holmes 2020.
4. On Egypt's current state of political exhaustion and demoralization, focusing on the place of silence, quietness, and sleep as aesthetic and political strategies, see Sprengel 2020.
5. For key critical and historical terminology concerning Abd al-Halim, I largely draw on historian Joel Gordon's work on Nasser-era figures and the nostalgia attached to them. The term "revolutionary melodrama" is taken from Gordon 2002, which projects the issue masterfully across the

entire panorama of Nasser-era cinema. Gordon 2007 deals with the question of nostalgia for Nasserite media icons. My own published writing on the subject comprises a discussion of Abd al-Halim's "sentimentalism" (Stokes 2006), a discussion of Abd al-Halim iconography (Stokes 2009), a discussion of the figure of the listener in Abd al-Halim films (Stokes 2010) and a discussion of his place in Egyptian and Arab modernism (Stokes 2020).

6. See Danielson's discussion of the mashaiyikh in which modern Egyptian singers such as Umm Kulthum would continue to ground their authenticity (Danielson 1997); Racy's discussion of tarab (enchantment) as the cardinal authenticating virtue of Arab art music (Racy 2003). My own questions about what happens when such a concept becomes debatable as applied to specific singers or performances, or to have reached some kind of historical limit, can be found in Stokes 2010.

7. Though I do not interpret it explicitly in these terms, a more detailed discussion of *Lahn al-Wafa* and its constituent motifs and gestures can be found in Stokes 2006. The "symphonic" and Beethovenian dimensions of this song took shape more actively in my mind with composer Peter Lam's re-orchestration of it and a performance, with symphony orchestra, at King's College London. See below.

8. The film is discussed in Gordon 2007. More needs to be said about its music, composed by Ali Shariai, than space permits here. It is an effort by an imaginative and knowledgeable film music composer to match the monumentalization of the film's visual style by an equivalent monumentalization of the Nasserite soundscape. Shariai steps only occasionally beyond brief quotations of well-known songs—a case less of nostalgic "monochroming" (Grainge 2002) than, arguably, an overenthusiastic "recoloring" of the black-and-white iconographic record.

9. On the revolutionary appropriations of old songs, see Sanders and Visonà (2012), specifically concerning the canonization of "Watani Habibi," originally to words by Ahmad Shafiq Kamil and music by Mohammed Abd al-Wahhab in 1958. Abd al-Halim Hafiz was the star of a song that included walk-on parts for various other vocalists, including Shadia and Sabah. Sanders and Visonà comment that "the core of the song lies in the focus on the word *watan*, which signifies 'homeland' or 'country'. Yet, this reappropriate process contextualizes it by evoking the word '*muwatin*' ('citizen'), thereby accenting the human aspect of the country, that is the people." (2012, 222–223). Interestingly, they start with Abd al-Halim, before going on to discuss other perhaps more obvious candidates, such as Sheikh Imam. Other songs discussed include Shadia's "Ya Habibti ya

Masr," Naguib Shihab al-Din's "Ya Masr Umi," Muhammad Mounir's "Ezzay?," Umm Kulthum's "Ana-l-sha'b," Ahmed Mekky's "January 25," and Ramy Essam's "Irhal" and "al-Gish al-'arabi fein?'" On Abd al-Halim imitators and satire concerning "Watani al-Akbar," see Stokes 2020b.

10. A presentation of Copenhagenize's core philosophy can be found in Colville-Anderson 2018. Ahmet Tarik al-Ahwal's 2017 contribution on Cairo to Copehagenize's blog, a small history of cycling in Egypt, can be found at http://www.copenhagenize.com/2017/06/egyptian-cycling-history-then-and-now.html (accessed 29 October 2021). It includes generous representation of Mikael Colville-Anderson's collection of old photographs of cycling and cyclists on Cairo's streets.

11. See note 10.

12. Though see Norcliffe 2015 on cycling cultures and histories. Outside Europe and North America his observations are mainly confined to China, and the question of postcolonialism is somewhat secondary to that of neoliberalism.

13. The date of the film, 1967, is also significant as regards the history of bicycle manufacture in Egypt. The colonial power, Britain, exported bicycles while it held sway. Nasser's turn to the Soviet Union for the construction of the Aswan dam meant the establishment of a significant quantity of Eastern Bloc industrial plants across Egypt. Czechoslovakia, for example, built thirty-five industrial installations between 1956 and 1961, including "power plants, sugar mills, water-treatment facilities, toy and bicycle factories, and shoe manufacturing" (L'Hommedieu 2008, 281). Agreements with other Eastern Bloc countries to manufacture bicycles were to follow, including with the German Democratic Republic in 1960. The United Arab Republic's first five-year plan (1960–1965) was an exercise in import-substituting industrialization; it marked the beginning, among many other things, of an Egyptian bicycle manufacturing industry. The film marks a moment in which this would have been a reality on Cairo's streets, in other words. As Ahmet Tarik Al-Ahwal remarks, pictures of the newly opened factories of the period often included the workers, men and women, assembled on their bicycles—images, it would seem, of speed, efficiency, health, and streets shared on the basis of equality between men and women. See note 10.

14. There is neither space nor (real) need for a comprehensive analysis. Roughly speaking, however, and for those for whom these are familiar terms, the sequence of maqam—modal—elements, identified by the main singer of each section, can be described as follows: (Abd al-Halim) *kord*—(Shadia) *hijaz*—(Abd al-Halim) reprise (kord)—spoken interlude (*ajam* in

background)—(Abd al-Halim and Shadia) duetting—ajam and *shahnaz*—(Abd al-Halim and Shadia duetting) *nahawand*—(Shadia short reprise) hijaz—(Abd al-Halim and Shadia in unison, full reprise) kord. The *iqa*—metrical scheme—is harder to characterize because of multiple changes of meter within sections, but, roughly, a medley of foxtrot, maqsum, and *mawwal*-like "free" meters. The shifting lyrical "perspectives" are those, separately, of him singing to her and her singing to him; of both imagining a (bewildering but joyful) present in terms of a (sad) past and vice versa; of the external world reflecting both joy and sadness back on them.

15. *Mu'id Gharam* was made in 1956 and *Dalila* later that same year.
16. On reflexivity, self-referentiality, and intertextual play in early Egyptian cinema, see especially Walter Armbrust's reflections on the Yusuf Wahbi film *Ghazal al-Banat* (Armbrust 2000).
17. See note 10.
18. See, for instance, Shadia's duet with another popular singer of the time, Karim Mahmoud, "Wahda wahda ya Biskileta," probably from the mid-1950s, which contrasts bicycle and car for amorous purposes, the former, obviously enough, their preference. The soundtrack can be found here: https://www.youtube.com/watch?v=nOmRnijAskI.
19. Such ways of thinking "implausibly propose(s) a society without the city" (Young 1986, 2). We need, rather, to start with our "positive experiences of city life to form a vision of the good society. Our political ideal is the unoppressive city." The modern city, and the citizenship that goes with it, means three things for Young. Firstly, the city possesses what she calls "physical historicity." It is an accumulation, a sedimentation, that has grown according to the complex currents of actually existing social histories rather than somebody's imposed vision of what that society ought to be. Secondly, it involves the necessity of intimate interaction with strangers, a necessity that imposes no demands or expectations on people to adopt the ways of others as their own. Thirdly, it involves the active constitution of public spaces, in which diverse city residents come together and dwell side by side, "sometimes appreciating one another, entertaining one another, or just chatting, always to go off again as strangers" (Young 1986, 21).
20. In Havana, as Robin Moore observes, revelry and revolution were conjoined (Moore 2006). On Shanghai see Farrar and Field 2015; on Kinsasha see White 2008; Vincenzo Perna offers a downbeat postlude to the period discussed in Moore's book, when nightlife was reduced to the desperate quest for tourist dollars during the implosion of the Cuban economy in the 1990s (Perna 2005).

21. On the introduction of CinemaScope in Egyptian cinema, and its economic, as well as aesthetic, challenges, see Vitalis 2000.
22. Joie de vivre might be translated into Egyptian Arabic as *hiffet dem* ("lightness of blood"). *Hiffet dem* remains a cardinal social virtue today. Abd al-Halim Hafiz's life was a study in it.
23. Slobin uses driving and road planning metaphors—traffic circles ("built to slow down the stream, make drivers think, offer them a choice of exits," Slobin 2020, 44), local traffic, border traffic, merging traffic, the rearview window—to organize his reflections on Detroit's music history.
24. Gorz's ironic "abolition" of the city would not, from Slobin's perspective, produce anything comparable. Anthropologist Marina Peterson's insightful studies of sound in Los Angeles might be located between these two poles. Peterson 2012, for instance, focuses on the attempts to reanimate its downtown music scene in the wake of a devastating process of suburbanization, and widely shared anxieties about what cars have done to civic life.
25. In social theoretical terms Abd al-Halim Hafiz was a contemporary of Henri Lefebvre, the subject of an observation in Glen Norcliff's book on the bicycle: "Cyclists demands for a safe place to ride are unambiguously a sub-set of Henri Lefevre's call for citizens to have a right to the city. . . . Lefevre defended the rights of citizens to be participants in the production of city spaces, to make the city a liveable space as well as an economic entity, and to occupy the city when those rights are denied or trampled on. Lefevre was writing in 1968 when the soixante-huitard's protests bought Paris to a halt as they asserted their collective opposition to several proposed modernist projects that would have fundamentally altered the character of the *City of Light*" (Norcliffe 2015, 231).
26. Gorz notes, in passing, the importance not just of restoring the joy of transport but of "love" for "one's own territory" as the key to the coming revolution (Gorz 1980, 76).
27. Metaphors of color seem obvious here but are potentially confusing. These songs have not so much been "monochromed" as, perhaps, having been first rendered in outline from a faded original and then heavy-handedly colored in using only primary colors. See note 7.
28. On Captain Sir Tom Moore's hundredth birthday celebrations, see https://www.bbc.co.uk/news/av/uk-52488385; on the recording of "You'll Never Walk Alone" with Michael Ball, see https://www.bbc.co.uk/news/av/entertainment-arts-52339204; for the recording itself, see https://www.youtube.com/watch?v=LcouA_oWsnU. There are many other sources of

information of course but the BBC reports give some sense of the official and public nature of the story at the time.
29. See, in *The Scotsman*, https://www.scotsman.com/news/people/watch-edinburgh-theatre-legend-allan-stewarts-musical-tribute-captain-tom-2618643.
30. Recall, briefly, another unassuming British icon, "Major Tim" Peake, who, as well as being the first British astronaut to conduct a spacewalk, has the unlikely distinction of being the first person to run a marathon for charity in space in 2016. See https://www.bbc.co.uk/news/science-environment-36112137.
31. See note 28.
32. Prolonged, indeed, beyond his death. When Captain Tom died early in the next year, Official Charts observed a surge in streaming and downloads of 1,864%, which also observed that it was likely far more people were listening to the song on radio and television, rather than using streaming apps. The song became a coronavirus anthem in the Netherlands. In football (soccer), it has been adopted as a club anthem by Twente, Feyernoord, and SC Cambuur football clubs.
33. The home supporters' end in the stands is named the 'Kop' in Liverpool, after the battle of Spion Kop in 1900—a Boer War reference.
34. See 1964's Panorama program: https://www.youtube.com/watch?v=XNboU_PbZMY. "You'll Never Walk Alone" is conspicuous by its absence here, perhaps because it was still new, not quite yet the iconic Liverpool song.
35. Liverpool FC being, largely, the "Catholic" club, Everton FC in Liverpool being, largely, the "Protestant" club. Catholicism in this context means Irish-identifying, migrant, "other": in other words, the poorer strata of the working class, victims of discrimination and violence.
36. Others include "Sign on, sign, with a pen in your hand, and you'll never work again," "Fuck off, Fuck off, with a hole in your arse, you'll never walk again." For a compilation of their most intense rivals, Manchester United's, parodies aimed at Liverpool FC and their fans, see https://www.prideofmanchester.com/sport/mufc-songs-liverpool.htm. For the most up-to-date and thoughtful discussion of British football chanting, cultures of fan rivalry and violence, their popular cultural hinterland, and the legal and other struggles to contain or curb them, see Millar, Power, Parnell, Widdop, and Carr 2021.
37. The song can be misused in other ways. Some used it to solicit sympathy with the police during the "Umbrella" protest movement in Hong Kong, which began in 2014. Liverpool fans took to Facebook to protest this use

of the song. See *The Liverpool Echo*'s report, https://www.liverpoolecho.co.uk/news/liverpool-news/liverpool-fc-anthem-youll-never-7960343.

38. It has some of the features of what Roland Barthes once described, with reference to photography, as a 'punctum' (Barthes 2000, 26): that is to say, a fragment seized, emotionally, by the imagination, disrupting, transforming, and recontextualizing the whole of which it was, until that moment, merely a 'part.' We do not need to share Barthes's preoccupation with the relationship between 'studium' and "punctum" in photography, between 'whole' and 'part,' a residue of structuralism, and one that requires a lot of translation into other media. But the term is useful in suggesting how a detail might overwhelm an assemblage of textual elements and become the emotional "point" of an image.

39. Elvis Presley and Frank Sinatra both extend the arch. It seems unlikely that the crowd is, as it were, "remembering" alternative versions, a fact that is I suspect hardly known these days by most.

40. Though interrupted by a goal, that extension is audible in 1970, Liverpool versus Everton. See https://www.youtube.com/watch?v=Dif7Y_gPzW0.

41. Consider, for instance, the use of recorded crowd singing of the song in Pink Floyd's 1971 album, *Meddle*, in the song "Fearless." Its citation here is, in context, nostalgic and haunting. Consider, too, its more upbeat citation in 2020 Netflix heist drama *La casa de papel*, in which the song, in its Gerry and the Pacemakers version, accompanies the appearance of crowds outside the Royal Mint in Madrid in solidarity with the gang and in defiance of the police.

42. For contrasting treatments of this issue, see Connor 2016 on the architectural affordances of the streets, bridges, and alleyways around Arsenal FC's stadium in North London and Castro 2011 on the acoustics of the street protests instrumental in the overthrow of Ferdinand Marcos in the Philippines in 1986.

43. The exercise can be undertaken with the following clips—though others can easily be found. An early 1970 version offers a distinct 𝄾, though with an interesting acceleration and lurch toward 𝄽 as the climax (and a goal) approaches. By 1973 (celebrating winning the 1973 Championship with Bill Shankley) it is an emphatic 𝄽. Powerful sound systems in the stadium have pulled the song back toward 𝄾 in recent years (hear, for instance, the end of https://www.youtube.com/watch?v=g8D0aBTyXgA), though the two conceptions of the song are still, in this particular instance, in sonic competition. For an example of when the crowd simply overpowers the stadium sound system, and the 𝄽 conception triumphs, see the outset of

Liverpool–Dortmund in 1974, https://www.youtube.com/watch?v=j72t BjGNlxI.

44. See track 6, "Tamssust," on *Maroc: Musiques berbère du Haut-Atlas* (Lortat-Jacob Bernard 1994).
45. The Union of European Football Associations, which is the governing body for football in Europe and umbrella organization for some fifty-five national associations.
46. See, for example, King 2008, which starts with a discussion of this scene.
47. "The audiovisual litany . . . idealizes hearing (and, by extension, speech) as manifesting a kind of pure interiority. It alternately denigrates and elevates vision: as a fallen sense, vision takes us out of the world. But it also bathes us in the clear light of reason" (Sterne 2003, 15).
48. For Tarde on the crowd, and its relation to the question of gestural mimesis, see Tarde 1901/1989 and Tarde 1890/1962; Brighenti 2010 puts it into a helpful critical and historical context. There is now, and probably as a consequence of Tarde's sociological rehabilitation, a profusion of crowd types and terms that have played out across sociology, critical theory, and cultural studies in recent years, including—among many others—the open and closed crowd, the rhythmic crowd, the stagnating crowd, the preindustrial crowd, the solitary crowd, the authoritarian crowd, the revolutionary crowd, the silent crowd, and the postmodern crowd, as well as in contemporary theorizations of the crowd as pack, crystal, swarm, mass, tribe, moral economy, information network, and the carnivalesque.
49. His gestural conception of mimesis plays an important part in Hardt and Negri's *Multitude* (Hardt and Negri 2004). Hardt and Negri felt compelled to distinguish multitudes from crowds, deeming only the former capable of recognizing difference and thus establishing a "commons." "The crowd" continues to represent the "dark matter" of sociological theory, as Mazzarella puts it, reflecting on Hardt and Negri's compulsion to make this distinction. Tarde himself did not. The crowd pulls not only on the traditional liberal subject but also on the "emergent horizons of a postliberal project" (Mazzarella 2010, 697).
50. Many examples could be chosen, but Jonathan Glancey's short BBC report (Glancey 2014) captures the tone of such discussions.
51. The "Old Oligarch," Berman tells us, "was fascinated by [the Athenian agora's] sloppiness. Here people dress down, social distance is minimized, one cannot even tell masters from slaves; Athens is the only city with a law forbidding masters to beat their slaves. The Old Oligarch is amazed that any city can hold together without a strictly visible social hierarchy. He concludes that informally defined spaces like Athens's agora, and

peaceable practices like shopping and related cultural activities, can make people feel comfortable with each other and nourish peaceable bonds between them, so that everybody learns both how to rule and how to obey" (Berman 2012, 200).

52. The relevant quotation, with its evocation of Hannah Arendt, is worth including in full. "The empty space then in haunted, populated by spirits that refuse to rest, collective and individual memories; a perception that leads toward an opposite reading of the empty space, and its transformation into a sign of potentiality, possibility, and plenitude, a democracy to come, with the empty public space awaiting a new festival and renewed occupation—a new 'space of appearance'" (Mitchell 2013, 112).

53. Historian Adam Mestyan usefully reminds us that the Khedive, the Ottoman viceroy, had to plot a precarious route between competing British and Ottoman demands on his loyalty, all the while maintaining an image of (progressive) independence. In spatial terms, this precarious independence was symbolized by the al-Azbekiyya gardens, constructed, along with a new opera house, on the site of an old barracks and parade ground in a liminal space between the old and new cities. It may have been "public," a space in which to see and be seen, but it represented a complex and conflicted history, not easily reduced to a singular "colonialism." See Mestyan 2017.

54. Samia Mehrez's volume, *Translating Egypt's Revolution* (see reference for Sanders and Visonà 2012), is a valuable example.

55. The most significant event in the square at the time of writing (2021) is the renovation of the Atatürk Kültür Merkezi. It was thought by many, and for years, that President Erdoğan would simply allow this prominent building, for a long time the citadel of cultural westernization in Turkey, to decay. It raises a question about my interpretation of the Davide Martello episode here, premised on exactly this assumption. Incorrect though it turned out to be, it certainly added important layers of meaning to the episode.

56. Others, indeed, have a historical (if not legal) claim on it. The northern part of the park was formerly the Pangaltı Armenian cemetery, attached to the nearby Surp Agop Hospital. The cemetery had been there since the sixteenth century and was indeed being used as such until the implementation of the Prost plan.

57. I draw mainly on my own memories in this section and continuous reading of the Turkish press, but these have been supplemented and perhaps modified by the various thoughtful accounts of Gezi Park's music that have appeared in recent years, notably Bianchi 2018; Jenzen, Erhart, Eslen-Ziya, Güçdemir, Korkut, and McGarry 2019.

58. For a classic text on "rough musicking" and its connections with charivari, see Thompson 1992.

59. It concludes with a traditional-sounding classical *gazel* (classical vocal improvisation), some words punningly modified, addressing the city: "O beloved Istanbul, lying ill-starred, her beauty ruined, what woe, what gas [i.e., tear gas], what grief is this? Everything is razed to the ground, whatever happened to you? Tell me; tell me; I don't want you this way" (translation my own). There was a ferocious campaign against the pots and pans at the time; the pro-government press managed to mobilize outrage in some quarters at the noisy balcony protests reminding readers and viewers that this was exam season, that children had a right to educational success and not to be prevented from accessing it by "politics." This was a riposte to the silent book-reading protests, insinuating, to some effect, that the protestors enjoyed educational privilege but were unwilling to extend it to others. The song in question, "Tencere Tava Havası," can be found here: https://www.youtube.com/watch?v=o-kbuS-anD4.

60. For a brief account of Davide Martello's earlier life, see https://www.dw.com/en/taksim-squares-piano-man-plays-for-peace/a-16938944. On his performance at the Bataclan, see https://www.theguardian.com/world/2015/nov/15/paris-attacks-john-lennon-imagine-pianist-davide-martello-klavierkunst. On the San Francisco incident, see https://sanfrancisco.cbslocal.com/2019/03/05/bicycle-pianist-loses-crashes-piano-san-francisco-hill. I am grateful to Davide Martello for kindly spending some time in responding to emails from me a few years ago.

61. See Eyerman and Jamison 1998 on the protest history of "We Shall Overcome" (Eyerman and Jamison 1998, 2). Originally a spiritual, it was adopted in the 1940s as a Union chant by the Tobacco Workers Union. Pete Seeger encountered in the 1950s as, already, a political anthem, fixing its title, adding new verses, and encouraging the improvisation of more, dependent upon context.

62. Eyerman and Jamison note that protest "may well occur in invisible waves and cycles, but there are also invisible links between the waves" (Eyerman and Jamison 1998, 47). Protest singing for them, to an extent, makes these links visible, or at least knowable to participants. Song, for them, is seen from a cognitive perspective, central to the production of meaning, knowledge, and *memory*. Their question, of making continuity, and fixing meaning, or, as they put it, "the struggle to define the situation" (Eyerman and Jamieson 1998, 19) is, however, not quite one I share. The approach I propose here is, in a sense, the reverse: the struggle to keep the

meanings of the moment open, and thereby constitutive of alliances and connections.
63. Their precise words concern the reluctance of social movement theory to theorize the "alteration of meaning, the struggle to define the situation" in protests (Eyerman and Jamison 1997, 19).
64. In this sense I would see this chapter as an extension and deepening of Ghosh's line of inquiry (Ghosh 2011)—which does not engage directly with music but suggests, to me, various ways in which it might have done so.

4

Conclusion

Early in 2016, I was invited to participate in a workshop at Royaumont, a ruined abbey just north of Paris, now a foundation supporting new music and musical scholarship. It was clearly a last-minute invitation, and it was going to be difficult to pull a paper together at short notice. But a concert, bearing the sparse title "99," had been announced for the evening after the workshop. It was to feature French Lebanese slam poet Marc Nammour, Iraqi American trumpeter Amir ElSaffar, multimedia composer Lorenzo Bianchi Hoesch, bansuri player Rashab Prasana, and bassist Jérôme Bolvin.[1] I knew ElSaffar, as it happened. We had met in Chicago at the beginning of the American-led Iraq invasion.[2] An established jazz trumpeter, he had turned to his father's record collection and had just begun to teach himself the Iraqi maqam tradition, concentrating on *santur* and vocals.[3] Many years had passed, and I was curious to see where this path had taken him. I put my misgivings aside, hastily concocted a paper, and jumped on Eurostar.

In classic anthropological fashion, I arrived late and missed most of the action. I did what I could to catch up over meals in the refectory, and in strolls around the gardens with participants, as and when the rain permitted. Fortunately, local ethnomusicologists had been enrolled to document the process. I was able, later, to fill in the gaps.[4] I learned that "99" is the number entered under "Department" on immigrants' identity cards. It is a bureaucratic fiction, in other words, informing the authorities that the bearer of the card was born outside France. I learned that the idea for the project first took shape in a performance by Nammour at the Avignon Festival in 2014. There he had attracted the attention of eminent musician and ethnomusicologist Frédéric Deval. Deval, it seems, was deeply immersed in Paul Zumthor's ideas about orality and poetics, and Jean-Luc Nancy's ideas about community, and these inspired a series of "transcultural" events at Royaumont that began in 2013 (Oleksiak 2020). They featured musical dialogue between distinguished world musicians, with a growing emphasis on what Deval referred to as *"paroles rythmique."* He saw rhythmic recitation as a kind of cultural universal, a fertile meeting ground for rappers, hip-hop artists, slam poets, and oral poets from around the world. Nammour was duly invited and the team for "99" assembled.[5]

I learned something about the creative process, too. Those writing about it tended, understandably enough, to focus on Nammour's poetry. He himself describes it as *"une écriture poussée qui privilegie moins le flow que le fond, tout en veuillant a donner de l'énergie"* ("a 'pushed' writing' that privileges less the 'flow' than the substance, wanting always to give it energy") attributing this "pushed" quality to his "accented French."[6] But, as I realized during the performance, it had something to do with the ensemble process, too. It seems that Hoesch would initiate this at the electronics with a sequence of *"ambiances sonores"*—grooves, chord sequences, textures. Prasana's bansuri and ElSaffar's santur were grafted on subsequently—Prasana, indeed, being a last-minute addition to the ensemble (Oleksiak 2016, 40).[7] The process comprised, then, a layering sounds and words, allowing each, as it were, to "push" the other. This could be noticed in various details. In the final number ("99 Is the Future"), for instance, the word 'ninety-nine' splits into three: the English "ninety-nine," the French *"quatre-vingt dix-neuf,"* and the Arabic *"tis'a wa tisa'in."* This delivered three contrasting metrical patterns that took their shape from the enveloping hip-hop groove, and then rippled outward into the surrounding soundscape.[8]

The performance itself was an assured display. Toward the end, Nammour's restless pacing gave way to seated, swaying recitation on a barstool.[9] The electronics slowly encroached on the voice, like a rising tide. If the words had been "pushing" the sounds, the sounds seemed at this point to pushing back, to be engulfing them. The choreography was simple but effective, its underlying messages clear, its emotional tone well judged. The audience, of the kind one often sees for new music in Paris—serious enough to make the journey out, wealthy (and White) enough to afford the tickets—took it in their stride. Nammour and his fellow musicians had, it seemed to me, understood the stage they were on, and the stakes of the event for their professional futures.

The critical response underlined that impression. Writing in the aftermath of the concert, Luigia Parlati concluded her description of the residency as follows:

> Once the 99-ers united, in Avignon, after having declined "the complexity of a multiple identity," Marc Nammour invites the public to join the 99, without crossing any border, without the need for papers, without needing to adopt any of the romantically already over-used definitions of "citizens of the world." As writer Patrick Chamoiseau puts it, "true citizenship in the world is multi-citizenship in multiple places," and 99, now part of this multiplicity, speaks to us of that (Parlatti 2016, 47).[10]

After several rereadings, it was the word 'true' that eventually struck me.[11] It betrayed, in the context of these sentences, the underlying anxiety. What is "truly" desired often reveals itself in negative terms—in this case, what "true citizenship" is *not*. Citizenship is *not*, for instance, a matter of "papers" supplied by the state. It has nothing to do, either, with the more philosophically loaded alternatives associated with identity politics or Kantian universalism. Parlatti steers us, instead, and inevitably rather vaguely, toward ideas prefixed by "multi-"; ideas, in other words, of citizenship as plurality and plenitude, as something somehow "more." The negative definition, then, is the source of the anxiety. We know only what it is not.

This broader intent of these sentences becomes clear if we widen the historical angle: because only a few decades ago, citizenship was understood by the political right across Western Europe as *too narrow* a concept to evoke meaningful political participation. Norman Tebbitt's notorious "cricket match" test in the United Kingdom serves as an illustration.[12] Tebbit, a vociferous ideologue in Margaret Thatcher's cabinet in the 1980s, wanted to know how many UK citizens supported Pakistan or India when these countries were playing against England at cricket matches. His intention was to introduce into British political discourse the idea of a line separating "real" citizens from those who were citizens in name only. Mere citizenship was clearly considered not enough to ensure participation in—or, at least, a baseline of compliance with—the aggressive process of neoliberal restructuring then taking place. Indeed, it was probably a hindrance. Margaret Thatcher had recently declared that "society does not exist."[13] Cultural nationalism would henceforth provide the fantasies of plurality and plenitude grounding authentic political belonging. In the United Kingdom these fantasies were to be summoned out of their dormancy by the Falklands War.[14]

As Yuval-Davies, Kannabiran, and Vieten suggest of Tebbit's "cricket match" test, these exhortations and veiled threats had complex effects (Yuval-Davies, Kannabiran, and Vieten 2006, 1–2). "Intimate" (i.e., White) society, turned in on itself, became hostile, defensive, and uncivil. The growing numbers of migrants and non-British-born people positioned outside it would be pushed toward alternative intimacies shaped by religion or race. But they were also pushed in the direction of cultural strategies to reinhabit and reimagine *their citizenship*—to extend and to invest more deeply in its meanings. Civility, increasingly opposed to the boorish and parochial uncivility of intimate society, would be configured across these spaces. It could be understood, in short, as a reaction to efforts to dismantle "society" by free-market ideologues in the 1980s and to supplant it with an aggressive cultural nationalism.

Efforts on the margins to rethink and rescale citizenship in such ways were always going to be rooted in the unstable terrain of political fantasy. The demands of religion, identity, and citizenship rarely line up neatly, for anybody. Modern political identity is necessarily, Yuval-Davies, Kannabiran, and Vieten show, a matter of narrative—of narrative whose constituent signs and symbols turn what might otherwise look contradictory and phantasmatic into spaces of felt coherence. One of the aims of this book has been to demonstrate that music is an important component of such narratives. As regards citizenship, it could be said indeed to have had a philosophically privileged role to play. Political society for Rousseau, as we saw in Chapter 1, depended upon conditions of audibility. These could never be taken for granted. There were questions about language; there were questions about space; there were questions about others (for instance, the Swiss mercenaries) intruding on the scene of listening, inviting speculation about why some might hear the same thing, but hear it in palpably different ways. In the early Enlightenment period, questions about political society evolved in tandem with questions about the ear, which had not yet become epistemologically suspect (Erlmann 2010). Music's ongoing place in discussions of citizenship rests, then, as I have been trying to stress throughout this volume, on old but still vibrant philosophical connections.

Such connections were subsequently to be weakened in the West by romantic ideologies of autonomous art. Music would become indeed the most autonomous of the autonomous arts. Habits of thought associating music with political community would be discredited. By the beginning of the twentieth century, music would be understood as needing to be "spoken for" if its civic lessons were to be publicly comprehensible. Critics, intellectuals, and academics stepped in, as we have seen. If the WAM tradition offered relatively little with which to think about democracy and progressive political community beyond Beethovenian clichés, writers and thinkers would be obliged to search in the pockets of experimentalism it still nourished, to look "down" the value hierarchy to jazz, pop, and rock; or to look "across" to other, non-Euro-American, worlds. Ethnomusicologists would develop their own distinct lines of inquiry here, as Chapter 2 has documented.

Parlatti's claims about "true citizenship" may involve a fantasy element, as already noted. But there are two aspects of her article that invite us to take these claims seriously. One is its postcolonial dimension. Readers will have already noted that the expression 'true citizenship' belongs not to Parlatti, but to Martiniquan author Patrick Chamoiseau. Chamoiseau's writing on *creolité* has drawn attention in France to the complexities of political belonging in its overseas departments. The inhabitants of Martinique and nearby Guadeloupe may be full French citizens, but the historical relationship between their islands and France has been determined by slavery and colonialism. Debates about independence continue, as a consequence, to be both lively and fraught across the Antillean archipelago. Chamoiseau has argued that independence will replace a known state of dependence only with another less clearly understood. What is required, in his view, is a new conception of "felt" political belonging, one no longer hobbled by concepts of territory and sovereignty. A "creole citizenship," as ethnomusicologist Jérôme Camal puts it, discussing Chamoiseau in his recent study of Guadeloupean gwoka (Camal 2019).

A Martiniquan philosopher of a slightly earlier generation, Édouard Glissant, had proposed a concept of the "creolization of the political" that helps contextualize and explain Chamoiseau's argument. Processes of colonial assimilation and mimesis might continue to drag Antillean political thinking toward the metropole. According to Glissant, these were probably inescapable. But a politics of "opacity, *détour* and *détournement*" (Camal 2019, 11) might interrupt them and put things on a different footing. *Détournement* would draw on practices by which slaves would make themselves "unreadable" to their masters, and thus outwit them in the small ways that would make life on the plantations somewhat manageable. The rejection of sovereignty, and the pursuit of a politics of departmental *citizenship* is, Camal remarks, itself a classic example of Glissant's *détournement*—a tricky move that wrong-foots the French state and gives its postcolonial subjects space and time to maneuver. Gwoka music in Guadeloupe, Camal observes, cultivates just such sensibilities.[15]

The stakes of these debates in France are high, as elsewhere. Those in the center are reluctant to recognize that the philosophical and political heritage of "*liberté, egalité, fraternité*" has assumed different shapes and forms in the former colonies. They are even more reluctant to recognize the variety of complex ways in which this philosophical and political heritage returns to the metropolis with migration. The migrant, in conventional liberal thinking, ascends a democratic gradient on their route to Europe or North America. Arriving at this particular summit, they are deemed ready to learn "true citizenship." This expectation is reflected, across Europe and North America, in the increasingly onerous citizenship rituals migrants are expected to undergo: the taking of citizenship courses and the passing of examinations, the renunciation of citizenship of countries whose democracy is implicitly understood to be wanting.[16] The idea that those in the metropolitan centers might have something to learn *from* migrants *about* citizenship is (in liberal reckoning) a contradiction in multiple terms. So Parlatti's deployment of Chamoiseau's expression is well judged and hits its target.

A second is its political context. The workshop, the concert, and the critical intervention all took place in the immediate aftermath of the Bataclan massacre on 13 November 2015. Amid multiple attacks by Islamist terrorists across Paris, 1,500 people attending a rock concert at the Bataclan Theatre were taken hostage. A hundred thirty people lost their lives in the ensuing carnage. Islamic State claimed responsibility for the attacks.[17] The French state had already begun to portray Islamist terrorism as an existential threat not just to France but also to "Europe" and "its values." It had already begun to draw sharp lines in the sand—outlawing all forms of veiling in public, banning all religious identifiers in schools, introducing new levels of surveillance and regulation in French mosques, beefing up the curriculum in school civics classes regarding secularism. Voices from the center of the State, moreover, had already begun to blur the distinction between 'Islam' (a framework, in its many varieties, for everyday life for millions of French citizens) and 'Islamism' (a political movement confronting the West). Indeed, it was the "soft power" of Islam in France that was beginning to pose, to some, the more serious threat—as illustrated by Michel Houllebecq's notorious novel *Submission*, which portrays, in dystopian terms, France under a democratically elected Islamic government (Houllebecq 2015).

Parlatti's claim for "true citizenship" on behalf of Nammour, an immigrant from the Arab world, and of "99," an artistic production that foregrounds the Arabic language and Arab musical instruments and sounds, was, then, a high-stakes operation. It was to mark out a distinct position in France's increasingly desperate culture wars. It was to ask, in pointed terms, why the neoliberal right across Europe was so aggressively conflating the concept of citizenship with 'Europe' and 'its values.' It was to point to the growing, and often intolerable, burdens being imposed on Muslims in France as they negotiate the terms of their political participation in the modern Republic. And it was to hint that their struggles might not only be recognized but also learned from.

Some of these lessons are, undoubtedly, extremely bleak. One of the Bataclan massacre's victims was a young ethnomusicologist at the Sorbonne, Kheireddine Sahbi, known to his friends as "Didine." He had been at a rehearsal of Arabo-Andalouse music, which he was researching, and was caught in the crossfire as he was walking back home.[18] He had begun his Arabo-Andalouse studies at the age of ten at his local music association in Algeria. These had to be curtailed due to the civil war in the 1990s. His parents, a civil servant and a French teacher, and his elder brother, Rafik, had encouraged him at home, leading him to a master's degree in musicology in Algiers, and then to an offer to study at the Sorbonne.

I had exchanged words of condolence with his Sorbonne professor, Jérôme Cler, before the concert at Royaumont. Years later I stumbled across Kheireddine Sahbi's obituary in *Le Monde*, which concluded with his brother Rafik's words:

> What I would like to say is that he will not be forgotten. He died with his violin in his hands, he had many projects on the go, he was a Muslim and he believed in the values of Islam. The Bataclan is already a name. But we would prefer a place dedicated to music which bears his name.[19]

I have already noted the somber mood of the "99" performance. This was probably the most significant dimension of it. I suspect Kheireddine Sahbi was known to at least some of the audience. I also suspect that some, and perhaps most, of the audience were wondering, like me, how things had reached this agonizing point. The choices now confronting young Arab Muslims in France seemed both crushingly pointless and entirely inescapable. The question in 2016 was no longer about the rights and wrongs of such choices. It was now one of what people like Kheireddine Sahbi, French citizens who "believe in the values of Islam," had to do to survive them.

Another bleak lesson to be drawn was how little music—painfully symbolized by the violin we must assume Kheireddine Sahbi held in his hands until the moment of his death—might protect us. "Arabo-Andalouse" music has long been thought of as a meeting place, a margin in which various abjected historical elements might accumulate, evidence of a "rhizomic" Mediterranean that eschews identity. It is rooted, after all, in the music of the Moriscos and Jews expelled in 1492, still bearing the name, in some cases, of the Iberian cities from which it originated. In Algeria, one of its most significant masters, Sheikh Raymond Leiris, was Jewish. Sheikh Raymond did not, himself, survive the Algerian civil war, but his nephew, Enrico Macias, did. Macias had much to say about this music and his restless quest for a (musical) identity as he moved between Algeria, France, and Israel. "Arabo-Andalouse" kept him on the move and focused his impatience with those who would try to capture it (and him) in identitarian terms (Swedenburg 2005).[20] It lies at the heart, too, of the way young musicians in Andalusia, in conversation with *andalucismo*'s long philosophical and philological heritage, try to cultivate a "feeling for history" that resists the binary codes (Christianity/Islam, Europe/Asia) that are insistently projected on their region's history (Hirschkind 2020, 1).

Many of the case studies in this book have concerned Muslim societies—in the Mediterranean world and the Middle East; in Central, South, and Southeast Asia; in North and West Africa; and in migrants from these parts of the world to European cities. This reflects, in part, the circumstances of my own research and fieldwork, which have, since about 1990, largely focused on modern Turkey and Egypt. It also reflects the fact that many European ethnomusicologists do their work in Muslim societies because of deeply rooted habits of regarding Muslims as "other," as where an inquiry into "others" might properly and legitimately start. The institutional and intellectual resources that have made such choices seem natural and self-evident— pushing young French scholars toward West and North Africa, young British scholars toward the Middle East and South Asia, young Dutch scholars toward Indonesia—have been extensively discussed in our field.[21] Questions about orientalism—and a commitment to decolonizing—could be described as infrastructural for an entire generation of ethnomusicologists and anthropologists.[22] But how might this regional emphasis bear on the question of music and citizenship? What might this vantage point help clarify; what might it distort or obscure?

Seen from such a vantage point, four things would seem to dominate the landscape. One is that the postcolonial Middle Eastern states wholeheartedly embraced music in their nation-building projects as one of the secular sciences that would offer their new citizens a route toward global modernity and enlightenment.[23] It appealed because it demarcated secular statecraft in unambiguous terms. It also appealed for technopolitical reasons. As we have seen, music seemed to invite control, regulation, measurement. The "old" and whatever it had come to signify (the weight of tradition, pain, sadness, melancholy, elite culture) might be moved off the public stage, and the "new" (faith in the future, happiness, optimism, energy, the true culture of "the people") ushered in. Such criteria were imprecise enough in music to ensure a mindset of continual revolutionary vigilance. Could we ever be sure, for instance, that "our music" had *finally and completely* been purged of its melancholy? Or *really* spoke for "the people"? Or that those charged with doing the job could really be trusted as opposed to pursuing their own agendas? If this is a familiar enough story elsewhere, in the Muslim-majority Middle East it is rather plainly a story about how the postcolonial nation-state sought to instill a sense of national belonging in their new citizens, a sense that could, in Mustafa Kemal Atatürk's own words, be *measured*. The connection between music and citizenship, for various historical reasons, lies close to the surface of public political discourse rather than being buried somewhere below it.

A second point is that instrumentalizing music in this way made it a vehicle for dissent and resistance. The very processes and materials of that instrumentalization tended, in other words, to expose the arbitrariness of the state's efforts to engineer the moods and sensibilities of the nation. When it comes to music, who is to say what counts as "happy" and what counts as "melancholy"? On the basis of whose knowledge and authority? What if "melancholy" makes people "happy"? And what is "modern," anyway? Such questions lay at the heart of Turkey's "Arabesk Debate" (Stokes 2021a), but they are familiar elsewhere.[24] They have attached music to the idea of popular voice, to co-feeling, civility, mutuality, and reciprocity. They have seen in one or another kind of music that the state has arbitrarily marginalized the terms of a more authentic democracy, a more participatory citizenship. It helped that the state would prove either incompetent, or easily distracted, or likely to change its mind about the institutions it itself had created, and, finally, absent itself in all but name from the entire scene. Music came, then, to assume a rather specific and clear set of associations with citizenly and democratic rights in the process of MENA postcolonial nation-building.

A third is the (obvious) observation that oil has made most of the MENA region a war zone for most of the last half of the twentieth century and the current one, too. The West has consistently preferred authoritarian governments in the Middle East, and a steady supply of oil, to democratically elected governments that might want to exercise some degree of control over it. Western governments have blamed Islam for the democracy deficit, and thereby persuaded the necessary majorities in their own countries to support the wars that have pushed these states toward authoritarianism, corruption, environmental collapse, and civil war. In Europe such projections are directed, with inordinate intensity, on the migrants and refugees who have fled these regimes and these wars. Muslims among them are considered, in the light of these projections, to have a particularly problematic relationship not just with democracy but with the basics of cosmopolitan civility as well. This consideration has exposed them in many Western countries to demands that they be "trained" or "schooled" in the civic skills they are held to lack, and that their newly acquired skills should constantly be on display.[25]

Music has played an interesting and uncomfortably revealing role here. "Good" migrants and refugees in Europe sing and play orchestral instruments, ideally under the tutelage of Western experts who can find a place for them in their multicultural ensembles, ideally at large charity events in the capital's concert halls, ideally in multicultural rock, pop, jazz, and hip-hop setups where Muslims can show that they "are able"' to play with their new neighbors, Black, White, Jewish, and other.[26] "Bad" migrants and refugees either dissent, or confine their music-making to local immigrant associations. The government occasionally steps in to provide expert help to jog such civilizing missions along. The fears fanned by populism that gather around Muslim migrants and refugees across Europe, and the efforts those migrants and refugees must make to prove themselves, are, in other words, exposed with an uncomfortable clarity around music.

This book has not, of course, been restricted to MENA-region case studies. Chapter 2, indeed, explored the issue of music and citizenship with reference to a broader, global literature. Area-studies paradigms are hard to escape whichever direction one looks, however. Their presence can certainly be felt in Chapter 2's accounts of musical citizenship—in the emphasis on social movements in Latin America, on "transition" in Central Asia and the former Eastern Bloc countries, on creolité and *mestizaje* in the Caribbean, on failing states in West Africa, for instance. The ghost of the Mediterraneanist "honor and shame" paradigm hovers over my discussion of "ideal citizen"

Zeki Müren in Turkey, no doubt, which frames all of Chapter 1. The connections between theory and region reflect worldviews fashioned in Western Europe and North America over a century or more. Their legacy is still quite palpable—and problematic, of course.

But other issues—climate crisis, authoritarianism, new media—bear on the question of citizenship today, and these are not so easy to parse in area-studies terms. That legacy is contested, too, by new dispositions toward fieldwork: less, these days, a matter of reporting to the metropolis, more a matter of "tasking" with our interlocutors in an increasingly globalized "field," as we have seen. One way or another, the question of citizenship can be approached on a global footing today, in ways that are attentive both to the complex optics of (post) colonialism and to emergent geopolitical realities. This book has been an attempt to demonstrate that, despite the pitfalls, the effort to do so is worthwhile.

It has also been an attempt to show that *music* provides a unique means of engaging with the question of citizenship. As I argued in Chapter 1, music and citizenship have entangled histories, at least in Enlightenment terms. Broad currents of thought about democracy, voice, audibility, sound, and song merged in the work of Rousseau and his contemporaries. My choice of the word music to gather my reflections on these broad currents of thought—as opposed, for example, to sound, aurality, chorality, or perhaps even song—is not unproblematic.[27] It is with Rousseau after all, as Tomlinson has pointed out, that song and music decisively parted company, the latter coming to assume the burden of representing Europe's "spiritual superiority" (Tomlinson 2012, 62), the former an exotic particularity in need of explanation. There are good reasons, as Tomlinson shows, to attempt to reverse this troubling move. And the case studies in Chapter 3—Abd al-Halim Hafiz's "Hagha Ghariba," the Liverpool Kop's "You'll Never Walk Alone," and Gezi Park's "Hey Jude," are, after all, studies of song.

But the term music is, nonetheless, the one you will find on the cover of this book. There are two reasons I have settled for this term. One, hinted at throughout, but worth stating more directly in conclusion, is that it might actually help reconnect us with the direct ways Rousseau and his contemporaries felt able to think about the relationship between music and democracy. The hierarchy he and his times established—we have music; they have song—has faded; we no longer find it difficult to believe that other people have music. This change might dispel some of the anxiety, defensiveness, and miscommunication that accumulates so quickly in our discussions of "the politics of music."[28] It might help us bridge institutional gaps, reach out across our own disciplinary field, and put our thinking, talking, and doing within reach of one another.[29]

The simple act of conjoining the terms music and citizenship might also help us think more actively and practically about the *crafting* of political community. Richard Sennett's discussion of the term 'craft' serves me well in conclusion (Sennett 2008). Craft, he showed, is the act of collective making in the shadow of industrial capitalism, involving social coordination and deliberation; improvisations linking hand and eye, learning by showing, and trying on the job. Though sequestered, socially, in new domains of professional expertise, craft builds on deeply rooted and widely shared capacities for play, and for pleasure in jobs done well. It is restorative of democratic hope and energy. It is a slightly odd word to attach to music-making, especially in the WAM tradition, wherein intense efforts are made to *hide* labor and material worlds. Most of us, particularly those of us who are musicians ourselves, recognize the craft dimensions of music easily enough, however. Democracy is crafted, too. We craft it in our everyday lives, with materials and techniques that have been handed down to us, which we make our own and pass on to others. We do so with that mixture of seriousness and playfulness, care and pride, patience and excitement, respect for the past and anticipation of better results in the future that is at always at play when we make things. It seems right to link the words citizenship and music in this way and to deepen the connections we find. Thought of in one another's terms, both might yet move forward.

Notes

1. It was also to have involved Egyptian poet Abdallah Miniawi, but circumstances at home prevented him from attending. See Parlatti 2016.
2. The invasion took place in 2003, combining troops from the United States, the United Kingdom, Poland, and Australia. It lasted just over a month,

initiating a prolonged and bloody occupation. The concert by ElSaffar's that I was recalling took place in Bloomington, probably in November that year, as well as another one at the University of Chicago early the following year. The latter memorably took place under the Ishtar Gate displayed in the museum in the University's Oriental Institute.
3. The santur is the Iraqi and Iranian hammered dulcimer. For English-language accounts of the Iraqi maqam tradition, see Simms 2004 and Hassan 2018. It was eclipsed by Ba'athist cultural policy, which valued a pan-Arab modernism more highly, until the fall of Saddam Hussain in 2003. The damage wrought on the country's cultural and intellectual infrastructures by the invasion and occupation was such that maqam continues to live an extremely precarious existence in Iraq, at best. It is still maintained to an extent in the cultural and intellectual life of the diasporas in Europe and the United States.
4. See, in particular, Parlatti 2016, Oleksiak 2016 and 2020, and Laborde 2020. I am grateful not only for these written accounts but their conversations with me during the event, and for their invitation of me to it.
5. Deval was, sadly, to pass away weeks before the event itself. He was not, in other words, to see this project come to fruition. An informative obituary by Patrick Labesse was published in Le Monde on 8 April 2016 (https://www.lemonde.fr/musiques/article/2016/04/05/frederic-deval-marieur-de-musiques-a-la-fondation-royaumont-est-mort_4896048_1654986.html).
6. Nammour himself walked vigorously around the stage while reciting, adding another dimension of physicality to this 'pushing'. Much of "99 is the Future", the culmination of the evening's set, was, I noticed, delivered, swaying, head down, from a bar stool centre stage, as the groove and electronics slowly but inexorably, like the tide, encroached on the words. I was not sure whether this was to be put down to exhaustion, or to signify closure or repose, or perhaps to underline the association between the words and the pacing.
7. Prasana was, I learned, able to participate only at the end of the two-week residency—a logistical matter that had significant implications for the sonic process. It marked the *bansuri*, though not the *santur*, as separate and somehow "other" throughout. On the other hand, the *santur*, as can be heard on the track "Refugee," is infrastructural, the source of various riffs that underpinning entire numbers.
8. Roughly speaking, the "ninety-nine" (pronounced as in American English, without the *t*s) was a swung two beats, the "*quatre-vingt-dix-neuf*" a swung four beats, and the "*tisa' wa tisa'in*" an ambiguous three-in-four. It is worth noting here, in passing, the metrical play on the key words translating "99"—worthy of a more detailed analysis than I have room for

now. Nammour's cipher for multitude was, as it were, itself rendered multitudinous and generative.

9. Parlatti notes the connection between the pacing and the ensemble process in interesting terms. "*Dans cette recherche, Marc Nammour avait un exigence, celle de faire respirer la parole. Ses textes étaient en partie esquissés, et l'écriture aurait dû démarrer et entrer dans la vif après ce travail de repérage, de connaissance, et de comprehension des autres et de leurs manières de jouer. La parole était là, commençant à prendre forme, et son corps aussi exprimait la même nécessité et envie de la dégager: autour des musiciens disposés en cercle dans la salle. Nammour dessinait chaque jour 'ses' cercles de déambulation, sa marche contribuant à mettre en mouvement la pensée*" (Parlatti 2016, 46–47) ("Marc Nammour had one requirement in this research process, that of allowing speech to breathe. His texts were only partly sketched, and the writing was intended to spring to life following the work of identifying, knowing, and understanding the others and their ways of playing. The words were there, beginning to take shape; his body, too, expressed the same need and desire to release them, [moving] around the musicians arranged in a circle in the room. Nammour constructed his own wandering circles every day, his walking helping to set thought in motion"). In the terms suggested in the text, above, this suggests a cumulative processes of hearing his words and modifying them in relation to successive layers.

10. "*Une fois les ninety-niners soudés, à Avignon, après avoir décliné toute la 'complexité d'une identité multiple,' Marc Nammour invite la public a rejoindre le 99, sans passer aucune frontière, sans besoin de papiers, sans besoin non plus de passer par les définitions déjà un peu usées romantiquement, de 'citoyens du monde.' Pour le dire avec l'écrivain Patrick Chamoiseau, 'le vrai citoyenneté au monde est la multiple citoyenneté dans les multiples lieux,' et 99, désormais partie de cette multiplicité, nous parle de cela*" (Parlatti 2016, 47).

11. It was, in fact, Michael Fend, following a spoken presentation of this material at King's College London in 2020, who first drew my attention to it. Always look out for the truth claims in political discourse, he suggested. It is an unfailing guide to where the underlying fantasies, fears, and anxieties lie.

12. The comment was made in April 1990 in an interview with the *Los Angeles Times*. The relevant portion of it reads as follows: "[a] large proportion of Britain's Asian population fail to pass the cricket test. Which side do they cheer for? It's an interesting test. Are you still harking back to where you came from or where you are?" I located the quotation eventually on an

educational website in "civic dilemmas" (https://www.facinghistory.org/civic-dilemmas/cricket-test). It is hard to overstate its provocative nature. Tebbit, for his part, doubled down on his claims, saying the "cricket test" would have helped avoid the 2007 London bombings. To this day, this notorious statement is still being angrily debated in the United Kingdom.
13. UK Prime Minister Margaret Thatcher declared that "there is no such things as society" in an interview with the magazine *Woman's Own* on 31 October 1987. "There are individual men and women, and there are families... [and] there is no such thing as entitlement, unless one has first met an obligation" (https://www.theguardian.com/politics/2013/apr/08/margaret-thatcher-quotes).
14. The Falklands War, as it is known in the United Kingdom, followed Argentina's invasion and occupation of the Falkland Islands (known in Argentina as Las Malvinas) on 2 April 1982. A ten-week war between the United Kingdom and Argentina followed. Mbembe's unsettling words spring to mind: "Today sees the principle of equality being undone by the laws of autochthony and common origin, as well as by divisions within citizenship, which is to say the latter's declension into 'pure' citizenship (that of the native born) and borrowed citizenship (one that, less secure from the start, is now not safe from forfeiture). Confronted with the perilous situations so characteristic of the age, the question, at least in appearance, is no longer to know how to reconcile the exercise of life and freedom with the knowledge of truth and solicitude for those different from oneself. From now on, it is to know how, in a sort of primitive outpouring, to actualize the will to power by means that are half-cruel, half-virtuous... Consequently, war is determined as end and necessity not only in democracy but also in politics and in culture" (Mbembe 2019, 3).
15. Gwoka is a form of recreational dance music that has become a kind of folk practice as pan-Antillean zouk continues to dominate the airwaves. It is cultivated at *lewoz* dance parties, where dancers engage in complex games of rhythmic disguise and misdirection with the musicians. Various forces (such as Intangible Cultural Heritage recognition) tug at this practice, but they are accommodated or resisted by those would keep it vibrant and able to press on the postcolonial debates of the moment (Camal 2019, 165–166).
16. These rituals are premised on the now-prevalent neoliberal dictum that, for newcomers, citizenly rights are bestowed only after an understanding of citizenly responsibility has been satisfactorily demonstrated. Margaret Thatcher's comment above (note 13) that "there is no such thing as entitlement, unless one has first met an obligation" spelled out that logic

unambiguously in 1987. It upended more familiar (liberal) conceptions of citizenship in which rights and duties are coterminous.
17. Islamic State, sometimes known as Islamic State of Iraq and the Levant, and sometimes by its Arabic acronym, DAESH, is the militant group that took shape in the aftermath of the American Iraq invasion, and, exploiting the Syrian civil war, controlled swathes of northern Iraq and Syria until the fall of its "capital," Raqqa, in 2017.
18. I adopt *Le Monde*'s nomenclature 'Arabo-Andalouse music' here, but it is more commonly referred to by ethnomusicologists as *andalusi* music, to indicate the (Andalusian) geographical and historical provenance of the most common urban art music practices of North Africa. It is known in different countries by a variety of more local names (al-Ala'a, ma'luf, and so forth), but they are closely related. For English-language ethnomusicological treatment, see in particular Glasser 2016, Reynolds 2021, and Davis 2004.
19. Charlotte Bonzonnet's obituary in *Le Monde* 26 November 2015 can be found online at https://www.lemonde.fr/attaques-a-paris/visuel/2015/11/26/kheireddine-sahbi-29-ans-enmemoire_4818065_4809495.html.
20. Such 'identitarian terms', anthropologist Ted Swedenburg helpfully emphasizes, include the ideologies of 'hybridity' in Mizrakhit culture in Israel today, and elsewhere. 'Anti-identity' identities are not an exception to the underlying rules of ethnic reckoning (that there will always be an excluded "other"). See Swedenburg 2005.
21. There is a huge literature here, but perhaps the earliest and most important book addressing the broader relationships of region and theory in anthropology is Fardon 1990. I am not aware of a companion volume in ethnomusicology, which (if I am right) strikes me as an interesting lacuna.
22. Key volumes in anthropology and ethnomusicology in this regard are, respectively, Clifford and Marcus 1986 and Barz and Cooley 2008.
23. On the embrace of andalusi music by the North African nation-states, see in particular Glasser 2016 and Davis 2004. On Syrian '*turath*' ("heritage"), see Shannon 2009. On Turkey, see Stokes 2020. Egypt, perhaps the most revealing case study in this regard, has, interestingly, been discussed only piecemeal, and often from a nostalgic perspective. See, however, the various contributors to Vigreux 1992 on the legacy of the 1932 Cairo Music Congress.
24. The mood is captured beautifully in Sinan Çetin's short film, *Be Happy! It's An Order*, showing soldiers intruding on a Turkish village festivity and ordering the villagers, at gunpoint, to stop playing folk music. A list of Western composers' names, hilariously mispronounced, are read out

at pointless length by the officer in charge to indicate the new direction of travel. The villagers ask why. Because this music is happy music, they are told. But so is ours, they reply, showing they smile when they play. Because this is universal music, they are told. So is ours, they reply, as one of the villagers strikes up first the theme of Mozart's Fortieth, and then Beethoven's Ninth on his *saz*. It can easily be found, at the time of writing, online (https://www.youtube.com/watch?v=cbW18HKWqzs). For ethnomusicological and anthropological work on how dissent and resistance take shape around popular music practices in the MENA region see, among others, Schade-Poulsen 1999, Levine 2008, Goodman 2005, and Gedik 2019.

25. Anthropologist Esra Özyürek's work on holocaust denial and Muslim migrants in Germany offers sharp lessons in this regard. Germany deems Muslim immigrants and their descendants to require a schooling in empathy for Jewish victims of the Holocaust. A rather particular conception of empathy is at play in these demands, one that in its implementation distances Muslim migrants, as she shows, from the civilizing mission of the German state. It is not to be confused with the rather complex, thoughtful, and no less empathetic ways many migrants and their descendants do, in fact, connect with Holocaust memorialization in Germany. See Özyürek 2018.

26. Eckhard Pistrick has studied Jordi Savall's musical initiatives with the Orpheus XXI orchestra and German immigrant and refugee musicians (Pistrick 2020). Kristine Ringsager has looked at government initiatives in Denmark to school immigrants and refugee musicians in rap (Ringsager 2017). I have written about some of the dynamics of the various Syrian and Iraqi refugee orchestras in the United Kingdom (Stokes 2021b).

27. The coordinates of this discussion are well known at this point and need little underlining. Sterne's vision of sound studies has been particularly influential (Sterne 2012), though critical views of sound studies are finally accumulating: principally, that it commodifies and bureaucratizes a field of study and imposes a problematic epistemological unity on its subject (Feld and Panopoulos 2015), that it focuses, unreflectively, on the West, its listening technologies and the myths that sustain them (Steingo and Sykes 2019). Ochoa Gautier's aurality, essentially an ontological move, helps us address the "richness of a multiplicity of variables among what different people consider the given and what they consider the made that come together in the acoustic" (Ochoa Gautier 2014, 22)—a "field," rather than a "network" of sonic relations in Camal's reading of the concept (Camal 2019, 8). Chorality has been discussed with reference to Steven Connor's

work in Chapter 3 of this book (Connor 2016). Gary Tomlinson's well-known arguments about song (see Tomlinson 2012), a means of reversing Rousseau's hierarchies discussed here, have recently been extended in the direction of "cantologies" (Denning and Tomlinson 2021).
28. Perhaps the most definitive analysis of this anxiety, defensiveness, and miscommunication, no less forceful for its age, is Bohlman 1993—the starting point for this entire project in many ways. I encountered Mondelli's illuminating work on Rousseau more recently, which puts the matter at hand very succinctly. "There is something peculiar about our tendency to talk about political music. It seems at first entirely natural.... Yet the very act of making such a distinction serves to delimit both music and politics. To speak of 'political music' is to imply both that music is inherently apolitical, and that politics is somehow abstracted from the activity of music-making" (Mondelli 2016, 143).
29. An early task, for instance, would be one of connecting ethnomusicology's "citizenship" turn with long-standing currents of thought about music and democracy in the study of rock, pop, jazz, improvisation, and new and experimental music. See in particular the contributions to Adlington and Buch 2020, *Finding Democracy in Music*.

Bibliography

Adlington, Robert, and Esteban Buch. 2020. "Introduction: Looking for Democracy in Music and Elsewhere." In *Finding Democracy in Music*, edited by Robert Adlington and Esteban Buch, 1–18. New York: Routledge.
Adorno, Theodor. 2002. *Essays on Music*. Selected with Introduction, Commentary and Notes by Richard Leppert. Berkeley: University of California Press.
Agamben, Giorgio. 1998. *Homo Sacer: Sovereign Power and Bare Life*. Stanford CA: Stanford University Press.
Ahmed, Sara. 2004. *The Cultural Politics of Emotion*. Edinburgh: Edinburgh University Press.
Aksoy, Ozan. 2019. "Kurdish Popular Music in Turkey." In *Made in Turkey: Studies in Popular Music*, edited by Ali Gedik, 149–166. New York: Routledge.
Alkabaani, Kareem, Wael Habbal, and Tom Western. 2020. "Active Citizenship in Athens." *Forced Migration Review*, https://www.fmreview.org/cities/alkabbani-habbal-western.
Allen, Warren Dwight. 1939. *Philosophies of Music History*. New York: American Book Company.
Anderson, Perry. 2021. *Ever Closer Union? Europe in the West*. London: Random House.
Andrisani, Vincent. 2015. "The Sweet Sounds of Havana: Space, Listening, and the Making of Sonic Citizenship." *Sounding Out!*, https://soundstudiesblog.com/tag/sonic-citizenship/.
Aparicio, Frances, and Candida Jacquez. 2003. "Introduction." In *Musical Migrations: Transnationalism and Cultural Hybridity in Latin America*, edited by Frances Aparicio and Candida Jacquez, 1–12. New York: Palgrave MacMillan.
Appiah, Kwame Anthony. 1991. "Is the Post- in Postmodernism the Post- in Postcolonial?" *Critical Inquiry* 17 (2): 336–357.
Arendt, Hannah. 1951. *The Origins of Totalitarianism*. New York: Harcourt.
Aretxaga, Begona. 2003. "Maddening States." *Annual Reviews of Anthropology* 32: 393–410.
Armbrust, Walter. 2000. "The Golden Age before the Golder Age: Commercial Egyptian Cinema before the 1960s." In *Mass Mediations: New Approaches to*

Popular Culture in the Middle East and Beyond, edited by Walter Armbrust, 292–328. Berkeley: University of California Press.

Aşan, Emine. 2003. *Rakipsiz Sanatkâr Zeki Müren*. Istanbul: Boyut.

Askew, Kelly. 2002. *Performing the Nation: Swahili Music and Cultural Politics in Tanzania*. Chicago: University of Chicago Press.

Aterianus-Owanga, Alice, and Pauline Guedj. 2014. "'On the Waves of the Ocean': Des musiques dans l'Atlantique noir." *Cahiers d'âtudes Africaines* 216 (4): 865–887.

Austerlitz, Paul. 1997. *Merengue: Dominican Music and Identity*. Philadelphia: Temple University Press.

Aksoy, Bülent. 2002. *Zeki Müren: 1955–63 Kayıtları/Recordings* (CD liner notes). Istanbul: Kalan.

Avelar, Idelber, and Christopher Dunn. 2011. "Introduction: Music as Practice of Citizenship in Brazil." In *Brazilian Popular Music and Citizenship*, edited by Idelber Avelar and Christopher Dunn, 1–27. Durham NC: Duke University Press.

Baily, John, and Michael Collyer. 2006. "Introduction: Music and Migration." *Journal of Ethnic and Migration Studies* 32 (2):167–182.

Baker, Geoffrey. 2015. *El Sistema: Orchestrating Venezuela's Youth*. New York: Oxford University Press.

Barthes, Roland. 2000. *Camera Lucida: Reflections on Photography*. London: Vintage.

Barz, Gregory, and Timothy Cooley, eds. 2008. *Shadows in the Field: New Perspectives for Fieldwork in Ethnomusicology*. Oxford: Oxford University Press.

Bhabha, Homi. 2004. *The Location of Culture*. New York: Routledge.

Beckles Willson, Rachel. 2013. *Orientalism and Musical Mission: Palestine and the West*. Cambridge: Cambridge University Press.

Begum, Rothna. 2018. "For Saudi Women, Freedom to Drive Masks New Crackdown." *Human Rights Watch*, https://www.hrw.org/news/2018/06/22/saudi-women-freedom-drive-masks-new-crackdown.

Bergeron, Katherine. 2008. *Voice Lessons: French Mélodie in the Belle Epoque*. New York: Oxford University Press.

Berlant, Lauren. 1997. *The Queen of American Goes to Washington City: Essays in Sex and Citizenship*. Durham NC: Duke University Press.

Berlant, Lauren. 2008. *The Female Complaint: The Unfinished Business of Sentimentality in American Culture*. Durham NC: Duke University Press.

Berlant, Lauren. 2011. *Cruel Optimism*. Durham NC: Duke University Press.

Berman, Marshall. 2012. "The Romance of Public Space." In *Beyond Zucotti Park: Freedom of Assembly and the Occupation of Public Space*, edited by Ron Shiffman, Rick Bell, Lance Jay Brown, and Lynne Elizabeth, with Anastassia Fisyak and Anusha Venkataraman, 197–206. Oakland CA: New Village Press.

Bianchi, Raffaella. 2018. "Istanbul Sounding like Revolution: The Role of Music in the Gezi Occupy Movement." *Popular Music* 37 (2): 212–236.
Biner, Zerrin Özlem. 2020. *States of Dispossession: Violence and Precarious Coexistence in Southeast Turkey*. Philadelphia: University of Pennsylvania Press.
Bohlman, Andrea. 2020. *Musical Solidarities: Political Action and Music in Late Twentieth-Century Poland*. New York: Oxford University Press.
Bohlman, Philip. 1993. "Musicology as a Political Act." *Journal of Musicology* 11 (4): 411–436.
Bohlman, Philip, and Ronald Radano. 2000. "Music and Race, Their Past, Their Presence." In *Music and the Racial Imagination*, edited by Philip Bohlman and Ronald Radano, 1–53. Chicago: University of Chicago Press.
Born, Georgina. 1998. "Anthropology, Kleinian Analysis and the Subject in Culture." *American Anthropologist* 100 (2): 373–386.
Born, Georgina. 2005. "On Musical Mediation: Ontology, Technology and Creativity." *Twentieth Century Music* 2 (1): 7–36.
Born, Georgina. 2012. "Music and the Social." In *The Cultural Study of Music: A Critical Introduction*, edited by Martin Clayton, Trevor Horn, and Richard Middleton, 261–274. New York: Routledge.
Born, Georgina, and Andrew Barry. 2018. "Music, Mediation Theories and Actor-Network Theory: Introduction." *Contemporary Music Review* 5–6: 443–487.
Bozonnet, Charlotte. 2015. "Kheireddine Sahby, 29 ans." *Le Monde*, November 26, 2015, https://www.lemonde.fr/attaques-a-paris/visuel/2015/11/26/kheireddine-sahbi-29-ans-enmemoire_4818065_4809495.html.
Braidotti, Rosi. 2013. *The Posthuman*. Cambridge: Polity Press.
Brighenti, Andrea. 2010. "Tarde, Canetti and Deleuze on Crowds and Packs." *Journal of Classical Sociology* 10 (4): 291–314.
Buford, Bill. 1992. *Among the Thugs*. London: Mandarin.
Burnham, Scott. 1995. *Beethoven Hero*. Princeton NJ: Princeton University Press. https://www.bundeskunsthalle.de/en/beethoven.html (accessed April 2, 2023).
Buchanan, Donna. 2005. *Performing Democracy: Bulgarian Music and Musicians in Transition*. Chicago: University of Chicago Press.
Buchanan, Donna. 2007. "'Oh Those Turks!' Music, Politics, and Interculturality in the Balkans and Beyond." In *Balkan Popular Culture and the Ottoman Ecumeme: Music, Image and Regional Political Discourse*, edited by Donna Buchanan, 9–54. Lanham MD: Scarecrow Press.
Butsch, Richard. 2008. *The Citizen Audience: Crowds, Publics, and Individuals*. New York: Routledge.
Butterworth, James. 2014. "The Ethics of Success: Paradoxes of the Suffering Neoliberal Self in the Andean Popular Music Industry." *Culture, Theory and Critique* 55 (2): 212–232.

Caeyers, Jan. 2020. *Beethoven: A Life*. Berkeley: University of California Press.
Çakırlar, Cüneyt. 2015. "Unsettling the Patriot: Troubled Objects of Masculinity and Nationalism." In *Queer Dramaturgies: International Perspectives on Where Performance Leads Queer*, edited by Alyson Campbell and Stephen Farrier, 81–97. London: Palgrave.
Camal, Jérôme. 2019. *Creolized Aurality: Guadeloupean Gwoka and Postcolonial Politics*. Chicago: University of Chicago Press.
Canetti, Elias. 1984. *Crowds and Power*, translated by Carol Stewart. New York: Farrar, Straus and Giroux.
Cassin, Barbara, Emily Apter, Jacques Lezra, and Michael Woods (eds.). 2014. *Dictionary of Untranslatables: A Philosophical Lexicon*. Princeton NJ: Princeton University Press.
Castro, Christi-Anne. 2011. *Musical Renderings of the Philippine Nation*. New York: Oxford University Press.
Cavicchi, Daniel. 2011. *Listening and Longing: Music Lovers in the Age of Barnum*. Middletown CT: Wesleyan University Press.
Çelik, Zeynep. 1992. *The Remaking of Istanbul: Portrait of an Ottoman City in the Nineteenth Century*. Seattle: University of Washington Press.
Chion, Michel. 1999. *The Voice in Cinema*. New York: Columbia University Press.
Clark, Gregory. 2015. *Civic Jazz: American Music and Kenneth Burke on the Art of Getting Along*. Chicago: University of Chicago Press.
Clarke, John, Stuart Hall, Tony Jefferson, and Brian Roberts. 1976. "Subcultures, Cultures and Class." In *Resistance through Rituals: Youth Subcultures in Postwar Britain*, edited by Stuart Hall and Tony Jefferson, 9–74. London: HarperCollins.
Clifford, James. 1986. "Introduction: Partial Truths." In *Writing Culture: The Poetics and Politics of Ethnography*, edited by James Clifford and George Marcus, 1–26. Berkeley: University of California Press.
Clifford, James, and George Marcus, eds. 1986. *Writing Culture: The Poetics and Politics of Ethnography*. Berkeley: University of California Press.
Cohen, Sara. 2007. *Decline, Renewal and the City in Popular Music: Beyond the Beatles*. Farnham: Ashgate.
Collier, Simon. 1986. *The Life, Music and Times of Carlos Gardel*. Pittsburgh: University of Pittsburgh Press.
Colville-Anderson, Mikael. 2018. *Copenhagenize: The Definitive Guide to Global Bicycle Urbanism*. Washington DC: Island Press.
Connor, Steven. 2016. "Choralities." *Twentieth-Century Music* 13 (1): 3–23.
Cook, Nicholas. 2008. "We Are All (Ethno)musicologists Now." In *The New Ethnomusicologies*, edited by Henry Stobart, 48–67. Lanham MD: Scarecrow Press.
Corte-Real, Maria de São José. 2010. "Introduction: Citizenship, Music and Migration." *Migrações* 7: 11–26.

Danielson, Virginia. 1997. *The Voice of Egypt: Umm Kulthum, Arabic Song, and Egyptian Society in the Twentieth Century*. Chicago: University of Chicago Press.

Dave, Nomi. 2019. *The Revolutions' Echoes: Music, Politics, and Pleasure in Guinea*. Chicago: University of Chicago Press.

Davis, Ruth. 2004. *Ma'luf: Reflections on the Arab Andalusian Music of Tunisia*. Lanham MD: Scarecrow Press.

Denning, Michael, and Gary Tomlinson. 2021. "Cantologies." *Representations* 154: 113–128.

Dent, Alex. 2009. *River of Tears: Country Music, Memory and Modernity in Brazil*. Durham NC: Duke University Press.

Dolan, Emily, and Alexander Rehding. 2021. "Timbre: Alternative Histories and Possible Futures for Music." In *The Oxford Handbook of Timbre*, edited by Emily Dolan and Alexander Rehding, 19–37. New York: Oxford University Press.

Dolar, Mladen. 1996. "The Object Voice." In *Voice and Gaze as Love Objects*, edited by Renata Salecl and Slavoj Zizek, 7–31. Durham NC: Duke University Press.

Dueck, Byron. 2013. *Musical Intimacies and Indigenous Imaginaries: Aboriginal Music and Dance in Public Performance*. New York: Oxford University Press.

Durkheim, Emile. 1893/1947. *The Elementary Forms of Religious Life*. New York: Free Press.

During, Jean. 1997. "Rhythmes ovoïdes et quadrature du cycle." *Cahiers des musiques traditionnelles* 10: 16–36.

El-Ghadban, Yara, and Kiven Strohm. 2013. "The Ghosts of Resistance: Dispatches from Palestinian Art and Music." In *Palestinian Music and Song: Expression and Resistance since 1900*, edited by Moslih Kanaaneh, Stig-Magnus Thorsen, Heather Bursheh, and David McDonald, 175–200. Bloomington: Indiana University Press.

el-Shawan Costelo-Branco, Salwa (see Shawan Costelo-Branco, Salwa, el-).

Eidsheim, Nina. 2019. *The Race of Sound: Listening, Timbre and Vocality in African American Music*. Durham NC: Duke University Press.

Englehardt, Jeffers. 2015. *Singing the Right Way: Orthodox Christians and Secular Enchantment in Estonia*. New York: Oxford University Press.

Erlmann, Viet. 2010. *Reason and Resonance: A History of Modern Aurality*. Cambridge, MA: Zone Books.

Ewell, Philip. 2021. "Music Theory's White Racial Frame." *Music Theory Spectrum* 43 (1): 324–329.

Eyerman, Ron, and Andrew Jamison. 1998. *Music and Social Movements: Mobilizing Traditions in the Twentieth Century*. Cambridge: Cambridge University Press.

Fardon, Richard (ed.). 1990. *Localizing Strategies: Regional Traditions of Ethnographic Writing*. Washington DC: Smithsonian Institute Press.

Farrar, James, and Andrew David Field. 2015. *Shanghai Nightscapes: A Nocturnal Biography of a Global City*. Chicago: University of Chicago Press.

Feld, Steven, and Panayotis Panopoulos. 2015. "Athens Conversation: On Ethnographic Listening and Comparative Acoustemologies," https://static1.squarespace.com/static/545aad98e4b0f1f9150ad5c3/t/5543bb7de4b0b5d7d7bb3d58/1430502269571/Athens+Conversation.pdf

Feld, Steven, Aaron Fox, Thomas Porcello, and David Samuels. 2004. "Vocal Anthropology: From the Music of Language to the Language of Song." *A Companion to Linguistic Anthropology*, edited by Alessandro Duranti, 321–345. Oxford: Blackwell.

Feldman, Martha. 2021. "Fugitive Voice." *Representations* 154: 10–22.

Feldman, Martha, and Judith Zeitlin. 2019. "The Clamor of Voices." In *The Voice as Something More: Essays towards Materiality*, edited by Martha Feldman and Judith Zeitlyn, 3–37. Chicago: Chicago University Press.

Fend, Michael. 2018. "From Immigrant Musician to State Employee: Cherubini's Career in Paris in the 1790s." In *Cherubini Studies: Atti del convegno Cherubini, Benevento 2018*, edited by Francesca Menchelli-Buttini, Maria Teresa Arfini, and Emilia Pantini, 263–278. Sinzig: Studio Verlag.

Fernandes, Sujatha. 2012. "Performing the African Diaspora in Mexico." In *Comparative Perspectives on Afro-Latin America*, edited by John Burdick and Kwame Dixon, 72–92. Cambridge: Cambridge University Press.

Flood, Alison. 2015. "President Obama Says Novels Taught Him How to Be a Citizen." *Guardian*, https://www.theguardian.com/books/2015/oct/28/president-obama-says-novels-taught-him-citizen-marilynne-robinson.

Foucault, Michel. 1979. *The History of Sexuality*. Harmondsworth: Penguin.

Garcia, Manuel Luis. 2015. "'At Home, I'm a Tourist': Musical Migration and Affective Citizenship in Berlin." *Journal of Urban Cultural Studies* 2 (1–2): 121–134.

Gedik, Ali. 2019. "Struggling with and Discussing a 'Republic' through Turkish Popular Music." In *Made in Turkey: Studies in Popular Music*, edited by Ali Gedik, 1–19. New York: Routledge.

Gellhorn, Marcia. 1929/2012. "Rudy Vallée: God's Gift to Us Girls." In *Music, Sound and Technology in America*, edited by Timothy Taylor, Mark Katz, and Tony Grajeda, 316–319. Durham NC: Duke University Press.

Gerwin, Marcin. 2018. *Citizens Assemblies: Guide to Democracy That Works*. Krakow: Otwarty.

Ghosh, Bishnupriya. 2011. *Global Icons: Apertures to the Popular*. Durham NC: Duke University Press.

Gilbert, Jeremy. 2020. "Editorial." *New Formations* 100–101 (Special Issue on Bureaucracy): 5–9.

Glancey, Jonathan. 2014. "The Violent History of Public Squares." December 3, 2014, https://www.bbc.com/culture/article/20141203-blood-on-the-streets.

Glasser, Jonathan. 2016. *The Lost Paradise: Andalusi Music in North Africa.* Chicago: University of Chicago Press.
Grainge, Paul. 2002. *Monochrome Memories: Nostalgia and Style in Retro America.* Westport CT: Greenwood.
Gray, Chris Hables. 2001. *Cyborg Citizenship: Politics in the Posthuman Age.* New York: Routledge.
Gray, Ellen. 2013. *Fado Resounding: Affective Politics and Urban Life.* Durham NC: Duke University Press.
Green, Andrew. 2019. "'What Will the Respectable Public Say?' Protest Musicianship and Class in 'Sexta' Events in Mexico City." In *Citizenship in the Latin American Upper and Middle Classes: Ethnographic Perspective on Culture and Politics*, edited by Fiorella Montero-Diaz and Franka Winter, 30–45. New York: Routledge.
Goodman, Jane. 2005. *Berber Culture on the World Stage: From Village to Video.* Bloomington: Indiana University Press.
Gordon, Joel. 2002. *Revolutionary Melodrama: Popular Film and Civic Identity in Nasser's Egypt.* Chicago: University of Chicago Center for Middle East Studies.
Gordon, Joel. 2007. "The Slaps Felt around the World: Family and National Melodrama in Two Nasser-Era Musicals." *International Journal of Middle East Studies* 39 (2): 209–228.
Gorz, André. 1980. *Ecology as Politics.* Montreal: Black Rose Books.
Guilbault, Jocelyne, with Gage Averill, Édouard Benoit, and Gregory Rabess. 1993. *Zouk: World Music in the West Indies.* Chicago: University of Chicago Press.
Hansen, Miriam. 1991. *Babel and Babylon: Spectatorship in American Silent Film.* Cambridge MA: Harvard University Press.
Hardt, Michael, and Antonio Negri. 2004. *Multitude: War and Democracy in the Age of Empire.* New York: Penguin.
Harkness, Nicholas. 2015a. "The Pragmatics of Qualia in Practice." *Annual Review of Anthropology* 44: 573–589.
Harkness, Nicholas. 2015b. "Voicing Christian Aspiration: The Semiotic Anthropology of Voice in Seoul." *Ethnography* 16 (3): 313–330.
Hassan, Scheherezade 2018. "Between Formal Structure and Performance Practice: On the Baghdadi Secular Cycles." In *Theory and Practice in the Music of the Islamic World: Essays in Honour of Owen Wright*, edited by Rachel Harris and Martin Stokes, 273–292. New York: Routledge.
Head, Matthew. 2013. *Sovereign Feminine: Music and Gender in Eighteenth-Century Germany.* Berkeley: University of California Press.
Hebdige, Dick. 1979. *Subculture: The Meaning of Style.* London: Methuen.
Hesmondhalgh, David. 2013. *Why Music Matters.* London: Wiley Blackwell.
Herzfeld, Michael. 1997. *Cultural Intimacy: Social Poetics in the Nation State.* New York: Routledge.

Hirschkind, Charles. 2020. *The Feeling of History: Islam, Romanticism and Andalucia*. Chicago: University of Chicago Press.

Holmes, Jessica. 2020. "'The Dress Clad, Out-Loud Singer of Queer Punks': Bradford Cox and the Performance of Disability." *Journal of the Society for American Music* 14 (3): 1–30.

Holst-Warhaft, Gail. 1983. *Road to Rembetika, Music of Greek Subculture: Songs of Love, Sorrow and Hashish*. Limni: Denise Harvey.

Houllebecq, Michel. 2015. *Submission*. London: Vintage.

Howard, Keith. 2012. "Introduction: East Asian Music as Intangible Cultural Heritage." In *Music as Intangible Cultural Heritage: Policy, Ideology and Practice in the Preservation of East Asian Traditions*, edited by Keith Howard, 1–22. New York: Routledge.

Human Rights Watch. 2020. "Saudi Arabia: Migrants Held in Inhuman, Degrading Conditions." *Human Rights Watch*, https://www.hrw.org/news/2020/12/15/saudi-arabia-migrants-held-inhuman-degrading-conditions.

Irigaray, Luce. 2001. *Democracy Begins with Two*. New York: Routledge.

Jensen, Olu, Itir Erhart, Hande Eslen-Ziya, Derya Güçdemir, Umut Korkut, and Aidan McGarry. 2019. "Music Videos as Protest Communication: The Gezi Park Protest on Youtube." In *The Aesthetics of Global Protest*, edited by Olu Jensen, Itir Erhart, Hande Eslen-Ziya, Derya Güçdemir, Umut Korkut, and Aidan McGarry, 211–231. Amsterdam: Amsterdam University Press.

Jones, Andrew. 2020. *Circuit Listening: Chinese Popular Music in the Global 1960s*. Minneapolis: University of Minnesota Press.

Kafadar, Cem. 2014. "How Dark Is the History of the Night, How Black the Story of Coffee, How Bitter the Tale of Love: The Changing Measure of Leisure and Pleasure in Early Modern Istanbul." In *Medieval and Early Modern Performance in the Eastern Mediterranean*, edited by Arzu Öztürkmen and E.B. Witz, 243–269. Turnhout: Brepols.

Kenyon, Nicholas. 2015. "The Triumph of a Musical Venture." *New York Review of Books* 24: 74–76.

King, Anthony. 2008. "English Fans and Italian Football: Towards a Transnational Relationship." In *Performing National Identity: Anglo-Italian Cultural Transactions*, edited by Manfred Pfister and Ralf Hertel, 265–285. Leiden: Brill.

Harris, Rachel. 2017. "The New Battleground: Sound-and-Dance in China's Muslim Borderlands." *World of Music* 6 (2): 35–56.

Hassan, Sheherezade, and Phillipe Vigreux (eds.). 1992. *Musique Arabe: Le Congrès du Caire de 1932*. Cairo: CEDEJ.

Honneth, Axel, and Nancy Fraser. 2003. *Redistribution or Recognition? A Political-Philosophical Exchange*. London: Verso.

Hoskins, Bryony, Jochen Jesinghaus, Massimiliano Mascherini, Giuseppe Munda, Michela Nardo, Michaela Saisana, Daniel Van Nijlen, Daniele Vidoni, and Ernesto Villalba. 2006. *Measuring Active Citizenship in Europe*. Luxembourg: European Commission Directorate-General Joint Research

Centre Institute for the Protection and Security of the Citizen, https://ec.eur opa.eu/jrc/sites/default/files/jrc-coin-measuring-active-citizenship-2006_ en.pdf.

Kabeer, Naila. 2005. "Introduction: The Search for Inclusive Citizenship; Meanings and Expressions in an Interconnected World." In *Inclusive Citizenship: Meanings and Expressions*, edited by Naila Kabeer, 1–27. London: Bloomsbury.

Kane, Brian. 2014. *Sound Unseen: Acousmatic Sound in Theory and Practice*. New York: Oxford University Press.

Kasinitz, Philip, and Marco Martiniello. 2019. "Music, Migration and the City." *Ethnic and Racial Studies* 42 (6): 857–864.

Keil, Charles, and Steven Feld. 1994. *Music Grooves: Essays and Dialogues*. Chicago: Chicago University Press.

Kenny, Michael. 1995. *The First New Left: British Intellectuals after Stalin*. London: Lawrence and Wishart.

Kidron, Michael. 2020. "Paradox upon Paradox: Fractal States and Their Making." *International Socialism* 164, http://isj.org.uk/paradox-upon-para dox-fractal-states-and-their-making/.

Klenke, Kerstin. 2019. *The Sound State of Uzbekistan: Popular Music and Politics in the Karimov Era*. New York: Routledge.

Kornhauser, Bronia. 1978. "In Defence of Krongcong." In *Studies in Indonesian Music*, edited by Margaret Kartomi, 104–183. Clayton: Center for Indonesian Studies, Monash University.

Kosnick, Kira. 2007. *Migrant Media: Turkish Broadcasting and Multicultural Politics in Berlin*. Bloomington: Indiana University Press.

Krüger, Simone, and Ruxandra Trandafoui. 2014. "Introduction: Touristic and Migrating Musics in Transit." In *The Globalization of Musics in Transit: Music Migration and Tourism*, edited by Simone Krüger and Ruxandra Trandafoui, 1–31. New York: Routledge.

Kutmaa, Kristin. 2018. "Inside the UNESCO Apparatus: Practices and Policies." In *Safeguarding Intangible Heritage: Practices and Politics*, edited by Natsuko Akagawa and Laurajane Smith, 68–83. New York: Routledge.

Labesse, Patrick. 2003. "Frédéric Leval, marieur de musiques à la Fondation Royaumont, est mort." *Le Monde*, April 8, 2016, https://www.lemonde.fr/ musiques/article/2016/04/05/frederic-deval-marieur-de-musiques-a-la- fondation-royaumont-est-mort_4896048_1654986.html.

Laborde, Denis. 2020. "L'idéal du musicien et l'âpreté du monde." *Gradhiva* 31: 10–23.

Lazar, Sian. 2013. "Introduction." In *The Anthropology of Citizenship: A Reader*, edited by Sian Lazar, 1–22. Malden MA: Wiley Blackwell.

Levi, Eric, and Florian Scheding. 2010. "Introduction." In *Music and Displacement: Diasporas, Mobilities and Dislocations in Europe and Beyond*, edited by Eric Levi and Florian Scheding, 1–11. Lanham MD: Scarecrow Press.

Levine, Mark. 2008. *Heavy Metal Islam: Rock, Resistance and the Struggle for the Soul of Islam.* New York: Three Rivers Press.
Levine, Mark. 2014. "The Revolution Never Ends: Music, Protest and Rebirth in the Arab World." In *Routledge Handbook of the Arab Spring: Rethinking Democratization*, edited by Larbi Sadiki, 392–403. New York: Routledge.
Levy, Claire. 2007. "Diversifying the Groove: Bulgarian Folk Meets the Jazz Idiom." *Journal of Interdisciplinary Music Studies* 1 (2): 25–42.
Lie, Siv. 2021. *Django Generations: Hearing Ethnorace, Citizenship, and Jazz Manouche in France.* Chicago: University of Chicago Press.
L'Hommedieu, Jonathan. 2008. "Czechoslovakia, Middle East Policy." In *The Encyclopedia of the Arab-Israeli Conflict: A Political, Social, and Military History*, edited by Spencer Tucker, 280–281. Santa Barbara CA: ABC-Clio.
Lipsitz, George. 1997. *Dangerous Crossroads: Popular Music, Postmodernism and the Poetics of Place.* London: Verso.
Locke, John. 1689/1988. *Two Treatises of Government.* Edited by Peter Laslett. Cambridge: Cambridge University Press.
Lortat-Jacob, Bernard. 1994. Liner Notes to *Maroc: Musiques berbère du Haut-Atlas.* Paris: Le Chant du Monde.
Manabe, Noriko. 2015–2016. *The Revolution Will Not Be Televised: Protest Music after Fukushima.* New York: Oxford University Press.
Marcus, George. 2002. *The Sentimental Citizen: Emotion in Democratic Politics.* University Park: Penn State University Press.
Marshall, T.H. 1950/1983. "Citizenship and Social Class." In *States and Societies*, edited by David Held, 248–260. Oxford: Martin Robertson/The Open University Press.
Martiniello, Marco. 2019. "Music and the Political Expression and Mobilization of Second and Third-Generation Immigrants in Urban Europe: Insights from Liège (Belgium)." *Ethnic and Racial Studies* 42 (6): 994–1012.
Mauss, Marcel. 1966. *The Gift: Forms and Functions of Exchange in Archaic Societies*, translated by Ian Cunnison. London: Cohen and West.
Mazzarella, William. 2004. "Culture, Mediation, Globalization." *Annual Reviews in Anthropology* 33: 345–367.
Mazzarella, William. 2010. "The Myth of the Multitude, or, Who's Afraid of the Crowd?" *Critical Inquiry* 36 (4): 697–727.
Mazzarella, William, Eric Santner, and Aaron Schuster. 2020. *Sovereignty Inc.: Three Inquiries in Politics and Enjoyment.* Chicago: Chicago University Press.
Mbembe, Achille. 2019. *Necropolitics.* Durham NC: Duke University Press.
McDonald, David. 2013. *My Voice Is My Weapon: Music, Nationalism and the Poetics of Palestinian Resistance.* Durham NC: Duke University Press.
Mestyan, Adam. 2017. *Arab Patriotism: The Ideology and Culture of Power in Late Ottoman Egypt.* Princeton NJ: Princeton University Press.
Middleton, Richard. 2006. *Voicing the Popular: On the Subjects of Popular Music.* New York: Routledge.

Millar, Stephen, Martin Power, Daniel Parnell, Paul Widdop, and James Carr. 2021. "Football and Popular Culture (Introduction)." In *Football and Popular Culture: Singing Out from the Stands*, edited by Stephen Millar, Martin Power, Daniel Parnell, Paul Widdop, and James Carr, 1–8. New York: Routledge.

Mitchell, Clyde. 1959. *The Kalela Dance: Aspects of Social Relationships among Urban Africans in Northern Rhodesia*. Manchester: Manchester University Press.

Mitchell, Timothy. 1991. *Colonising Egypt*. Berkeley: University of California Press.

Mitchell, Timothy. 2002. *Rule of Experts: Egypt, Technopolitics, Modernity*. Berkeley: University of California Press.

Mitchell, W.T.J. 2013. "Image, Space, Revolution: The Arts of Occupation." In *Occupy: Three Inquiries in Disobedience*, edited by W.J.T. Mitchell, Bernard Harcourt, and Michael Taussig, 93–130. Chicago: University of Chicago Press.

Moehn, Frederick. 2011. "'We Live Daily In Two Countries': Audiotopias of Post-dictatorship Brazil." In *Brazilian Popular Music and Citizenship*, edited by Idelber Avelar and Christopher Dunn, 109–130. Durham NC: Duke University Press.

Montero-Diaz, Fiorella. 2019. "'Marginal Like You!': Constructing Citizenship through Fusion Music in the Peruvian Traditional Upper Classes." In *Citizenship in the Latin American Upper and Middle Classes: Ethnographic Perspective on Culture and Politics*, edited by Fiorella Montero-Diaz and Franka Winter, 62–79. New York: Routledge.

Mookherjee, Monica. 2005. "Affective Citizenship: Feminism, Postcolonialism, and the Politics of Recognition." *Critical Review of International Social and Political Philosophy* 8 (1): 31–50.

Moore, Robin. 2006. *Revelry and Revolution: Cultural Change in Socialist Cuba*. Berkeley: University of California Press.

Moten, Fred. 2003. *In The Break: The Aesthetics of the Black Radical Tradition*. Minneapolis: University of Minnesota Press.

Mondelli, Peter. 2016. "The Phonocentric Politics of the French Revolution." *Acta Musicologica* 88 (2): 143–164.

Morcom, Anna. 2013. *Illicit Worlds of Indian Dance: Cultures of Exclusion*. New York: Oxford University Press.

Navaro-Yashin, Yael. 2002. *Faces of the State: Secularism and Public Life in Turkey*. Princeton NJ: Princeton University Press.

Neveu Kringelbach, Hélène. 2013. *Dance Circles: Movement, Morality and Self-Fashioning in Urban Senegal*. Oxford: Berghan.

Nooshin, Laudan. 2016. "Happy Families? Convergence, Antagonism and Disciplinary Identities or 'We're All God Knows What Now' (Cook 2016)." Paper presented at the City Debate, "Are We All Ethnomusicologists Now?"

City University London, https://openaccess.city.ac.uk/view/creators_id/l=2Enooshin.html.

Norcliffe, Glen. 2015. *Critical Geographies of Cycling: History, Political Economy and Culture*. Farnham: Ashgate.

Norton, Barley. 2018. "Filming Music as Heritage: The Cultural Politics of Audiovisual Representation." In *Music as Heritage: Historical and Ethnographic Perspectives*, edited by Barley Norton and Naomi Matsumoto, 79–101. New York: Routledge.

Norton, Barley, and Naomi Matsumoto. 2018. "Introduction: Historical and Ethnographic Perspectives on Music as Heritage." In *Music as Heritage: Historical and Ethnographic Perspectives*, edited by Barley Norton and Naomi Matsumoto, 1–17. New York: Routledge.

Novak, David. 2017. "Project Fukushima! Performativity and the Politics of Festival in Post-3/11 Japan." *Anthropological Quarterly* 90 (1): 225–253.

Nussbaum, Martha. 2001. *Upheavals of Thought: The Intelligence of Emotions*. Cambridge: Cambridge University Press.

Nussbaum, Martha. 2013. *Political Emotions: Why Love Matters to Justice*. Cambridge MA: Harvard University Press.

Ochoa Gautier, Ana Maria. 2014. *Aurality: Listening and Knowledge in Nineteenth-Century Colombia*. Durham NC: Duke University Press.

O'Leary, Naomi. 2019. "The Myth of the Citizens Assembly: It Worked in Ireland but It Won't Solve Brexit." *Politico*, June 18, 2019, https://www.politico.eu/article/the-myth-of-the-citizens-assembly-democracy/.

O'Toole, Michael. 2014. "Sonic Citizenship: Music, Migration, and Transnationalism in Berlin's Turkish and Anatolian Diasporas." PhD Dissertation, University of Chicago.

O'Toole, Michael. 2022. "Rehearsing Publics, Sounding Citizens: Classical Turkish Music and Diasporic Citizenship in Berlin." In *Encounters in Ethnomusicology: Essays in Honor of Philip V. Bohlman*, edited by Michael Figueroa, Jamie Jones, and Timothy Rommen, 227–243. Zurich: Lit.

Oleksiak, Julie. 2016. "99 pour un monde meilleur." *Haizebegi* 3: 38–43.

Oleksiak, Julie. 2020. "La musique contre la violence du monde? Une art de la programmation transculturelle." *Hermès* 86 (1): 36–42.

Ong, Aihwa. 1999. *Flexible Citizenship: The Cultural Logics of Transnationality*. Durham NC: Duke University Press.

Oransay, Gültekin. 1985. *Atatürk ile Küğ: Belgeler ve Veriler*. Izmir: Küğ Yayını.

Özışık, E. 1963. *Musıki Sanatı*. Istanbul. Nurgök.

Özyürek, Esra. 2006. *Nostalgia for the Modern: State Secularism and Modern Politics in Turkey*. Durham NC: Duke University Press.

Özyürek, Esra. 2018. "Rethinking Empathy: Emotions Triggered by the Holocaust among the Muslim-Minority in Germany." *Anthropological Theory* 18 (4): 456–477.

Pamuk, Orhan. 2001. *My Name Is Red*. London: Faber and Faber.

Park, Robert. 1974. "The Crowd and the Public." In *The Crowd and the Public and Other Essays*, edited by Henry Elsner, 3–81. Chicago: University of Chicago Press.

Parlatti, Luigia. 2016. "Compter jusqu'à 99." *Haizebegi* 3: 44–47.

Pasler, Jann. 2009. *Composing the Citizen: Music as Public Utility in the Third Republic France*. Berkeley: University of California Press.

Petryna, Adriana. 2002. *Life Exposed: Biological Citizens after Chernobyl*. Princeton NJ: Princeton University Press.

Pennanen, Risto. 2010. "Melancholic Airs of the Orient: Bosnian *Sevdalinka* Music as an Orientalist and Nationalist Symbol." In *Music and Emotions*, edited by Risto Pennanen, 76–90. Helsinki: Helsinki Collegium for Advanced Studies.

Perna, Vincenzo. 2005. *Timba: The Sound of the Cuban Crisis*. Farnham: Ashgate.

Peterson, Marina. 2012. *Sound, Space and the City: Civic Performance in Downtown Los Angeles*. Philadelphia: University of Pennsylvania Press.

Philips-Hutton, Ariana. 2020. *Music Transforming Conflict*. Cambridge: Cambridge University Press.

Pilzer, Joshua. 2012. *Hearts of Pine: Songs in the Lives of Three Korean Survivors of the Japanese "Comfort Women."* New York: Oxford University Press.

Pilzer, Joshua. 2015. "The Study of Survivors' Music." In *The Oxford Handbook of Applied Ethnomusicology*, edited by Svanibor Pettan and Jeff Todd Titon, 481–510. New York: Oxford University Press.

Pistrick, Eckehard. 2020. "Dangerous Fields: Existentiality, Humanity, and Musical Creativity in German Refugee Camps." *Violence: An International Journal* 1 (2): 332–353.

Plummer, Christopher. 2003. *Intimate Citizenship: Private Decisions and Public Dialogues*. Seattle: University of Washington Press.

Preciado, Paolo. 2020. "Learning from the Virus." *Artforum*, https://www.artforum.com/print/202005/paul-b-preciado-82823.

Putnam, David. 2000. *Bowling Alone: The Collapse and Revival of American Community*. New York: Simon and Schuster.

Racy, Ali Jihad. 2003. *Making Music in the Arab World: The Culture and Artistry of Tarab*. Cambridge: Cambridge University Press.

Rahaim, Matthew. 2017. "Otherwise Than Participation: Unity and Alterity in Musical Encounters." In *Music and Empathy*, edited by Elain King and Caroline Waddington, 175–193. New York: Routledge.

Ramnarine, Tina. 2007. "Musical Performance in the Diaspora: Introduction." *Ethnomusicology Forum* 16 (1): 1–17.

Rasmussen, Anne K., Angela Impey, Rachel Beckles Willson, Ozan Aksoy, Denise Gill, and Michael Frishkopf. 2019. "Call and Response: SEM President's Roundtable 2016, 'Ethnomusicological Responses to the Contemporary Dynamics of Migrants and Refugees.'" *Ethnomusicology* 63 (2): 279–314.

Reily, Suzel. 1992. "Música Sertaneja and Migrant Identity: The Stylistic Development of a Brazilian Genre." *Popular Music* 40 (1): 337–358.

Reily, Suzel. 1994. "Macunaíma's Music: National Identity and Ethnomusicological Research in Brazil." In *Ethnicity and Identity: The Musical Construction of Place*, edited by Martin Stokes, 71–96. Oxford: Berg.

Reynolds, Emma. 2018. "The Agony of Sophia, the World's First Robot Citizen Condemned to a Lifeless Career in Marketing." *Wired*, https://www.wired.co.uk/article/sophia-robot-citizen-womens-rights-detriot-become-human-hanson-robotics.

Reynolds, Dwight. 2021. *The Musical Heritage of Al-Andalus*. New York: Routledge.

Rice, Timothy. 1994. *May It Fill Your Soul! Experiencing Bulgarian Music*. Chicago: University of Chicago Press.

Rice, Timothy. 2017. *Modeling Ethnomusicology*. New York: Oxford University Press.

Ringsager, Kristine. 2017. "'Featuring the System': Hip Hop Pedagogy and Danish Integration Policies." *Suomen Antropologi* 42 (2): 75–93.

Rosenfeld, Sophia. 2011. "On Being Heard: A Case for Paying Attention to the Listening Ear." *American Historical Review* 116 (2): 316–334.

Rouget, Gilbert. 1985. *Music and Trance: A Theory of the Relations between Music and Possession*. Chicago: University of Chicago Press.

Rousseau, Jean-Jacques. 1762/1968. *The Social Contract*. Translated by Maurice Cranston. Harmondsworth: Penguin.

Rousseau, Jean-Jacques. 1781/1993. *Essai sur l'origine des languages*, edited by Catherine Kintzler. Malesherbes: GF Flammarion.

Sanders, Lewis, IV, and Mark Visonà. 2012. "The Soul of Tahrir: Poetics of a Revolution." In *Translating Egypt's Revolution: The Language of Tahrir*, edited by Samia Mehrez, 213–248. Cairo: American University of Cairo Press.

Savigliano, Marta. 1995. *Tango and the Political Economy of Passion*. Bounder CA: Westview Press.

Schade-Poulsen, Marc. 1999. *Men and Popular Music in Algeria: The Social Significance of Raï*, Austin: University of Texas Press.

Scheding, Florian. 2018. "'Who Is British Music?' Placing Migrants into National Music History." *Twentieth Century Music* 15 (3): 439–492.

Sennett, Richard. 2008. *The Craftsman*. New Haven CT: Yale University Press.

Shannon, Jonathan. 2009. *Among the Jasmine Trees: Music and Modernity in Contemporary Syria*. Middleton CT: Wesleyan University Press.

Shawan Costelo-Branco, Salwa, el-. 1980. "The Socio-Political Context of Al-Musiqa Al-'Arabiyyah in Cairo, Egypt: Politics, Patronage, Institutions and Musical Change (1927–77)." *Asian Music* 12 (1): 86–128.

Shay, Anthony. 2002. *Choreographic Politics: State Folk Dance Companies*. Middletown CT: Wesleyan University Press.

Silver, Michael. 2018. *Voices of Drought: The Politics of Music and Environment in Northeastern Brazil*. Urbana: University of Illinois Press.

Silverman, Carole. 2012. *Romani Routes: Cultural Politics and Balkan Music in Diaspora*. New York: Oxford University Press.
Silverman, Kaja. 1988. *The Acoustic Mirror: The Female Voice in Psychoanalysis and Cinema*. Bloomington: Indiana University Press.
Simonett, Helena. 2001. *Banda: Mexican Musical Life across Borders*. Middletown CT: Wesleyan University Press.
Simms, Robert. 2004. *The Repertoire of Iraqi Maqam*. Lanham MD: Scarecrow Press.
Slobin, Mark. 1996. "Introduction." In *Retuning Culture: Musical Changes in Central and Eastern Europe*, edited by Mark Slobin, 1–13. Durham NC: Duke University Press.
Slobin, Mark. 2020. *Motor City Music: A Detroiter Looks Back*. New York: Oxford University Press.
Solomon, Thomas. 2013. "The Oriental Body on the European Stage: Producing Turkish Cultural Identity on the Margins of Europe." In *Empire of Song: Europe and Nation in the Eurovision Song Contest*, edited by Dafni Tragaki, 173–202. Lanham MD: Scarecrow Press.
Sonevytsky, Maria. 2019. *Wild Music: Sound and Sovereignty in Ukraine*. Middletown CT: Wesleyan University Press.
Sprengel, Darci. 2020 "'Loud' and 'Quiet' Politics: Questioning the Role of 'the Artist' in Street Art Projects after the 2011 Egyptian Revolution." *International Journal of Cultural Studies* 23 (2): 208–226.
Stanyek, Jason, and Benjamin Piekut. 2010. "Deadness: Technologies of the Intermundane." *Drama Review* 54 (1): 14–38.
Steingo, Gavin, and Jim Sykes. 2019. "Remapping Sound Studies in the Global South." In *Remapping Sound Studies*, edited by Gavin Steingo and Jim Sykes, 1–36. Durham NC: Duke University Press.
Steintrager, James, with Ray Chow. 2019. "Sound Objects: An Introduction." In *Sound Objects*, edited by James Steintrager and Ray Chow, 1–19. Durham NC: Duke University Press.
Sterne, Jonathan. 2003. *The Audible Past: Cultural Origins of Sound Reproduction*. Durham NC: Duke University Press.
Sterne, Jonathan. 2012. "Sonic Imaginations." In *The Sound Studies Reader*, edited by Jonathan Sterne, 1–36. New York: Routledge.
Stirr, Anna. 2017. *Singing across Divides: Music and Cultural Intimacy in Nepal*. New York: Oxford University Press.
Stoever-Ackermann, Jennifer. 2011. "Reproducing American Citizenship in 'Blackboard Jungle': Race, Cold War Liberalism, and the Tape Recorder." *American Quarterly* 63 (3): 781–806.
Stokes, Martin. 2006. "Adam Smith and the Dark Nightingale: On Twentieth-Century Sentimentalism." *Twentieth-century Music* 9 (3): 201–219.
Stokes, Martin. 2009. "Abd al-Halim's Microphone." In *Music and the Play of Power in the Middle East, North Africa and Central Asia*, edited by Laudan Nooshin, 55–73. Farnham: Ashgate.

Stokes, Martin. 2010a. "Listening to Abd al-Halim." In *Global Soundtracks: Worlds of Film Music*, edited by Mark Slobin, 309–336. Middletown CT: Wesleyan University Press.

Stokes, Martin. 2010b. *The Republic of Love: Cultural Intimacy in Turkish Popular Music*. Chicago: University of Chicago Press.

Stokes, Martin. 2017. "Musical Ethnicity: Affective, Material and Vocal Turns." *World of Music* 6 (2): 19–34.

Stokes, Martin. 2020a. "Music and Migration." *Music Research Annual* 1: 1–24.

Stokes, Martin. 2020b. "Sentimental Gesture and the Politics of 'Shape' in the Performances of Abd al-Halim Hafiz." In *Investigating Musical Performance: Theoretical Models and Intersections*, edited by Gianmario Borio, Giovanni Giuriati, Alessandro Cecchi, and Marco Lutzu, 185–197. New York: Routledge.

Stokes, Martin. 2021a. *The Arabesk Debate: Music and Musicians in Modern Turkey* (second edition). Oxford: Oxford University Press.

Stokes, Martin. 2021b. "On the Beach: Musicology's Migrant Crisis." *Representations* 154: 113–128.

Straw, Will. 2014. "The Urban Night." In *Cartographies of Place: Navigating the Urban*, edited by Michael Darroch and Janine Marchessault, 185–200. Montreal: McGill-Queens University Press.

Straw, Will. 2015. "Media and the Urban Night." *Articulo: Journal of Urban Research* 11, https://journals.openedition.org/articulo/3098.

Swedenburg, Ted. 2005. "Against Hybridity: The Case of Enrico Macias/Gaston Ghrenassia." In *Palestine, Israel and the Politics of Popular Culture*, edited by Rebecca Stein and Ted Swedenburg, 231–256. Durham NC: Duke University Press.

Sykes, James. 2018. *The Musical Gift: Sonic Generosity in Post-War Sri Lanka*. New York: Oxford University Press.

Sykes, James. 2020. "The Anthropocene and Music Studies." *Ethnomusicology Review* 22 (2), https://ethnomusicologyreview.ucla.edu/journal/volume/22/piece/1030.

Tarde, Gabriel. 1890/1962. *The Laws of Imitation*. Gloucester MA: Peter Smith.

Tarde, Gabriel. 1901/1989. *L'Opinion et la foule*. Paris: Presses Universitaires de France.

Taylor, Timothy. 2018. "General Introduction." In *Music, Sound and Technology in America*, edited by Timothy Taylor, Mark Katz, and Tony Grajeda, 1–28. Durham NC: Duke University Press.

Taylor, Timothy, Mark Katz, and Tony Grajeda (eds.). 2018. *Music, Sound and Technology in America*. Durham NC: Duke University Press.

Thompson, Emily. 2002. *The Soundscape of Modernity: Architectural Acoustics and the Culture of Listening in America, 1900–1933*. Cambridge MA: MIT Press.

Thompson, E.P. 1992. "Rough Music Reconsidered." *Folklore* 103 (1): 3–26.

Tochka, Nicholas. 2016. *Audible States: Socialist Politics and Popular Music in Albania*. New York: Oxford University Press.
Toynbee, Jason, and Byron Dueck. 2011. "Migrating Music." In *Migrating Music*, edited by Jason Toynbee and Byron Dueck, 1–17. New York: Routledge.
Tomlinson, Gary. 2012. "Music, Anthropology, History." In *The Cultural Study of Music: A Critical Introduction*, edited by Martin Clayton, Trevor Herbert, and Richard Middleton, 59–72. New York: Routledge.
Tragaki, Dafni. 2007. *Rebetika Worlds: Ethnomusicology and Ethnography in the City*. Cambridge: Scholars Press.
Tragaki, Dafni. 2013. "Introduction." In *Empire of Song: Europe and Nation in the Eurovision Song Contest*, edited by Dafni Tragaki, 1–33. Lanham MD: Scarecrow Press.
Tragaki, Dafni. 2019. "Music and the Political: A Dialogue with Martin Stokes." *Rast Musicology Journal* 7 (2): 2181–2186, https://doi.org/10.12975/pp2 181-2186.
Treece, David. 2013. *Brazilian Jive: From Samba to Bossa and Rap*. London: Reaktion Books.
Trilling, Daniel. 2019. "How the Media Contributed to the Migrant Crisis." *The Guardian*, August 1, 2019, https://www.theguardian.com/news/2019/aug/01/media-framed-migrant-crisis-disaster-reporting.
Trnka, Susanna, Christine Dureau, and Julie Park. 2013. "Introduction: Senses and Citizenships." In *Senses and Citizenships: Embodying Political Life*, edited by Susanna Trnka, Christine Dureau, and Julie Park, 1–32. New York: Routledge.
Tucker, Joshua. 2013. *Gentleman Troubadours and Andean Pop Stars: Huayno Music, Media Work, and Ethnic Imaginaries in Urban Peru*. Chicago: University of Chicago Press.
Turino, Thomas. 2000. *Nationalisms, Cosmopolitans, and Popular Music in Zimbabwe*. Chicago: University of Chicago Press.
Turino, Thomas. 2008. *Music as Social Life: The Politics of Participation*. Chicago: University of Chicago Press.
Tunbridge, Laura. 2020. *Beethoven: A Life in Nine Pieces*. London: Viking.
Van Zoonen, Lisbet. 2005. *Entertaining the Citizen: When Politics and Popular Culture Converge*. Lanham MD: Rowman and Littlefield.
Virolle, Marie. 2000. *La chanson raï: De l'Algérie profonde à la scène internationale*. Paris: Karthala.
Vitalis, Bob. 2000. "American Ambassador in Technicolor and CinemaScope: Hollywood and Revolution on the Nile." In *Mass Mediations: New Approaches to Popular Culture in the Middle East and Beyond*, edited by Walter Armbrust, 269–291. Berkeley: University of California Press.
Wade, Peter. 2010. *Race and Ethnicity in Latin America*. London: Pluto Press.
Washabaugh, William. 1996. *Flamenco: Passion, Politics and Popular Culture*. Oxford: Berg.

Webster-Kogen, Ilana. 2018. *Citizen Amari: Making Ethiopian Music in Tel Aviv*. Middletown CT: Wesleyan University Press.

Weintraub, Andrew. 2010. *Dangdut Stories: A Social and Musical History of Indonesia's Most Popular Music*. New York: Oxford University Press.

Western, Tom. 2020. "Listening with Displacement: Sound, Citizenship, and Disruptive Representations of Migration." *Migration and Society*, 3 (1): 294–309.

White, Bob. 2006. *Rumba Rules: The Politics of Dance Music in Mobutu's Zaire*. Durham NC: Duke University Press.

Wilford, Steven. 2017. "'We Are All Algerian Here': Music, Community and Citizenship in Algerian London." *Ethnomusicology Review* 22 (2), https://ethnomusicologyreview.ucla.edu/content/"we-are-all-algerian-here"-music-community-and-citizenship-algerian-london.

Yalçınkaya, Fisun. 2016. "Zeki Müren de Bizi Duyuyor!" *Milliyet*, February 3, 2016, https://www.milliyet.com.tr/gundem/zeki-muren-de-bizi-duyuyor-2188458.

Yano, Christine. 2003. *Tears of Longing: Nostalgia and the Nation in Japanese Popular Song*. Cambridge MA: Harvard University Press.

Yetkin, Mutlu. 2014. "The End of Cool Istanbul: Culture in Turkey before and after Gezi." *Qantara*, January 31, 2014, https://en.qantara.de/content/culture-in-turkey-before-and-after-gezi-the-end-of-cool-istanbul.

Young, Iris Marion. 1986. "The Ideal of Difference and the Politics of Community." *Social Theory and Practice* 12 (1): 1–26.

Yurchak, Alexei. 2005. *Everything Was Forever Until It Was No More: The Last Soviet Generation*. Princeton NJ: Princeton University Press.

Yuval Davies, Nira, Kalpana Kannabiran, and Ulrike Vieten. 2006. "Situating Contemporary Politics of Belonging." In *The Situated Politics of Belonging*, edited by Nira Yuval-Davies, Kalpana Kannabiran, and Ulrike Vieten, 1–13. New York: Routledge.

Žižek, Slavoj. 1996. "There Is No Sexual Relationship." In *Voice and Gaze as Love Objects*, edited by Renata Salecl and Slavoj Žižek, 208–249. Durham NC: Duke University Press.

Index

For the benefit of digital users, indexed terms that span two pages (e.g., 52-53) may, on occasion, appear on only one of those pages.

Figures are indicated by *f* following the page number

Abd al-Halim Hafiz, 85n.39, 88–102, 118–19, 129–31nn.5–9, 151
acoustics, 1–2, 18, 77, 109–10, 135n.42, 157–58n.27. *See also* citizenship: acoustic
activism, 20–21, 39, 53–57, 74, 77–78, 80n.10, 80–81n.11, 118–19, 128
Adlington, Robert, 41n.10, 129n.1, 158n.29
Agamben, Giorgio, 34–35, 36
agora, 116–17, 117n.51, 118–19, 127
Algeria, 71–72, 85nn.35–36, 146–47
Appiah, Anthony, 91–92
arabesk, 20, 84n.32, 86n.43, 149
'Arab Spring', 39, 117–18
audience, 7, 14–20, 44n.29, 54–55, 72–73, 88–89, 97–98, 101, 141, 147
aurality, 151, 157–58n.27. *See also* listening
authoritarianism, 5, 10–11, 20, 39, 50–51, 66–67, 70–71, 84n.32, 116, 124, 149–50, 151
Avelar, Idelber, 50–52

Bakhtin, Mikhail, 30–31, 32
Baldwin, James, 91–92
Bataclan, 138n.60, 145–48
Beethoven, Ludvig Van, 3–4, 40–41nn.6–7, 50, 88–89, 130n.7, 144, 156–57n.24
Berlant, Lauren, 69–71, 76–77, 129n.2
Berman, Marshall, 117, 127, 136–37n.51
Bhabha, Homi, 9
Black Aesthetics, 26–27, 30, 46n.42

Bohlman, Philip, 79n.3, 129n.3, 158n.28
Born, Georgina, 22, 29–30
Brazil, 10–11, 50–51, 82–83n.19, 84n.32
Buford, Bill, 111–13
Bulgaria, 58–59, 82n.17
Burke, Kenneth, 25–27
Butsch, Richard, 17–18, 19, 43–44nn.26–27

Cairo, 20, 38, 89–91, 94, 96–97, 99–100, 101, 118, 131n.10, 131n.13
Camal, Jérôme, 144, 145, 157–58n.27
Canetti, Elias, 108–9
cassettes, 20, 21–22, 23–24, 44–45n.31
censorship, 15–16, 57–58
Chamoiseau, Patrick, 142, 144–45, 154n.10
Cherubini, Luigi, 4
chorality, 114–15, 151, 157–58n.27. *See also* voice
cinema 12–13, 18, 19, 23, 28–29
 Egyptian, 89–90, 91–92, 95, 97–98, 99, 132n.16, 133n.21
Citizens' Assemblies, 1, 40n.2
citizenship
 acoustic, 74
 anthropology of, 5–7, 42n.14
 biopolitical 47–48n.52
 cultural, 50–51, 54–55, 84n.28
 cyborg, 20–21, 45n.34
 iconography of, 87–88
 intimate, 9–10, 67–76
 sentimental, 69–70
 sonic, 49, 79n.1
 technocracy and, 50–51, 57–67

178 INDEX

city, 14, 19, 67, 95, 96–99, 102, 108–9, 110–11, 115–18, 119–20, 123, 129n.1, 132n.19, 133n.24, 133n.25, 136–37n.51
  See also space: urban; space, public
civility 1–2, 10, 12, 36, 99, 110–11, 149–50
  and the crowd 115–17
  and migrancy 80n.8, 143, 149–50
  and nightlife 96–97
  and race 98–99
  'sly' 9
  and voice 31–32
Clark, Gregory, 25–27
climate crisis, 5, 34–35, 86n.44, 151
Connor, Steven, 30, 107–8, 114–15, 135n.42, 157–58n.27
Coronavirus pandemic, 35–36, 134n.32
counterpublic, 69–70, 84–85n.33
creolité, 144, 150–51
crowd, 14–15, 17, 18–20, 39, 87–88, 97, 102–16
cycling, 88, 89–93, 94

dangdut, 42n.19, 71, 72–73
Dave, Nomi, 61–64, 82–83n.19, 83n.21
Declaration of the Rights of Man and of the Citizen (1789), 4
democracy, 2–3, 4, 5–6, 7, 16, 63–64, 66, 68, 75, 95, 106, 114, 145, 149, 152
  and the city, 95 (*see also* space: urban; space, public)
  and criticism 25–27
  and crowds, 14–15, 115
  and Islam, 145–46, 149–50
  and music study, 5, 33, 144, 158n.29
  and postcolonialism, 66–67, 118
  and Rousseau, Jean-Jacques, 14–15, 151–52
  and subcultural theory, 23, 135n.39
  and transition, 58–59
  and war, 155n.14
détournement, 145
Deval, Frédéric, 140–41, 153n.5
disability, 39, 86n.44, 87, 128–29, 129n.3
Dunn, Stuart, 50–52
Durkheim, Emile 112–13

Egypt, 70, 72, 81n.16, 85n.39, 88–102, 116, 118–19, 128, 129n.4, 129–31nn.5–11, 131–32nn.13–18, 148, 152n.1, 156n.23. *See also* cinema: Egyptian
El-Ghadban, Yara, 65–66
emotion, 6–7, 8, 10–11, 18, 67, 87, 96–97, 100, 112, 127, 141. *See also* emotives; sentiment
emotion, political 24–25, 69–70, 75, 77–78, 86n.43, 116
'emotional turn' 46n.41
  and hermeneutics 135n.38
emotives, 85n.40. *See also* emotion
Erdoğan, Recep Tayyip, 42n.23, 119, 120, 137n.55
estrada, 59–61, 67
ethnicity, 50–52, 54. *See also* identity
eudaimonia, 2–3, 25
Eurovision Song Contest, 69, 73–74, 84n.31
Exposition Universelle, 16, 17

Facebook, 21, 44n.29, 134–35n.37. *See also* social media
football, 92–93, 104–6, 109–11, 115, 125–26, 134nn.32–36, 135–36nn.42–43, 136n.45
Foucault, Michel, 34–35, 47–48n.52
France, 16–17, 53–56, 68–69, 71–72, 112–13, 140–42, 144–48. *See also* Revolution: in France
Frankfurt School, 20–21, 45n.32
French Revolution. *See* revolution: in France

Gezi Park, 116, 119–27, 128, 137n.57, 138n.59, 151. *See also* Istanbul: Turkey
Gorz, André, 98, 99, 133n.26
Greece, 42n.19, 68, 82n.17
Guinea, 59, 61–63

Harkness, Nicholas, 31–33, 47n.49
Herzfeld, Michael, 68–69
Hesmondhalgh, David, 2–3, 25

identity, 16–17, 49, 50–57, 75–76, 79n.5, 142, 143–44, 147–48. *See also* ethnicity; multiculturalism
  and identity cards 127, 140–41

multiple, 142, 156n.20
national, 4, 73, 110–11
queer 69 (*see also* queer theory)
racial 30–31 (*see also* race)
theories of, 28–29, 77–78, 79n.4 (*see also* postcolonialism)
Indonesia, 10–11, 42n.19, 71, 72–73, 75, 84n.32, 85n.37, 148
intimacy, 34, 42n.16, 49, 67–76, 95, 120, 127, 143. *See also* citizenship: intimate
Islam, 9, 39, 61, 71–72, 118, 120, 124, 145–46, 147–50, 157n.25. *See also* Islamophobia
Islamophobia, 39
Israel, 39, 52–53, 65, 70, 80n.7, 84n.29, 89, 147–48, 156n.20
Istanbul, 20, 57, 96–97, 116–17, 119–24, 138n.59. *See also* Gezi Park; Turkey

jazz, 25–27, 52, 53–55, 58–59, 92, 99–100, 101, 140, 144, 158n.29
jeliya, 61–63

Klenke, Kirsten, 59–61

Lacan, Jacques, 28, 29–30
Lazar, Sian, 5–7
liberalism 87, 116. *See also* neoliberalism
Lie, Siv B., 53–56
listening, 1, 2–3, 7, 15, 17, 18, 19–20, 27, 29, 30–31, 37–38, 61, 74, 107–8, 112, 143–44. *See also* 'aurality'
democratic 29
mass mediated 25
regressive 19
Liverpool Football Club, 104–5, 106, 107–8, 109–11, 134nn.35–36
Lortat-Jacob, Bernard 110, 110*f*, 136n.44
love, 11, 46n.45, 72, 85n.37, 92–93, 95, 102

Manabe, Noriko, 86n.44, 125
Marshall, T.H., 41n.11, 50–51, 67–68
Martello, Davide, 122–23, 124, 126, 128, 137n.55, 138n.60
Mbembe, Achille, 34–35, 47–48n.52, 155n.14

mediation, 7, 13–14, 19–20, 21–23, 26–27, 37–38, 45–46n.39, 118–19, 128. *See also* cassettes; cinema; radio; television; social media
and the critic 25–27
and neo-Aristotelian theory 24–25
and subcultural theory 23–24
melancholy, 9–10, 75, 148–49
MENA region, 39, 56, 92, 118, 148–51, 156–57n.24
microphone, 10, 27–29, 99–100
Middle East. *See* MENA region
migrant aesthetics, 80n.8
'migrant crisis', 56
migrants, 45n.35, 56–57, 64–65, 71, 75, 79n.1, 79n.5, 140–41, 143, 145, 146, 148, 149–50
migration, 10–11, 34–35, 52, 71, 80nn.8–10, 84n.26, 85n.35, 96–97, 110, 145
Moore, Captain Sir Thomas, 102, 103–4, 133–34n.28
multiculturalism, 50, 50n.5
Müren, Zeki, 8–14, 20, 21–22, 27–28, 33–34, 39, 41n.7, 43n.24, 70, 71, 74, 75, 85n.39, 150–51

Nammour, Marc, 140–42
nationalism, 10–11, 64–65, 102, 142–43
neoliberalism, 25, 50–51, 65–66, 67, 83n.20, 124, 131n.12. *See also* liberalism
nightlife, 96–97, 132n.20
Novak, David, 125–26
Nussbaum, Martha, 24–25, 46n.40, 66–67

Özyürek, Esra, 34, 157n.25

Palestine, 39, 65–66, 84n.28
Park, Robert, 113–14
Pasler, Jan, 16–17
Plummer, Ken, 9–10, 67–68, 69–70, 75–76
populism, 36, 72–73, 150
postcolonialism, 91, 131n.12. *See also* state: postcolonial
Preciado, Paolo, 35–36
protest, 39, 40n.1, 71–72, 89, 115–16
and festivalization, 126
and social media, 21, 121, 125
and song, 106, 121–22, 124

public, 17, 18, 26–27, 31, 67–
    68, 114, 137n.53. *See also*
    counterpublics; space
  good, 19
  health, 5, 35
  kissing in, 120
  listening, 17
  utility, 16–17

queer theory, 30

race, 25, 30–31, 39, 53–54
radio, 1, 2, 18, 19, 21–22, 23–24, 29,
    44n.29, 57, 93, 134n.32
  Egyptian, 20
  Turkish, 27
rai, 71–72, 75–76, 85n.35
rebetika, 42n.19, 59, 84n.32
resonance, 15, 17, 18, 75, 78–79, 108–9
revolution, 19–20, 21, 44n.29, 59, 61–62,
    69–70, 100, 116–17, 148–49
  in China, 96–97
  and crowds, 115, 128
  in Cuba, 132n.20
  in Egypt, 87–89, 90–91, 95, 96, 99, 102,
    118, 128, 129–30n.5, 130–31n.9
  in France 2–3, 15–17, 20–21,
    43n.25, 117–18
  and love, 133n.26
rhetoric, 8, 26–27, 62, 90, 115
Rice, Timothy, 58–59, 77–78, 82n.17
Rousseau, Jean-Jacques, 14–15, 16,
    41n.11, 43n.25, 47n.49, 151–52,
    158n.28

secularism, 9, 34, 120, 121, 123, 124, 125–
    26, 127, 145–46, 148–49
sentiment, 15, 42n.20, 69–70, 95,
    103, 106. *See also* citizenship:
    sentimental; emotion;
    sentimental crowd
sentimental crowd, 87–88, 115–16, 128
Slobin, Mark, 82n.17, 98–99,
    133nn.23–24
soccer. *See* football
social media, 19, 21, 103, 115–16, 121,
    122–23, 125, 127. *See also* Facebook

social movements, 5–6, 69–70, 86n.44,
    87–88, 125–26, 128, 139n.63, 150–51
Sonevytsky, Maria, 37, 70–71, 73–74,
    75, 82n.17
sovereignty, 7, 33, 34–38, 47n.51, 70–71,
    144, 145
state, 5, 6–7, 8–9, 13, 16, 20, 34–37, 57–76,
    117–18, 122–23, 127, 142, 145–46
  of exception, 34–35, 36
  in MENA region, 149–50
  postcolonial, 49, 50–51, 58, 61–62,
    63, 66–67, 75, 148–49 (*see also*
    postcolonialism)
space, public, 14–15, 16, 18, 67–68, 95, 97,
    115–16, 127, 132n.19, 137n.52
  urban 40n.1, 97–98, 108, 115–16 (*see
    also* city)
Sterne, Jonathan, 44n.28, 112, 136n.47,
    157–58n.27
Strohm, Kiven, 65–66
subcultural theory, 23–24, 45–46n.39

Tahrir Square, 88, 89, 90–91, 118–20,
    125, 127
tarab 88–89, 100, 101, 130n.6. *See
    also* Cairo
Tarde, Gabriel, 112–14, 136nn.48–49
television, 104–5, 134n.32
  in Turkey 8–9, 12–13, 19, 23, 27
timbre, 30–31, 47n.49
Trump, Donald, 36–37, 48n.53
Turkey, 8–14, 21–22, 29–127, 44–45n.31,
    81n.16, 85n.39, 148. *See also* Gezi
    Park; Istanbul

Ukraine, 37, 70–71, 73–74, 75,
    82n.17, 116
Umm Kulthum, 70, 88–89, 96, 130n.6,
    130–31n.9
UNESCO Intangible Cultural Heritage
    (ICH) programme 64, 155n.15
United Kingdom, 1–2, 102–12, 115–16,
    128, 142–43

Virolle, Marie, 71–72, 85n.35
vocal studies, 10, 27, 28–33, 37–38. *See
    also* voice

voice 37–38, 86n.42, 128–29, 141, 149, 151. *See also* vocal studies
  choral 114–15 (*see also* chirality)
  and citizenship 27–33
  in crowds 107–10 (*see also* crowd)
  in film 29, 46–47nn.46–47
  and intimacy 70–72, 73–76 (*see also* intimacy; voice: intimate)
  and Lacanian theory 28–30, 46n.44
  and postcolonialism 70–71, 75, 84n.32 (*see also* postcolonialism)
  and race 27, 30–31 (*see also* race)
  revolutionary 14–16, 19–20, 117–19 (*see also* Rousseau, Jean-Jacques)
  and timbre 31, 47n.49
  and voicing 32–33
  of Zeki Müren, 10–11, 13–14, 20

Webster-Kogen, Ilana, 52–53, 56
Weintraub, Andrew, 42n.19, 71, 72–73, 84n.32, 85n.37
whiteness, 50, 87, 129n.3. *See also* race
World Music, 52, 53–54, 71–72, 75–76, 83n.21, 140–41

"You'll Never Walk Alone," 102, 103–8, 109–10, 109f, 133–34n.28, 134n.32, 134n.34, 151
Young, Iris Marion 95, 132n.19

The manufacturer's authorised representative in the EU for product safety is Oxford
University Press España S.A. of El Parque Empresarial San Fernando de Henares,
Avenida de Castilla, 2 – 28830 Madrid (www.oup.es/en or product.safety@oup.com).
OUP España S.A. also acts as importer into Spain of products made by the manufacturer.

Printed in the USA/Agawam, MA
May 9, 2025

887224.001